An Ex-Colored Church

Rev. Alexander Minor,

With love, respect, and
appreciation for a CME
colleague and brother.
Peace & Justice,

Raymond R. Sommerville Jr

4-16-04

VOICES OF THE AFRICAN DIASPORA

This series presents the development of the intellectual tradition of the African diaspora. The series will bring together a variety of disciplines, including literary and social/cultural criticism, anthropology, sociology, religion/philosophy, education, political science, psychology, and history—by publishing original critical studies and reprints of classic texts. The reprints will include both nineteenth- and twentieth-century works. The goal is to make important texts accessible and readily available both to the general reader and to the academic.

CHESTER J. FONTENOT, JR.
SERIES EDITOR

Other Titles in the Series

Chester Fontenot, Mary Alice Morgan, and Sarah Gardner, ed. *W. E. B. Du Bois and Race: Essays Celebrating the Centennial Publication of The Souls of Black Folk*

Rufus Burrow, Jr., *God and Human Responsibility: David Walker and Ethical Prophecy*

An Ex-Colored Church

Social Activism in the CME Church, 1870–1970

Raymond R. Sommerville Jr.

Mercer University Press
Macon, Georgia

ISBN 0-86554-903-6
MUP/P280

First Edition.

∞The paper used in this publication meets the minimum requirements of American National Standard for Information Sciences—Permanence of Paper for Printed Library Materials, ANSI Z39.48-1992.

Library of Congress Cataloging-in-Publication Data

Sommerville, Raymond R., 1958-
An ex-colored church : the evolution of social activism in the CME Church, 1870-1970 / Raymond R. Sommerville Jr.
    p. cm.
Includes bibliographical references and index.
ISBN 0-86554-903-6 (pbk. : alk. paper)
1. Christian Methodist Episcopal Church—History. 2. Christianity and politics—Christian Methodist Episcopal Church—History. I. Title.
BX8463.S66 2004
287'.83--dc22

2003027449

CONTENTS

Abbreviations

ACMHR	Alabama Christian Movement for Human Rights
AME	African Methodist Episcopal Church
AMEZ	African Methodist Episcopal Church
CME	Christian [Colored] Methodist Episcopal Church
CORE	Congress of Racial Equality
COCU	Consultation on Church Union
FCC	Federal Council of Churches of Christ
FCNC	Fraternal Council of Negro Churches
ICAA	International Committee on African Affairs
ITC	Interdenominational Theological Center
MC	Methodist Church
MEC	Methodist Episcopal Church
MECS	Methodist Episcopal Church, South
MIA	Montgomery Improvement Association
NCLC	Nashville Christian Leadership Conference
NCNC	National Committee of Negro Churchmen
NAACP	National Association for the Advancement of Colored People
NCC	National Council of Churches of Christ
NUL	National Urban League
SCLC	Southern Christian Leadership Conference
SNCC	Student Nonviolent Coordinating Committee
SRC	Southern Regional Council
TCA	Tuskegee Civic Association
WCC	World Council of Churches
WMC	World Methodist Council

Preface

I am a fourth-generation minister in the Christian Methodist Episcopal Church, formerly known as the Colored Methodist Episcopal Church in America. Until I went to seminary in 1980, it was the only church I really knew; it was and remains my spiritual home. But it was my traumatic move from the North to the New South in 1970 that first introduced me to the historical and physical origins of the CME Church. It was this migration back south that prompted me to ask the following questions: First, if the CME Church is an indigenous church rooted in the South, what was its role in the in the modern Civil Rights movement—a mass movement that was religiously based in African-American churches and led by African-American clergy? Second, who were the principal leaders and advocates of Civil Rights activism in the CME Church? Third, how did the denominational name change from "Colored" to "Christian" reflect a shift in the church's social consciousness and social location in the Jim Crow South?

These are difficult historical questions that defy simple answers; some of the answers lay buried in dusty archives and fading memories. However, in the post-Civil Rights era there has been a tendency to exaggerate the role of African-American clergy and churches' involvement in the movement. It is one thing to say that African-American churches and clergy overwhelming supported the movement's goal of freedom, but it is entirely different to say that they put their lives on the line for this cause. Because of the radical and dangerous consequences of this goal, even Martin Luther King Jr. had a difficult time recruiting participants from African-American churches, including his own National Baptist Convention. This was particularly the case with the CME because of its roots in the post-Civil War South and its ambivalent relationship with its parent church, the socially conservative Methodist Episcopal Church, South. Consequently, CME social consciousness and activism evolved differently than its counterparts in the African Methodist Episcopal (AME) and African Methodist Episcopal Zion (AMEZ) churches.

Taking a long view, this social biography delineates some of the social and theological factors that contributed to the maturation of CME social thought activism from 1870 to 1970, as it became a leading supporter and advocate of the Civil Rights movement.

This project could not have been completed without a circle of family, mentors, colleagues, students, and friends from various communities who provided ongoing critique and encouragement. First, I owe a debt of gratitude to my family for their countless sacrifices and emotional support throughout this pilgrimage, especially to my wife, Sharon, and my children, Raymond III and Maya. They have been at my side from beginning to end, continuously embracing me as husband and daddy. This book is dedicated to the memory of my parents, the Reverend Raymond R. Sommerville Sr. and Barbara Hoye Sommerville, who both died before its completion but not before passing on to me their blessings and encouragement. They were shining exemplars of the Christian faith and dedicated workers in the CME Church.

Moreover, I am grateful to my siblings and relatives in Atlanta, Birmingham, and New York for hosting me on numerous research trips, especially Kevin and Sherrie Sommerville, Mark and Karen Sommerville, Anthony and Palmetta Hodges, Anita McGrew, and Kevin McGruder. I was also sustained through the prayers and support of extended family in the CME Church, especially Oliver DeWayne Walker, Thomas Hoyt, Paul and Earleen Stewart, W. Clyde and Elaine Williams, and the members of Thirgood CMEC in Birmingham and Phillips Temple CMEC in Indianapolis.

Second, I wish to thank my mentors, colleagues, and students at several academic institutions, beginning with C. Eric Lincoln, William C. Turner, Clarence G. Newsome, and Charles Long at Duke University for planting and nurturing the seed for this project. Next, I thank Jimmie Franklin, Dennis C. Dickerson, Eugene TeSelle, and Dorothy Parks of Vanderbilt University for their commitment to my development as a church historian and to the completion of this project. I am especially indebted to my advisor, Lewis V. Baldwin, for his keen oversight and diligent support over the long haul.

Furthermore, I thank my colleagues and students at Christian Theological Seminary for their generous support and encouragement, especially Richard Dickinson, Edward Wheeler, Newell Williams, and Clark Williamson for providing research and writing opportunities, and for my colleague-mentor Rufus Burrow for persistently admonishing me to "keep at it." Without the technical assistance and moral support of CTS staff members Joyce Krauser, Karen Kelm, and Laura Isenthal this project would have died a thousand deaths.

Finally, I owe a debt of gratitude to all my former students at Fisk University and CTS for their relentless questioning and patient endurance in anticipation of my completion of this project.

CHAPTER 1

Introduction

In December 1870, the Colored Methodist Episcopal Church in America (CMEC) became one of the first new denominations to emerge from the smoldering ashes of the Civil War. However, as the first independent African-American denomination founded in the postwar South, the CME Church faced a peculiar predicament. As a product of both southern white Methodist paternalism[1] and African Americans' quest for freedom, the church's early identity was largely shaped by its relationship with the Methodist Episcopal Church, South (MECS). How were colored Methodists going to navigate the troubled waters between these poles?[2] At the founding conference of the CME

---

[1]By paternalism I mean the guiding conviction on the part of white southerners that they knew what was best for African-American slaves and freed people. Rooted in southern patriarchical norms and notions of providential design, paternalism assumed a hierarchical relationship between a superior party over an inferior one, involving mutual obligations for the promotion of social order and harmony. Scholars have employed the following models to understand the complex relationship between whites and blacks in the South: parent-child, doctor-patient, teacher-student, and benevolent dictator-benefactor. For a discussion of these models in relation to slavery, see Howard McGary and Bill E. Lawson (*Between Slavery and Freedom* [Bloomington: University of Indiana Press, 1992] 16–34), who emphasize the coercive nature of paternalism and its denial of African-American autonomy; see also Eugene D. Genovese, *Roll, Jordan, Roll: The World the Slaves Made* (New York: Vintage Books, 1976) 5–7, 658–61; George M. Fredrickson, *The Black Image in the White Mind: The Debate on Afro-American Character and Destiny, 1817–1914* (New York: Harper & Row, 1971) 68–78.

[2]For an in-depth treatment of the origins of the CME Church, see Othal H. Lakey, *The History of the CME Church* (Memphis: CME Publishing House, 1985);

Church in 1870, the MECS bequeathed to its former slave members its doctrines and polity, with only minor modifications.[3] Thus this parent-child relationship not only militated against CME involvement in Reconstruction politics,[4] but also resulted in keen competition from northern Methodist bodies—the African Methodist Episcopal Church (AMEC), the African Methodist Episcopal Zion Church (AMEZC), and the Methodist Episcopal Church (MEC)—for "colored" members and property of the MECS. Seeing themselves as the legitimate redeemers of their southern sisters and brothers, these northern bodies stigmatized the CME Church as the "rebel church," or the "Democrats' church," or "the old slavery church."[5]

While such charges, made in the fervor of missionary competition, obscure the commitment of the CME Church to African-American survival and uplift, they do contain an element of truth. In their compromise with the MECS, the leaders of the CME Church publicly committed the church to a policy of political neutrality and accommodation, thus forcing the young church into the awkward position of defending its racial credentials while still maintaining a symbiotic relationship with the MEC, South. It is not surprising, then, that in comparison to the other African-American

---

Harry V. Richardson, *Dark Salvation: The Story of Methodism as It Developed among Blacks in America* (Garden City NY: Anchor/Doubleday, 1976).

[3]Among these modifications was the adoption of the MECS Discipline's excision of the prohibition of "slaveholding; buying or selling of slaves" from John Wesley's General Rules, a compendium of moral guidelines first drawn up by Wesley in 1739 (revised in 1743) and adopted by the founding conference of American Methodism in 1784.

[4]For an interpretation of these tensions involving the freedpeople and Reconstruction politics, see William B. Gravely, "The Social, Political and Religious Implications of the Formation of the Colored Methodist Episcopal Church (1870)," *Methodist History* 18 (October 1979): 3–25; Katharine L. Dvorak, *An African-American Exodus: The Segregation of the Southern Churches* (Brooklyn: Carlson Publishing, 1991); Clarence E. Walker, *A Rock in a Weary Land: The African Methodist Episcopal Church During the Civil War and Reconstruction* (Baton Rouge: Louisiana State University Press, 1982); see chapter 4 in Love Henry Whelchel Jr., *Hell without Fire: Conversion in Slave Religion* (Nashville: Abingdon Press, 2002).

[5]Lakey, *The History of the CME Church*, 239.

denominations in the South, very few of these colored Methodists became activists or politicians during the Reconstruction era. As a result, CME social and religious activism was suppressed during the latter quarter of the nineteenth century as the denomination struggled to forge its identity in an already scorched religious and social landscape.

Having been shaped in this crucible, the CME Church was poised to enter the twentieth century as a major contributor to race relations in the South. More specifically, there was a marked shift in the denomination's racial consciousness and social activism as it responded to social and religious movements in the twentieth century. Among these were two crucial twentieth-century movements: the ecumenical movement and the modern Civil Rights movement.[6] The purpose of this study is to examine CME involvement in these movements and to assess their impact on the CME Church's evolving

---

[6]The terms "ecumenism" and "ecumenical" derive from the Greek word *oikoumene*, meaning the "whole inhabited world." These three movements converged in their emphasis on racial justice, although this emphasis was not an early focus of the ecumenical movement. This movement developed chiefly an effort to unify and renew Christian churches at local, national, and international levels. The movement had its roots in the nineteenth-century missions movement, especially the 1910 World Missionary Conference in Edinburgh, Scotland. This conference spurned several other ecumenical conferences and ventures that in 1948 became the World Council of Churches (WCC). On the history of the WCC and global ecumenism, see Ruth Rouse and Stephen Neill, eds., *A History of the Ecumenical Movement, 1517–1948* (Philadelphia: Westminster Press, 1967); Nicholas Lossky et al., eds., *Dictionary of the Ecumenical Movement* (Grand Rapids MI: William B. Eerdmans, 1991). The ecumenical concern in the denominationally diverse United States actually preceded global developments, emerging first through participation in voluntary, non-denominational bodies (e.g., the American Bible Society and the Student Volunteer Movement) and leading to the 1908 founding of the Federal Council of Churches of Christ (FCC); see Samuel M. Cavert, *The American Churches in the Ecumenical Movement, 1900–1968* (New York: Association Press, 1968) and *Church Cooperation and Unity in America: A Historical Review: 1900–1970* (New York: Association Press, 1970). The CME Church and other African-American Methodist churches were among the charter members of both the FCC and WCC, as well as other ecumenical bodies like the World Methodist Council (WMC) and the Consultation of Church Union (COCU). I use CME ecumenism to refer to CME efforts to engage in mutual dialogue and cooperative missions with other Methodist and Christian bodies at local, regional, national, and global levels.

social and ecumenical consciousness. I will argue that CME involvement in these movements precipitated a painful but invigorating shift in denominational identity, ecumenism, and social activism. Though CMEs were not the most visible leaders of these movements they were represented at all levels: as participants in national and regional ecumenical organizations like the National Council of Churches (NCC) and the Southern Christian Leadership Conference (SCLC), as advocates in denominational meetings and conferences, and as grassroots leaders and participants in local campaigns. Moreover, their participation in the Civil Rights movement of the 1950s and 1960s was preceded by decades of involvement in local and regional struggles for racial justice throughout the South. This involvement at times placed them at odds with their white Methodist counterparts and in solidarity with other African-American Methodists, especially on such volatile issues as racial desegregation and the role of social protest in religion. Consequently, the Civil Rights movement was a watershed event for the CME Church, leading to new self-understandings and ecumenical relationships.

For millions of African Americans across the United States, the Civil Rights movement of the 1950s and 1960s marked a watershed experience in the country's checkered racial history. Regarded by many African Americans as the "Second American Reconstruction," the modern movement sought to overturn decades of de jure segregation and to fulfill the broken promises of the first Reconstruction era.[7] Although initially sparked by a series of momentous events in 1954 and 1955—the Emmett Till murder in Money, Mississippi; the 1954 *Brown v. Board of Education* Supreme Court decision; and the 1955–1956 Montgomery bus boycott—the

---

[7]For continuities between the Civil Rights movement and prior protest movements, see Aldon D. Morris, *The Origins of the Civil Rights Movement: Black Communities Organizing for Change* (New York: Free Press, 1984); Manning Marable, *Race, Reform, and Rebellion: The Second Reconstruction in Black America, 1945–1990*, 2d ed. (Jackson: University Press of Mississippi, 1991); V. P. Franklin, *Black Self-Determination: A Cultural History of African-American Resistance* (New York: Lawrence Hill Books, 1992).

modern Civil Rights movement was a continuation of earlier protest movements initiated by African Americans and their allies, beginning with their importation to North America in the seventeenth century. Earlier examples of this collective thrust for freedom include the Negro Convention movement of the antebellum period, the Radical Reconstruction of the South of the nineteenth century, and the Marcus Garvey movement in the early twentieth century. Because of its social location in the Jim Crow South and its conservative social philosophy, the CME Church was only minimally involved in these movements.

Colored Methodists, like other African-American churches in the South, largely responded to the collapse of the Radical Reconstruction and the rise of Jim Crow[8] by channeling their energy and resources into missionary expansion, educational development, and denominational maintenance. The majority of church leaders, it seems, adopted some form of Booker T. Washington's pragmatic social philosophy of accommodation to the new social order. Few were attracted to the emigrationist strategy advocated by AME bishop Henry McNeal Turner and other black nationalist leaders, although a growing numbers of CMEs would later join the masses of African Americans who migrated out of the rural South.

---

[8]The term "Jim Crow" was popularized in the early nineteenth century by a white minstrel performer named Thomas "Daddy" Rice, who imitated the dance and demeanor of an African-American stable worker belonging to a Mr. Crow. Scholars are not clear as to when the term became synonymous with the system of racial segregation that emerged in the post-emancipation South, but many agree that by the 1890s "the term took on the additional force and meaning to denote the subordination and separation of black people in the South, much of it codified, much of it enforced by custom and habit" (Leon F. Litwack, *Trouble in Mind: Black Southerners in the Age of Jim Crow* [New York: Alfred A. Knopf, 1998] xiv-xv). For other treatments of the origins of Jim Crow segregation in the New South, see C. Vann Woodward, *The Strange Career of Jim Crow*, 3rd rev. ed. (New York: Oxford University Press, 1974) and *Origins of the New South, 1877–1913* (Baton Rouge: Louisiana State University Press, 1971); George B. Tindall, *The Emergence of the New South, 1913–1945* (Baton Rouge: Louisiana State University Press, 1967); Edward L. Ayers, *The Promise of the New South: Life after Reconstruction* (New York: Oxford University Press, 1992); Howard N. Rabinowitz, *Race Relations in the Urban South, 1865–1890* (Urbana IL: Univeristy of Illinois Press; 1980.).

But for the overwhelming majority of colored Methodists who, for varying reasons, chose to remain in the New South, little had changed in their daily lives. The quality of their lives was still adversely affected by a system of racial domination (economic, political, and social), predicated on the doctrine of white supremacy and buttressed by racial violence. This system contributed to a vacuum of southern African-American protest leaders and organizations during the period before the advent of the modern Civil Rights movement.[9] This vacuum was particularly conspicuous among African-American churches and clergy, who were more preoccupied with daily survival, middle-class respectability, and otherworldly spirituality. There were, of course, some notable exceptions to this trend, such as clergy active in local protests and Civil Rights organizations like the NAACP, but they were unable to mobilize or sustain a mass movement in the South.

By the mid-1950s a number of factors converged to produce a viable protest movement to challenge racial oppression in the South. These factors included a more widespread mood of African-American insurgency as a result of urbanization and participation in two world wars, a revitalization of African-American churches as organizational centers of protest activity and ideology, the influence of anticolonial struggles in India and Africa, and improved communication technology. At the center of this vortex of activism was a young pastor named Martin Luther King Jr., who was unexpectedly thrust into the leadership of the 1955–1956 Montgomery bus boycott. As the movement evolved, King creatively drew upon his cultural and

---

[9]For a critical interpretation of this phenomenon, see Gayraud S. Wilmore (*Black Religion and Black Radicalism: An Interpretation of the Religious History of Afro-American People*, 2d rev. ed. [Maryknoll NY: Orbis Books, 1983]), who characterizes the retreat of mainline African-American churches from civil rights advocacy as the "deradicalization of the Black Church"(chapter six); for some exceptions to this general thesis, see Ralph E. Luker, *The Social Gospel in Black and White: American Racial Reform, 1885–1912* (Chapel Hill: University of North Carolina Press, 1991); Edward L. Wheeler, *Uplifting the Race: The Black Minister in the New South, 1865–1902* (Lanham MD: University Press of America, 1986); Randall K. Burkett, *Black Redemption: Churchmen Speak for the Garvey Movement* (Philadelphia: Temple University Press, 1978).

prophetic roots in the African-American religious tradition, as well as his exposure to liberal Christian thought and colonial resistance struggles, to mobilize African-American church people to confront racial segregation with the strategies of nonviolent direct action.

While not all African-American religious bodies and leaders supported King and his Southern Christian Leadership Conference (SCLC), King nonetheless captivated the religious imagination of the masses of African-American church people, including CMEs. Like most black denominations, the CME Church was initially reluctant to endorse King's protest strategies, but several denominational leaders, ministers, and laypeople took an active role in the SCLC's local and regional campaigns. For example, in King's own hometown of Atlanta, SNCC (Student Nonviolent Coordinating Committee) activist Ruby Doris Smith emerged as a key leader, and attorney Donald Hollowell served as a movement attorney. In Birmingham, King's childhood classmate Nathaniel Linsey spearheaded a contingent of CMEs in the historic 1963 campaign, while Miles College president Lucius Pitts worked as a conciliatory force there. Like CMEs in other movement centers, these CMEs joined preexisting or newly created ecumenical bodies committed to racial justice.

Like King, many of these southern-born leaders had grown impatient with the slow pace of racial reform, and their experiences in such organizations as the National Council of Churches (NCC), the World Methodist Council (WMC), and the World Council of Churches (WCC) fomented both new conceptions of and alliances for social ministry. Following in the legacy of Channing Tobias, a CME executive with the YMCA and Phelps-Stokes Fund, a younger generation of CME leaders sought to respond to the urgent social crises of their times. Their involvement in this movement would set the agenda for the emergence of a new church, signified in 1954 by its name change from the "Colored" to the "Christian" Methodist Episcopal Church.

Beginning with Carter Woodson's pioneering study *The History of the Negro Church*[10] in 1921, a number of studies have explored selected aspects of African Methodism—its historical origins, ministry, social activism, ecumenism, and theology.[11] While many of these studies stress the separate origins of individual Methodist bodies in the eighteenth and nineteenth centuries, their reliance on a consensus model of African-American denominations tends to obscure the evolving social, political, and theological diversity of these bodies, as well as their distinctive regional and cultural characteristics.[12] For example, the fact that the CME Church was founded in the former Confederate South by former slaves and slaveholders suggests a different context of development than that of the African Methodists in the North, who experienced a relatively longer period of freedom and autonomy. The same could be said of African-American Methodists in the former central jurisdiction of the Methodist Episcopal Church who, until 1968, were confined to a caste system within the predominantly white Methodist Church for an even longer period of time.

Thus, beginning with the assumption that the CME Church entered the twentieth century with a distinctive denominational, regional, and cultural history, this study seeks to answer the following questions: What effect did the CME Church's social location and sense of place in the New South have on its evolving sense of identity, theology, and social mission? What role did its earlier and ongoing relationship with southern white Methodists have on its involvement in Civil Rights activism? Was there a dialectic tension between the denominational hierarchy and local leaders/churches on

---

[10]Carter G. Woodson, *The History of the Negro Church* (Washington DC: Associated Publishers, 1921).

[11]See, for example, Richardson, *Dark Salvation*; C. Eric Lincoln and Lawrence H. Mamiya, *The Black Church in the African-American Experience* (Durham NC: Duke University Press, 1990); Mary R. Sawyer, *Black Ecumenism: Implementing the Demands of Justice* (Valley Forge PA: Trinity Press International, 1994).

[12]For an elaboration of this critique, see Laurie F. Maffly-Kipp, "Denominationalism and the Black Church," in *Reimagining Denominationalism*, ed. Robert Bruce Mullin and Russell E. Richey (New York: Oxford University Press, 1994) 58–73.

such issues as support of and participation in the movement? How did the ideas and cultural forces unleashed by the movement affect individual leaders, churches, and the larger denomination?

Chapter 2, "When We Were Colored: The Formative Years of the CME Church, 1870–1900," provides an overview of the place of the CME Church within the broader spectrum of American Methodism, with particular emphasis on its roots in southern Methodism and African-American religious culture.

Having established the historical background for the emergence of a "colored" Methodism in the New South, chapter 3, "The 'Paine College Ideal': CME Responses to Racial Injustice during the Jim Crow Era, 1900–1954," examines the CME Church's responses to the problem of racial injustice during the era leading up to the Civil Rights movement. Although CMEs expressed support for Booker T. Washington's accommodationist philosophy and strategies, they developed their own distinctive approach to racial progress, a strategy that combined educational reform, ecumenism, and Civil Rights activism. Paine College, in Augusta, Georgia, emerged as the main proponent of this distinctive approach and produced a generation of leaders committed to the "Paine College Ideal," with Channing Tobias as its most visible representative and advocate. This chapter also reveals that as CMEs weaned themselves from the paternalistic ties to southern Methodists, they formed new alliances with more progressive ecumenical bodies like the Fraternal Council of Negro Churches (FCNC) and more vigorously pursued organic merger with other African-American Methodist bodies.

The next three chapters present case studies of CME participation in movement centers in southern cities during the Civil Rights movement: Memphis, Tennessee; Tuskegee, Alabama; Nashville, Tennessee; Atlanta, Georgia; and Birmingham, Alabama.

Chapter 4, "The CME Church and the Birth of the Civil Rights Movement, 1954–1960," examines CME responses to the 1954 Supreme Court decision that outlawed segregation in public schools. Coincidentally, the decision was handed down the same year the denomination entertained a proposal to change its name from "Colored" to "Christian" Methodist Episcopal Church. Although this proposal was not a direct result of the Supreme Court's decision, the two became historically linked as turning points for the CME Church. Together, they propelled the denomination into deeper levels of activism and ecumenism, especially after the 1955 Montgomery bus boycott led by Martin Luther King Jr. This chapter explores the immersion of two CME leaders in the earliest phases of the movement: Henry Bunton in Memphis, Tennessee, and Charles Gomillion in Tuskegee, Alabama. Largely without the sanction of the denominational hierarchy, these two local leaders set a precedent for subsequent church involvement in Civil Rights campaigns and electoral politics.

With this heightened sense of social and ecumenical consciousness during the 1960s, a number of CMEs in the South took the initiative to participate in the Civil Rights movement and to encourage their local congregations to do likewise. Chapter 5, "The Sacred Call to Activism: CMEs and the Student Activism of the 1960s," focuses on movement centers in Nashville and Atlanta during the rise of student activism. For several reasons these centers produced an inordinate share of Civil Rights organizations, strategies, and leaders. This chapter further examines the distinctive contributions of three diverse CME figures: seminary professor Joseph Johnson, student-activist Ruby Doris Smith, and Civil Rights attorney Donald Hollowell.

In many ways the 1963 Civil Rights campaign in Birmingham, Alabama, and the March on Washington can be regarded as the zenith of CME Civil Rights activism. Chapter 6, "There Is a Balm in Birmingham: The CME Church and the Birmingham Movement, 1961–1964," discusses how the campaign in Birmingham not only revitalized the movement as a whole, but also transformed the CME Church into an active supporter of the movement. At the center of this transformation was President Lucius Pitts of Miles College, whose negotiating skills contributed to a breakthrough in the Birmingham crisis. Joining him were countless other CME ministers and laypeople who attended mass meetings, marched in the streets, and were thrown into jails. After Birmingham and the March on Washington, the Civil Rights movement evolved into more of an interracial, ecumenical, interfaith movement, especially as liberal churches and ecumenical bodies placed the struggle for racial justice on their agenda.

With its strategic location in the South and its long history of ecumenical involvement, the CME Church moved to the forefront of this emerging ecumenical Civil Rights activism. The participation of CMEs in the Birmingham campaign paved the way for wider CME participation at local, regional, and national levels. Chapter 7, "'Implementing Justice and Righteousness': The Apex of CME Activism and Ecumenism, 1964–68," examines the responses of the CME Church at these multiple levels between 1964 and 1968, the apex of the movement and CME involvement. The chapter first explores how CME involvement in national and global ecumenical bodies contributed to the church's social consciousness and activism, leading to the adoption of a CME social creed and social action commission. Second, the chapter discusses how CME Civil Rights ecumenism led to a revival of merger dialogue with the AME and AMEZ churches. The chapter closes with a discussion of CME responses to the rise of the black power movement in the late 1960s during the denouement of the Civil Rights movement.

Finally, the conclusion summarizes the major findings and assesses the impact of the Civil Rights movement on CME social activism and ecumenism. Although the achievements and legacies of the Civil Rights movement were significant, it produced some bittersweet fruits for African-American Methodists in the post-Civil Rights era.

CHAPTER 2

When We Were Colored: The Formative Years of Colored Methodism, 1866–1900

The experience of Lucius Holsey of Georgia, an early leader and bishop in the Colored Methodist Church in America (CMEC), is in some ways representative of the colored remnant that remained within the Methodist Episcopal Church, South (MECS) after the Civil War. Born near Columbus, Georgia, in 1842, Holsey was the product of his slave mother, Lousia, and her white owner, James Holsey. In a rare disclosure of his African lineage, which highlights his own double-consciousness, Holsey acknowledged that his mother was "of pure African descent," the daughter of a slave named Alex, "an African of Africans."[1] James Holsey provided a stark contrast to his mother's "pure African descent": "He was a gentleman of classical education dignified in appearance and manner of life, and represented that old antebellum class of Southern aristocracy."[2]

Although young Lucius was eventually sold by this genteel southerner to a cousin in Sparta, Georgia, his status as a "mulatto" shielded him from some of the harsher aspects of plantation life and afforded him closer social contact with southern whites. He spent

---

[1]Lucius H. Holsey, *Autobiography, Sermons, Addresses, and Essays of Bishop L. H. Holsey, D.D.* (Atlanta: The Franklin Printing and Publishing Company, 1899) 17.

[2]Ibid.

most of his early life as a domestic slave, working as a house servant, gardener, body servant, and carriage driver. As a loyal and trusted servant, Holsey voluntarily chose to remain a slave an additional year beyond emancipation with his last owner, Richard Malcolm Johnston, a planter and professor at Franklin College in Athens. In his autobiography, Holsey candidly disclosed the depth of his loyalty to his owner: "In all things I was honest and true to him and his interests. Though young, I felt as much interest in his well-being as I have felt since in my own. I made it a special point never to lie to him or deceive him in any way. I felt I could not be false even to those who appeared to be my enslavers and oppressors, and I have never regretted this course in after years."[3]

Just as revealing as his interpretation of the slave-master relationship is Holsey's post-emancipation assessment of the positive value of slavery for himself and other African-American slaves: "The training I have received in the narrow house of slavery has been a minister of correction and mercy to me in all these years of struggle, trial, labor, and anxiety. I have no complaint against American slavery. It was blessing in disguise to me and to many. It has made the Negro race what it could not have been in its native land."[4]

Holsey's description of slavery as "a minister of correction and mercy" and a "blessing in disguise" suggests the major influence of a particular variant of American Christianity on Holsey: southern, evangelical Methodism. Holsey's identity as a colored Methodist was deepened by his close relationship to Bishop George Pierce of the MECS, who officiated at three major religious events in Holsey's life: his marriage to Pierce's servant Harriet Turner on 8 November 1862, his examination and licensure as a minister in the MECS, and his ordination as a deacon and appointment to his first pastorate.

This symbiotic and hierarchical relationship between a southern Methodist bishop and an ex-slave minister came to symbolize the rather ambiguous relationship of the CME Church with the MECS after emancipation. This chapter traces the roots of this complex

---

[3]Ibid., 18.
[4]Ibid.

relationship in the antebellum period by discussing three distinctive elements of colored Methodism in the South that distinguished it from African Methodists in the North and contributed to its more conservative social and political consciousness. The first is the legacy of an African sacred cosmos, which provided second- and third-generation slaves in the nineteenth century with a religious-cultural ethos that was more African than European in orientation. The second is the distinctive Wesleyan heritage and influence African Americans were introduced to by their exposure to Methodist preachers and missions. The third is the wider theological ethos of southern evangelicalism that influenced white and colored Methodists' views on the church's role in society. I conclude with a descriptive analysis of the emergent social and political consciousness of the first generation of CMEs during the Reconstruction era, one that was constrained by southern paternalism, evangelicalism, and social location.

The emergence of the CME church during the smoldering aftermath of the Civil War has been interpreted by one church historian as the "grafting of two conflicting institutions growing on American soil: American Methodism and American slavery."[5] But for the vast majority of former slaves who constituted this new denomination, it was American Methodism, not American slavery, that shaped their religious and social identity. More specifically, it was the pervasive influence of southern Methodism that would stamp an indelible imprint on colored Methodism, one that would prove to be a mixed blessing for colored Methodists, especially during the turbulent years of national and regional reconstruction.

This emphasis on Methodist identity was clearly evident at the organizational conference in December of 1870 in Jackson, Tennessee, where forty-six colored delegates joined white representatives from the MECS to organize the CME Church. Several

---

[5]Othal H. Lakey, *The History of the CME Church* (Memphis: CME Publishing House, 1985) 73. Lakey's denominational history probes the symbiotic relationship between the CME Church and the MECS and generally assesses that relationship as either positive or ambiguous.

years later, Holsey, a delegate from Georgia and future bishop of the CME Church, reflected on the changed state of affairs portended by the conference: "The asperities of the now defunct institution (slavery) were...mitigated by the beautiful and lavish hand of Christian charity and evangelistic labors bestowed upon the sons and daughters of Ham by the Southern Methodist people."[6]

The opening report of the conference by the Committee on Church Organization set a tone that would characterize the new relationship between southern white and colored Methodists for years to come. In an effort to forge a denominational name and identity, the committee carefully underscored the blessings and benefits of familial relations with the MECS:

> Whereas the Methodist Episcopal Church in America was the first name given to the Methodist Church in the United States; and
>
> Whereas we are part of that same Church, never having seceded or separated from the Church; but in the division of the Church by the General Conference in 1844 we naturally belonged to the South, and have been in that division ever since; and now, as we belong to the "colored" race....
>
> Resolved, 1. That our name be the "Colored Methodist Episcopal Church in America."
>
> 2. That while we thus claim for ourselves an antiquity running as far back as any branch of the Methodist family on this side of the Atlantic Ocean...we shall for ever hold in grateful remembrance what the Methodist Episcopal Church, South, has done for us; we shall forever cherish the kindliest feeling toward the bishops and General Conference for giving to us all that they enjoy of religious privileges, the ordination of our deacons and elders, and at this conference our bishops

---

[6]Lucius H. Holsey, *Autobiography, Sermons, Addresses, and Essays* of Bishop L.H. Holsey, D.D. 2nd ed. (Atlanta: The Franklin Printing and Publishing Company, 1899.) 243.

will be ordained by them to the highest office known in our Church....

3. That we request the bishops to organize our General Conference on the basis of the Discipline of the Methodist Episcopal Church, South, in its entire doctrine, discipline and economy, making only such verbal alterations and changes as may be necessary to conform it to our name and the peculiarities of our condition.[7]

On the surface, these resolutions not only reveal the conciliatory spirit of colored Methodists, but a strong attachment to the southern Methodist church—its doctrines, polity, and leadership. For instance, there is no hint of repressed rage or angry denunciation on the part of colored Methodists over the MECS's condoning of slavery or its support of the Confederacy. This conciliatory rhetoric and posture of colored Methodists invited conjecture about their motives at the organizational conference. Was it a sincere display of gratitude and good will by newly freed slaves? Or was it a more guarded attempt at conciliation, an interim strategy until a more autonomous colored church could be established?

To their contemporary Methodists in the North, colored Methodists' motives, no matter how sincere or guarded, were viewed with outright suspicion and hostility. Abolitionist churches like the biracial Methodist Episcopal Church (MEC) and exclusively African-American ones like the African Methodist Episcopal (AME) and the African Methodist Episcopal Zion (AMEZ) churches openly condemned colored Methodists for choosing to remain in a caste system that merely substituted one form of bondage for another. An editorial in MEC's *New Orleans Christian Advocate* offered this dire diagnosis of the infant colored church:

The Colored Methodist Episcopal Church of America, South...or whatever it may be called, has the rickets, spinal

---

[7]Quoted in Charles Henry Phillips, *History of the Colored Methodist Episcopal Church* (Jackson TN: Publishing House of the CME Church, 1898) 35.

complaint, and consumption. Instead of Gospel milk and meat, it has been fed upon Confederate politics, hatred to Yankees and official vanity till the poor thing is too dyspeptic to digest wholesome food and too blind to find it.... Poor thing! It is a fit place for nobody but such as prefer to be in slavery and ignorance rather than free and educated, and so has but a narrow and not widening field for operation.[8]

Church historians have also offered explanations for the conciliatory rhetoric and posture of colored Methodists at the 1870 organizing conference. Methodist historian Hunter Farish stressed the continuing patterns of Southern paternalism as a major factor in the relationship between the two races.[9] Pioneered by Methodist evangelist William Capers in South Carolina and Presbyterian evangelist Charles Colcock Jones in Georgia, proslavery missionaries promulgated a mission strategy based on mutual obligation and reciprocal duties between slaves and masters.[10]

Even after the Civil War abolished slave owners' proprietary rights over their slaves, southern Methodists slowly and painfully conceded that emancipation did not absolve them of all responsibilities to their colored members. In fact, it was their Christian obligation to continue to provide spiritual oversight, moral instruction, and material support to the masses of freed people, who were considered too childlike to fend for themselves or to stave off the aggressive proselytizing of Northern Methodists.

---

[8]*New Orleans Christian Advocate,* 30 July 1870.

[9]Hunter D. Farish, *The Circuit Rider Dismounts: A Social History of Southern Methodism, 1865–1900* (Richmond VA: The Dietz Press, 1938) 163–72.

[10]For a discussion of slave missions, see especially chapter 4 in Donald G. Mathews, *Religion in the Old South* (Chicago: University of Chicago Press, 1977); Donald G. Mathews, "The Methodist Mission to the Slaves, 1829–1844," *Journal of American History* 51 (March 1 *Journal of the General Conference,* (MECS) 1866, 15–21.965): 615–31; Albert J. Raboteau, *Slave Religion: The "Invisible Institution" in the Antebellum South* (New York: Oxford University Press, 1978) 152–80. Mathews suggests that the missions failed largely because of slaves' refusal to accommodate to racial subservience and the missionaries' exaggerated view of what the mission could accomplish (*Religion and the Old South,* 48–150).

In their episcopal address of 1866, southern bishops reminded members how the MECS had provided for colored members in the past: "Heretofore the colored people within our bounds have deserved and received a large share of our labors. We have expended our means and strength liberally and patiently for many years for their salvation and improvement."[11] At the same time, the bishops cautioned members about the possibility of the departure of colored members to the AME and ME churches, "while others, notwithstanding extraneous influences and unkind misrepresentations of our Church, will remain with us."[12] It was for this loyal remnant of colored Methodists that the 1866 General Conference adopted a plan for the organization of separate colored circuits, missions, district and annual conferences.[13]

While there is little doubt that southern paternalism was a major factor in the relationship between white and colored Methodists, it was not the only factor.[14] Such an interpretation obscures the agency

---

[11] *Journal of the General Conference* (MECS) 1866, 15-21.

[12]Ibid. Of the 200,000 slave members reported in 1860, only 78,742 of these "colored members" could be accounted for in 1866; for a statistical analysis of this decline, see Othal H. Lakey, *The Rise of "Colored Methodism: A Study of the Background of the Beginnings of the Christian Methodist Episcopal Church"* (Dallas: Crescendo Book Publications, 1972) 58–62; Lakey, *The History of the CME Church*, 108–14.

[13]It should be noted, however, that not all African-American members of the MECS joined the CME Church; some were attracted to the AME, AMEZ, and ME churches while an even smaller remnant chose to remain with the MECS. In 1939, with the reunification of the MEC and MECS, this smaller remnant was absorbed into the Central Jurisdiction—a segregated conference for African Americans within the United Methodist Church; see Grant S. Shockley, ed., *Heritage and Hope: The African-American Presence in United Methodism* (Nashville: Abingdon Press, 1991); James S. Thomas, *Methodism's Racial Dilemma: The Story of the Central Jurisdiction* (Nashville: Abingdon Press, 1992).

[14]For a perceptive treatment of the slave owners' paternalism employing Marxist analysis to explain its distinctiveness and pervasiveness as a product of a prebourgeois society, see Eugene D. Genovese, *Roll, Jordan, Roll: The World the Slaves Made* (New York: Pantheon Books, 1974) 4–7. But paternalism contained its own seed of destruction by fueling slaves' solidarity and resistance: "Paternalism's insistence upon mutual obligation—duties, responsibilities, and ultimately even rights—implicitly recognized the slaves' humanity.... Thus the slaves found an

of African-American freed people in securing their own rights and organizing their own institutions independent of white oversight and control. In other words, colored members did not sit idly by waiting on their white benefactors from either the North or South to determine their destiny. Nor did they allow their many detractors to alter their intentions of proceeding with their own church. They cautiously, yet strategically, moved to organize autonomous churches and conferences within the fragmented bond of southern paternalism, which would ultimately lead to a separate denomination.

Several denominational studies on the roots of colored Methodism have sought to penetrate beyond the public rhetoric of colored and white leaders to suggest how the colored members acted on their own interests, while simultaneously acquiescing to white control and paternalism.[15] Historian Othal Lakey, for example, points to several initiatives taken by colored Methodists prior to the 1870 organizational conference to organize racially separate churches and conferences as evidence of their desire for freedom from white control. Within a span of four years (1866–1870) colored Methodists had assisted MECS officials in the organization of five annual conferences and forty-five district conferences across the South with about 40,000 members, along with the recruitment of colored presiding elders and preachers. Thus, by the 1870 General Conference, colored members had exceeded the minimum criteria established by the 1866 General Conference for the formation of a separate colored body.[16]

As early as 1867, colored Methodists' endeavors began to reap a promising harvest. In west Tennessee alone, Reverend Thomas

---

opportunity to translate paternalism itself into a doctrine different from that understood by their masters and to forge it into a weapon of resistance" (5).

[15]For perspectives on the self-agency of colored Methodists, see especially Lakey, *The Rise of "Colored Methodism"* and *The History of the CME Church*; Katharine L. Dvorak, *An African-American Exodus: The Segregation of the Southern Churches* (Brooklyn: Carlson Publishing, 1991); and William B. Gravely, "The Social, Political and Religious Implications of the Formation of the Colored Methodist Episcopal Church (1870)" *Methodist History* 18 (October 1979): 3–25.

[16]Lakey, *The History of the CME Church*, 118.

Taylor, the white general superintendent of the Colored Work, reported the organization of a colored conference that included 10,000 members and 120 ministers.[17] By December of 1870, a total of eight annual conferences had been organized in the former confederate states of Tennessee, Mississippi, Alabama, Virginia, Georgia, South Carolina, Arkansas, and the border state of Kentucky. This rapid growth of colored Methodist conferences was assisted by the exodus of colored members from the MECS to join the AME, AMEZ, and ME churches, which had all dispatched missionaries to the South to organize new churches.

Like their southern Methodist benefactors, colored Methodists in the South were not oblivious to the attention they were receiving from northerners. At the 1870 General Conference of the MECS, colored Methodist leaders responded with their own petition at the 1870 General Conference, staking their own claims for autonomy: "We believe that the time has now come when a General Conference can be organized for our race; under the circumstances it might be advisable to wait until our ministers were better educated. But in order that there should be no alienation on the part of our people we ask that you form at once and authorize the organization of a Colored General Conference."[18]

In addition to the initiative of colored Methodists themselves, the spectacular growth of colored churches and conferences within the MECS can be attributed to several other factors that would profoundly affect the relationship between white and colored Methodists in the South. First, the cataclysmic social and political changes wrought by emancipation had direct implications for African-American religion in the South, including the evolving religious cosmos of colored Methodism. Second, the initial response of southern white Methodists to emancipation, which ranged from shock to ambivalence, created a space for colored Methodism to sprout and grow. Third, the emergence of a new social and political climate in the South during the Reconstruction era further heightened the tension between

---

[17]*Nashville Christian Advocate*, 23 January 1869.
[18]Reported in *Daily Christian Advocate*, 28 May 1870.

southern white and colored Methodists. Thus the evolution of a distinct colored Methodist religious identity and social consciousness can be seen as a "dialogic" tension between southern Methodist paternalism and colored Methodist autonomy—a tension that would remain unresolved well into the twentieth century.[19] The roots of this tension can be traced to the antebellum encounter between African Americans and white Methodists in the slave South, from which a distinctive form of African-American Christianity developed.

THE SACRED COSMOS OF COLORED METHODISM

The precise origins of African-American Christianity in British North America, of which colored Methodism was a vital expression, remains elusive to scholars. It is elusive because British colonists (for example, Anglicans, Congregationalists, Presbyterians, and Catholics) made little concerted effort to christianize African slaves until the early eighteenth century. Even then, the majority of slaves in the North American colonies remained only marginally affected by European Christianity.[20] Scholars can only speculate on the barest of documentary evidence the survival of African religious beliefs and practices among slaves prior to more intensive efforts to christianize them in the eighteenth century. How, then, do we account for this time lag in evangelizing slaves who, at the beginning of the eighteenth century, constituted a relatively small but conspicuous presence?

---

[19]See Evelyn Brooks Higginbotham (*Righteous Discontent: The Women's Movement in the Black Baptist Church, 1880–1920* [Cambridge MA: Harvard University Press, 1993] 15–16) for a distinction between "dialogic" and "dialectic" tension. Colored Methodists would maintain a close working relationship and dialogue with the MECS, although rarely as equal partners.

[20]Some notable exceptions during the colonial period include Cotton Mather, John Eliot, and Samuel Hopkins, in New England, and John Woolman among the Quakers; see especially chapter 3 in Raboteau's *Slave Religion*; Milton C. Sernett, *Black Religion and American Evangelicalism: White Protestants, Plantation Missions, and the Flowering of Negro Christianity, 1787–1865* (Metuchen NJ: Scarecrow Press, 1975); Forrest G. Wood, *The Arrogance of Faith: Christianity and Race in America from the Colonial Era to the Twentieth Century* (New York: Alfred A. Knopf, 1990).

One reason for the delay was the absence of a clearly defined mission strategy targeting non-Europeans, especially Indians and Africans, as potential converts. Such an omission might be considered highly ironic considering that a number of English immigrants migrated for avowedly religious purposes: to escape religious persecution (Pilgrims and Quakers), to found "reformed" churches (Puritans and Congregationalists), and to plant the church in new territories (Catholics and Anglicans). Another factor was the severe shortage of clergy and absence of denominational hierarchies in North America, which constrained pastoral outreach and ministry to Anglo-American communities, much less to Indian and African populations.

Perhaps the major reason for the delayed mission to Africans in colonial North America was the divided mind of Europeans on the conversion of Africans, now complicated by increasing European involvement in and justification of the institution of slavery. English attitudes of Africans as the "other" precipitated theological debate about the legitimacy of slave missions. Some proslavery apologists even debated whether slaves had souls worthy of redemption or sufficient intelligence to comprehend the gospel.[21] Since the majority of English colonists had little previous contact with Africans, either as slaves or as freed people, their attitudes were based largely on ethnocentric biases and racist perceptions. Thus, by the beginning of the eighteenth century, many Christians in the North American colonies were still negotiating the peculiar "otherness" of Africans.

Even in 1701 when British mission bodies like the London-based Society for the Gospel in Foreign Parts targeted Africans for conversion in the early eighteenth century, most Africans rejected a religious system that appeared alien to their religious cosmos and inimical to their social and spiritual well-being. Short of outright

---

[21]For a discussion of this debate, see especially Winthrop D. Jordan, *White Over Black: American Attitudes toward the Negro, 1550–1812* (Chapel Hill: University of North Carolina, 1968) and H. Shelton Smith, *In His Image, But...: Racism in Southern Religion, 1780–1910* (Durham NC: Duke University Press, 1972); Wood, *The Arrogance of Faith*; George M. Fredrickson, *The Black Image in the White Mind: The Debate on Afro-American Character and Destiny, 1817–1914* (New York: Harper & Row, 1971).

coercion, it appears that the majority of first- and second-generation Africans in North America did not easily, or completely, abandon their "African religious cosmos" to embrace European Christianity.

By the mid-nineteenth century, however, those Africans who were identified as colored Methodists had come to inhabit a religious cosmos that was shared by hundreds of thousands of other Christians in the South, the overwhelming majority of whom were affiliated with Methodist and Baptist churches. It was a religious cosmos dually shaped by African and Euro-American religions, mixed in the crucible of slavery in North America. While the memory and influence of Africa did gradually fade as subsequent generations of African Americans were acculturated into the North American system of slavery, much of the African worldview was transformed into a new religious phenomenon—African-American Christianity.[22]

Although colored Methodists seldom referred to their African past or to African influences in their religious development, they shared common elements of the distinctive form of African-American Christianity that had evolved by the late eighteenth and early nineteenth centuries. Among those elements were the reality of a unified spiritual universe, with no sharp dichotomies between the sacred and the secular; an emphasis on harmony within the cosmos and community as the highest good; the pervasiveness of the divine and ancestral spirits as animating forces in the cosmos; the continuation of certain African traditional leadership roles (for example, priests/priestesses, elders, diviners); and the continuation and modification of certain African religious beliefs and rituals (for example, conceptions of deities, the afterlife, sacrifice, and the importance of music performance).[23]

---

[22]For the debate on the presence of African retentions in African-American religion and culture in the nineteenth century, see Raboteau, *Slave Religion*, 48–75; Sterling Stuckey, *Slave Culture: Nationalist Theory and the Foundations of Black America* (New York: Oxford University Press, 1987); Margaret Washington Creel, *"A Peculiar People": Slave Religion and Community Culture among the Gullahs* (New York: New York University Press, 1988).

[23]Sociologists C. Eric Lincoln and Lawrence Mamiya (*The Black Church in African-American Experience* [Durham NC: Duke University Press, 1986] 2–7) have

While many of these African retentions persisted in permutated forms, by the mid-nineteenth century colored Methodists were more likely to describe their religious cosmos with Christian (specifically, Wesleyan) rather than African categories. Through time, the African continuum eventually receded as a primary referent for either religious or historical identity and replaced with the more ambiguous referent "colored Methodist." Though the designation "colored Methodist" was originally intended to be descriptive, it also came to signify a quest for a usable past that would legitimate a new religious status.

THE WESLEYAN HERITAGE AND INFLUENCE

In 1870, when colored Methodists claimed for themselves "an antiquity running as far back as any Methodist body on this side of the Atlantic," they were asserting their ecclesiastical identity as authentic heirs of John Wesley and the Wesleyan movement in England.[24] In effect, they articulated a phenomenon historian W. E. B. Du Bois would later describe as "double consciousness": the tension of being both "an American, a Negro; two souls, two thoughts, two unreconciled strivings; two warring ideals in one dark body whose dogged strength alone keeps it from being torn asunder."[25] But for

---

delineated these and other elements as constitutive of a "Black Sacred Cosmos," a worldview by which Africans in the "New World" selectively incorporated African sensibilities, meanings, and practices for the purposes of survival and meaning-making in an alien cultural context. Raboteau, *Slave Religion*; Sobel, *Trabelin' On*; Creel, *"A Peculiar People"*; Stuckey, *Slave Culture*; Lawrence W. Levine, *Black Culture and Black Consciousness: Afro-American Follk Thought from Slavery to Freedom* (New York: Oxford University Press, 1977).

[24]*Minutes of the CME General Conference*, 1870. This assertion also served to refute the charge of Northern Methodist bodies that the formation of the CMEC was "irregular" since it was facilitated by a schismatic MECS, which, in 1844, parted with the MEC over the issue of slavery.

[25]W. E. B. Du Bois, "Of Our Spiritual Strivings," *The Souls of Black Folk*, in *W. E. B. Du Bois: Writings*, ed. Nathan L. Huggins (New York: Library of America, 1986). For Du Bois, the concept of "double-consciousness" referred to the following three issues: (1) the problem of self-definition, resulting from a society pervaded with negative stereotypes about African Americans; (2) African-American separateness as

colored Methodists there was a third dimension not fully articulated in Du Bois's poignant description: their triple consciousness as colored, Methodist, and American, now encapsulated in their own self-designation as the "Colored Methodist Church in America."[26] Thus, even before these newly freed slaves were granted full citizenship rights as U.S. citizens, they pointed to their unbroken lineage as Wesleyans and to the consecration of their two bishops by southern Methodists as legitimation of their identity.

In the hopeful but volatile aftermath of slavery, colored Methodists embraced their Methodist roots and identity rather than their African past or their present status as freed people in the United States. Since much of their Wesleyan self-identity and knowledge of Methodism was influenced by the MECS, it is appropriate, then, to inquire about the content of Methodism transmitted to colored Methodists during and after their enslavement, and how it was appropriated selectively by colored Methodists to legitimate their peculiar Wesleyan identity.

Given the paternalistic ideology that prevailed throughout much of the slave-owning South, it is not surprising that Methodist slave owners presented to slaves a highly selective version of Methodist history and doctrine, especially concerning the contentious issue of slavery within the Methodist church. The primary intent of the plantation missions, inaugurated by southern Christians in the eighteenth century, was to produce dutiful and responsible Christians who questioned neither the authority of their owners nor the

---

a result of exclusion from American institutions; and (3) internal psychic conflict between one's African self and American identity.

[26]This is not to infer that Du Bois was unaware of the influence of religion in African-American life and culture. In *The Souls of Black Folk* and other writings, Du Bois addressed the history and role of African-American churches as social and cultural institutions. Although he was raised a Congregationalist in New England and claimed no denominational affiliation, Du Bois's understanding of African-American churches was enriched by his exposure to these churches as a student and university professor in the South; see, for example, Du Bois, ed., *The Negro Church* (Atlanta: Atlanta University Press, 1903)

legitimacy of the slave order.[27] So while John Wesley was remembered for his efforts to reform the Anglican Church and his promotion of scriptural holiness, stories of his opposition to slavery and involvement in the abolitionist crusade were completely expunged from slave catechisms.[28] Similarly, slaves heard little or nothing of the anti-slavery stance taken by early Methodist conferences in the colonies, a stance strongly communicated by the denomination's first superintendents (bishops), Thomas Coke and Francis Asbury, and clearly stipulated in the first American Methodist *Discipline*, which required slave-owning members to free slaves or to risk expulsion.[29] Further, southern Methodists attempted to shield their slave members from exposure to northern African-American Methodist denominations, which were originally founded to protest racial

---

[27]See, for example, Holland T. McTyeire, C. F. Sturgis, and A. Holmes, *Duties of Masters to Servants: Three Premium Essays* (Charleston: 1851).

[28]Between 1736 and 1737, John Wesley and his brother Charles served as Anglican missionaries in the new colony of Georgia under the auspices of the Society for the Propagation of the Gospel in Foreign Parts; for various reasons, their brief mission failed to stir English colonists, Indians, or Africans; see Wesley's *Thoughts on Slavery*, vol. 11 of *The Works of John Wesley*, ed. Thomas Jackson (Oxford: Clarendon Press, 1975–1983) 59–79. Wesley's treatise drew freely from an earlier work by French Quaker Anthony Benezet, *Some Historical Account of Guinea: Its Situation, Produce and the General Disposition of Its Inhabitants* (1771); see also Warren Thomas Smith, *John Wesley and Slavery* (Nashville: Abingdon Press, 1986).

[29]*Minutes of the Annual Conferences of the Methodist Episcopal Church, for the Years 1773–1828* (New York, 1840), I, 12. The 1780 conference condemned slavery as "contrary to the laws of God, man, and nature, and hurtful to society," but merely advised slave owners to manumit their slaves. The 1784 spring conference enacted even more stringent legislation, threatening to expel any member who bought or sold a slave; to suspend local preachers who refused to emancipate their slaves, while granting a year's amnesty to local preachers in Virginia; and to discontinue traveling preachers who similarly refused to free their slaves. While these stipulations were upheld later that year at the historic Christmas conference in Baltimore, American Methodism's anti-slavery stance would gradually weaken under the pressure of pro-slavery advocates in the South and North, culminating in denominational division in 1844; for an account and interpretation of Methodism's retreat from its early anti-slavery stance, see especially Donald G. Mathews, *Slavery and Methodism* (Princeton NJ: Princeton University Press, 1965); Smith, *In His Image, But...*, 36–47; C. C. Goen, *Broken Churches, Broken Nation: Denominational Schisms and the Coming of the War* (Macon GA: Mercer University Press, 1985).

discrimination in the Methodist Church.[30] Methodist slave owners and preachers indeed had good reason to conceal these radical aspects of their history in their catechisms and sermons. Had they not, the whole mission strategy could have been undermined, as was the case in 1822 when the Reverend Morris Brown and members of his AME church in Charleston, South Carolina, were implicated for their involvement in the Denmark Vesey slave conspiracy.[31]

SOUTHERN METHODISM'S MISSION TO SLAVES

Between 1784 and 1804, Methodists' views on slavery in both the North and South underwent a gradual transformation, shifting the emphasis from abolishing slavery to evangelizing slaves. In the South, where the majority of Methodists resided, Methodists joined other evangelical churches in the early nineteenth century in a concerted effort to evangelize the growing slave population. This mission was

---

[30]It is not clear whether colored Methodists were familiar with efforts by the AMEC to organize congregations in the slave-owning states prior to emancipation; the most notable congregation was established in Charleston but was closed in the wake of the 1821 Denmark Vesey slave conspiracy. It is clear, though, that during the Civil War colored Methodists encountered African Methodist missionaries and joined newly formed AME and AMEZ congregations in the South. In fact, the first two CME bishops, William H. Miles and Joseph Beebe, were ordained ministers in the AMEZ Church in Kentucky and North Carolina, respectively. On the spread of African Methodists in the South, see Daniel Alexander Payne, *History of the African Methodist Episcopal Church* (New York: Arno Press, 1969); David H. Bradley, *A History of the AME Zion Church, 1796–1968* (Nashville: Parthenon Press, 1956–1970); Clarence E. Walker, *A Rock in a Weary Land: The African Methodist Episcopal Church During the Civil War and Reconstruction* (Baton Rouge: Louisiana State University Press, 1982); Reginald F. Hilderbrand, *The Times Were Strange and Stirring* (Durham NC: Duke University Press, 1995).

[31]Morris Brown, a free African American born in Charleston, served as pastor to disaffected African-American Methodists in the city. His independent African Association comprised three congregations with several thousand members, mostly slaves. For studies of this conspiracy that emphasize religion as the critical component, see Gayraud S. Wilmore, *Black Religion and Black Radicalism: An Interpretation of the Religious History of Afro-American People*, 2d rev. ed. (Maryknoll NY: Orbis Books, 1983) 81–87; Vincent Harding, *There Is a River: The Black Struggle for Freedom in America* (New York: Harcourt Brace Jovanovich, 1981) 65–74; Creel, *"A Peculiar People,"* 150–60.

fueled by three crucial factors: slaves' response to the southern phase of the Second Great Awakening, or the Great Revival (1800–1805); southern churches' defensiveness in response to the mounting criticism of northern abolitionists; and the pervasive fear of slave conspiracies and rebellions. Together, these factors forced southern Presbyterians, Methodists, and Baptists to carefully refine their proslavery arguments and hone strategies to evangelize slaves.

Slaves responded enthusiastically to the fervent preaching of evangelical preachers during the Great Revival, which was ignited in June 1800 by Presbyterian sacramental revivals in Logan County, Kentucky, and spread like a brush fire throughout the South.[32] After initially joining Presbyterian and Baptist revivalists, southern Methodists gradually incorporated the camp meeting as an institutionalized feature of their conferences and missions, with the circuit rider as its most visible representative. Taking place outdoors, under the canopy of brush arbors or wooden sheds, these protracted services featured emotional, evangelical preaching, gospel singing, and the Lord's Supper. In 1833 the Reverend James Gwen in Nashville enthusiastically reported that "the work of the Lord has greatly increased this mission among colored people the last quarter. Our campmeeting for this state closed last Thursday, about a thousand colored people attended."[33] Gwen's observations suggest just how effective these highly charged religious services were in capturing the attention, if not the religious imaginations, of African Americans in the South.

Two notable features of the southern revivals were their interdenominational make-up (predominantly Presbyterian, Baptist,

---

[32]For the origins of these revivals, see especially John H. Boles, *The Great Revival: 1787-1805 The Origins of the Southern Evangelical Mind,* (Lexington: University of Kentucky Press, 1972); Dickson D. Bruce Jr., *And They All Sang Hallelujah: Plain-Folk Camp-Meeting Religion, 1800–1845* (Knoxville: University of Tennessee Press, 1974); Paul K. Conkin, *Cane Ridge: America's Pentecost* (Madison: University of Wisconsin Press, 1990). For information about African-American participation in the revival, see Raboteau, *Slave Religion,* 129–50.

[33]Quoted in W. P. Harrison, ed., *The Gospel among Slaves: A Short Account of Missionary Operations among the African Slaves of the Southern States* (Nashville: Publishing House of the ME Church, South, 1893) 187.

and Methodist) and their biracial composition.[34] In camp meetings across the South, African Americans and whites often exhibited similar responses to the fervent preaching, including dramatic conversion experiences and ecstatic behavior (for example, singing, crying, shouting, and dancing).[35] These shared responses to the revival resulted in a rather unexpected and ironic blessing: the fostering of a spiritual egalitarianism among all those sharing the new birth experience. For African-American converts, though, with their holistic worldview, the notion of spiritual egalitarianism had even more radical implications: it conferred on them a measure of social worth and implied equality in other areas of life—moral, social, and political.

THE FRUIT OF METHODIST REVIVALISM

Methodist involvement in the southern phase of the Second Great Awakening yielded a bountiful crop of African-American converts, especially in Maryland, Virginia, North Carolina, and South Carolina. There were several aspects of Methodism that proved especially attractive to African-American slaves and freed people. First, Methodism's early condemnation of slavery struck a responsive chord with slaves. Second, the emotional intensity of Methodist preaching and worship appealed to African-based spirituality and spoke in their vernacular.

---

[34]By the 1830s, however, the interdenominational character of southern revivalism would be severely challenged by denominational competition and schisms, conflicting church polities, and the routinization of revivals into denominationally sponsored camp meetings and weeklong revival services; see Boles, *The Great Revival*, 143–64.

[35]These shared experiences within the revivals, however, should not be interpreted as a sign of complete freedom and equality for African Americans. The seating of the meetings was often racially segregated, as was as the administration of the Lord's Supper. According to Dvorak, the most constitutive elements of southern religion were the sermon and the Lord's Supper; segregated seating and reception of the Lord's Supper "served as a means of social control in "a hierarchical and white-dominated society, and as constituting a 'racial etiquette' " (*An African-American Exodus*, 17).

Third, southern Methodism offered slaves a highly organized structure of conferences, circuits, revivals, and class meetings, and limited access to leadership as class leaders, exhorters, and local preachers. Few colored preachers in the South, however, became circuit riders prior to emancipation. The widespread fear of slave revolts in the wake of the 1822 Denmark Vesey conspiracy and the 1831 Nat Turner rebellion drastically limited the mobility of slave preachers. Historian Donald Mathews has noted, "Among all Evangelicals, Methodist circuit riders were the most aggressive in seeking out Africans, who were often more responsive to Methodist preaching than were whites. In considering their exotic charges, Methodist preachers revealed a sentimental but compelling sensitivity to the 'sons and daughters of oppression,' 'poor distressed Africans,' 'the poor Negroes,' and 'poor Africans.'"[36]

THE DEVELOPMENT OF PLANTATION MISSIONS

In 1829 William Capers, a convert from a wealthy planter family in Charleston, South Carolina, organized the first Methodist slave mission in the South Carolina Conference with the support of planter Charles Pinckney. The next year the Methodist Church inaugurated a system of plantation missions consisting of regular preaching, worship, and catechetical instruction by traveling missionaries. In 1840 Capers was appointed secretary of the southern department of the church's missionary work, expanding the missions from two in 1829 to sixty-eight in 1844 and including almost 22,000 slave members. Moreover, his popular *Catechism for the Use of Methodist Missions* served as both an apology for slavery and a manual for the oral instruction of slaves.[37]

---

[36]Donald G. Mathews, *Slavery in the Old South*, 66.

[37]The 1847 catechism was an expansion of Capers's earlier and shorter *Catechism for Little Children* (1843), which included lessons on salvation and duty, the Lord's Prayer, and three hymns; see also McTyeire, Sturgis, and Holmes, *Duties of Masters to Servants*; Mathews, "The Methodist Mission to the Slaves, 1829–1844," 615–31.

Continuing the pattern of Methodist catechisms written by John Wesley and Richard Watson, Capers included the Lord's Prayer, the Ten Commandments, twelve question-and-answer lessons, and an appendix of Scripture passages regarding slaves' duty to God and master. With the exception of Romans 4:2–3, which deals with the doctrine of justification by faith, these passages were selected more for the purpose of prescribing appropriate slave behavior rather than teaching doctrinal standards. For example, Capers included passages that stress obedience as a religious duty (Ephesians 5:22–26:4 and 1 Timothy 6:1–2), forbid sexual immorality (Matthew 5:27–28), condemn lying (Zechariah 5:3 and James 5:12), stress Sabbath observation (Numbers 15:32–36), and condemn drunkenness and stealing (1 Corinthians 5:9–10 and Revelation 21:7–8).[38]

Relying on a carefully crafted oral method to reach largely illiterate slave converts, Capers devised a simple question-and-answer format in which the teacher would first pose the question, state the answer, and then have the class repeat both question and answer: "Q. What is a servant's duty to his master and mistress? A: To serve them with a good will heartily and not with eye-service."[39]

While it is questionable how effective Capers' slave mission and catechisms were in molding a dutiful and converted slave population, they nonetheless had some measurable impact by increasing the slave membership in the Methodist Church. From 1846 to 1861 the MECS reported an increase of colored members from 118,904 to 209,836.[40] Moreover, slave missions exerted a powerful influence on colored Methodists' expanding religious and social consciousness, largely succeeding in the quest of uniting white and colored Methodists into a religious unity shaped by a southern, Protestant, evangelical ethos. At the core of this evangelical ethos was, first, an individual experience of salvation, often witnessed by an intense conversion experience and buttressed by an Arminian-Wesleyan theology of grace.

---

[38]*Catechism for the Use of Methodist Missions*, appendix.
[39]Ibid.
[40]Reported in Raboteau, *Slave Religion*, 176.

A second shared element was the authority of the Bible, which was regarded as an authoritative guide to faith and behavior. Although colored Methodists remained entrenched in the orality of African modes of communication, they were increasingly becoming a "people of one book," even if that book was a "talking book."

A third element of this shared evangelical ethos was the pursuit of the experience of Wesleyan sanctification ("scriptural holiness") as a subsequent experience of grace. In their 1885 report on the status and work of the church, CME bishops Miles, Holsey, and Lane issued this final exhortation: "Dear brethren, wake! stir yourself! and let us do all we can to maintain the dignity of the church and 'spread scriptural holiness over these lands.'"[41] The propagation of "scriptural holiness" was closely tied to the fourth element in the evangelical ethos: a commitment to evangelism—zealously sharing one's faith with one's immediate kin, neighbors, and even owners.

A fifth element of their evangelical worldview was its extreme spiritualizing of religious experience and social ethics, which had important social implications for an understanding of the church's relationship with the world. This distinction was underscored by C. H. Phillips in an 1887 address to the Grand Order of the Odd Fellows at Collins Chapel CME Church in Memphis. "Christianity is spiritual in its object," he stressed. "Its great purpose is to save souls, to scatter that religion taught by Christ in all the world. The work of societies is temporal."[42]

It is perhaps this last element—the spiritualizing of religious experience and social ethics—that distinguishes colored Methodists in the South from their African Methodist counterparts in the North. Both groups accepted the Wesleyan doctrine and experience of sanctification but applied it differently within their respective social contexts. Likewise, both groups were deeply committed to the ultimate goals of freedom and racial uplift but advocated different strategies for how these goals could be achieved, ranging from accommodation to electoral politics to separatism and emigration.

---

[41]*Christian Index*, 1 July 1885.
[42]"Sermon on Christian Unity," *Christian Index*, 19 March 1887.

Consequently, even with their subtle rejection of the most anti-egalitarian and dehumanizing aspects of Methodist missions and paternalism, colored Methodists seemed to have internalized much more of the southern evangelical ethos, social ethic, and paternalistic ideology than their northern counterparts. Like their white Methodist counterparts, colored Methodists emphasized personal holiness, sexual restraint, deference to hierarchical authority, and a strict dichotomy between the church and the world.

Given their attachment to this evangelical ethos and to their own quest for freedom, colored Methodists faced a peculiar dilemma at the end of the Civil War: should they reject the proslavery and paternalistic southern Methodist Church that had spurned and nurtured them? Or should they respond to the invitation to join the emancipationist churches of northern Methodists?

Their response to this dilemma was further compounded by the ambivalence of southern Methodists about retaining those colored members who chose to remain with the MECS. At the 1866 General Conference, the southern Methodists reported a colored membership of 78,742, a precipitous decline from the 207,766 reported in 1860.[43] In August 1865, MECS bishops published a "Pastoral Letter" staunchly defending the missionary enterprise to slaves but painfully conceding that an exodus of colored members was already underway. The bishops reminded a war-torn, demoralized church of its commitment to the spiritual welfare of the freed people:

> The interest of the colored population should engage your serious attention. Heretofore the colored people within your bonds have deserved and received a large share of your labors. We have expended our means and strength liberally and patiently for many years for their salvation and improvement.... It is grateful to our feelings to know that if the colored people do not remain under our pastoral care, their departure reflects no discredit upon our labors [on behalf

---

[43]Lakey, *The Rise of "Colored Methodism,"* 59; *Minutes of the Annual Conference, 1866* (MECS).

of their welfare]. Many of them will probably unite with the African M. E. Church, some with the Northern Methodists, while others, notwithstanding extraneous influences and unkind misrepresentations of our Church, will remain with us.[44]

Despite this open admission of the defection of colored members, the MECS was either reluctant to perceive the full implications of freedom for their colored members or unwilling to accommodate the changed status of its colored membership.[45] With their denominational survival at stake and a new generation of leadership at the helm, southern Methodists were divided about the best course of action to take with their colored remnant. An editorial in the Richmond *Episcopal Methodist* by George Williams and Holland McTyeire counseled political realism: "As respects religion, ecclesiastical independence is bound to follow the civil. They will leave us."[46] Bishop George Pierce and other moderates, however, advocated a more cautionary stance, that is, to patiently await the return of colored members. At no point, however, did any faction within the church seriously entertain the possibility of full ecclesiastical and social equality of colored Methodists in the reconstructed MECS. On the eve of the 1866 General Conference in New Orleans, James Evans of Columbus, Georgia, succinctly expressed

---

[44]*Journal of the General Conference of the Methodist Episcopal Church, South Held at New Orleans,* 1866, 18.

[45]Dvorak offers the following summary of how MECS paternalism affected the church's responses to "the exodus" of it's colored members:

Initially, at war's end, whites were not so much hostile as hurt—and confused to the point of paralysis. Thus contemporary accounts by whites may mask the story of the exodus partly because of antebellum self-perceptions still operative in their thinking. Whites still thought of themselves as the masters of society, even when they had no slaves. Slaves were their children. How could these creatures, when freed, initiate and carry on the monumental task of institutional building? Thus accounts of whites are skewed by mechanisms of apparent denial and projection (*An African-American Exodus,* 73–74).

[46]15 November 1865.

the consensus view on the implications of freedom for colored members: "Public opinion and the social relations of the two races in the South preclude the ideas of such equality in a common organization with the whites."[47] Consequently, by the time of the 1866 General Conference, southern Methodist leaders had concluded that a plan of separation was needed, one that would maintain the precarious balance between white paternalism and colored autonomy.

GENERAL CONFERENCE IN NEW ORLEANS, 1866

How to preserve this balance was a major issue confronting the 1866 General Conference. The conference addressed the issue by entertaining four reports from the Committee on the Religious Interest of the Colored People, chaired by Evans. The first report called for the establishment of day schools for colored people ,"under proper regulations and trustworthy teachers."[48] Conceding that the status of colored people had changed with emancipation, the report maintained that the "interests of the white and colored people are materially dependent upon the intelligence and virtue of this race, that we have had and must continue to have among us."[49]

It was with the second report, though, that the General Conference more openly and realistically addressed the future of its remaining colored remnant. The report called for specific actions: the authorization of separate colored pastoral charges and quarterly conferences under colored leadership and control; the licensing and full ordination of colored ministers; the formation of districts headed by colored presiding elders; and the organization of colored annual conferences by the College of Bishops. Granting that a minimum of two or more colored annual conferences could be organized, the committee further called for the organization of a "separate General Conference jurisdiction for themselves, if they desire, and the bishops deem it expedient."[50]

---

[47]*Southern Advocate*, 15 June 1866.
[48]*General Conference Minutes, 1866* (MECS).
[49]Ibid.
[50]Ibid.

The ensuing debate on the conference floor, however, reveals conference delegates' conflicting interpretations of the reports. For example, they disagreed on the issue of whether the organization of "separate pastoral charges" could take place without dividing the southern church and whether it would result in the formation of a new colored denomination.[51] Clearly at issue was the prospect of either supporting self-separating groups of colored members or reabsorbing them on the basis of social and ecclesiastical equality.

The committee's final two reports addressed requests by the AMEC for church property reserved for colored members. The committee flatly rejected the request, partly because it contradicted the thrust of the previous report on colored separation and partly because of the MECS's apprehensions about the political motives of the AMEC. Nonetheless, report three was modified to allow transfer of church property to the AME Church under certain conditions (for example, when whole congregations left the MECS). Underpinning the debate over church property was southern Methodism's theological understanding of the spiritual nature of the church,[52] which was now being reiterated to limit colored Methodist

---

[51]For a full discussion of the debate, see William B. Gravely, "The Social, Political and Religious Implications of the Formation of the Colored Methodist Episcopal Church (1870)" *Methodist History* 18 (October 1979–July 1980): 3–25.

[52]This understanding of the church was developed more formally by Presbyterian theologians like James H. Thornwell (1812–1862) but was a widely accepted doctrine of southern evangelicals across denominations. Basically, the doctrine held that the church is limited by the authority of Scripture in identifying various social and political causes with the will of God. For example, in an 1861 address before the General Assembly of the Presbyterian Church in the Confederate States of America, Thornwell declared, "We have no right, as a Church, to enjoin it as a duty, or to condemn it as a sin.... The social, civil, political problems connected with this great subject transcend our sphere, as God has not entrusted to his Church the organization of society, the construction of Government, not the allotment of individuals to their various stations" (quoted in Goen, *Broken Churches, Broken Nation*, 165). As the Civil War became more imminent, southern evangelicals experienced more difficulty in consistently applying this doctrine to slavery and the war. Thornwell himself did not support the idea of secession until 1860, when he became a vigorous supporter of the Confederate cause until his death in 1862.

participation in Reconstruction politics—a fateful decision that could damage the credibility of the new church.

THE SOCIAL WORLD OF COLORED METHODISM

On 15 December 1870, forty-six colored Methodist delegates, representing eight annual conferences in former Confederate and border states, convened in Jackson, Tennessee, to organize a new Methodist denomination and the first independent African-American denomination in the South.[53] They were joined by a committee representing the MECS, which included Senior Bishop Robert Paine; Bishop Holland McTyeire; and three white elders, Alex L. P. Green of Nashville, Samuel Watson of Memphis, and Thomas Taylor of Jackson. These representatives came to Jackson to assist in the birthing of a new denomination for colored members, to consecrate its first bishops, and to ensure its continuity with MECS doctrine and polity. In turning over the supervision of the conference to the newly elected colored bishops, William Miles and Richard Vanderhorst, Bishop Paine reminded them of their cordial relations and filial ties: "There is no strife between us—let there never be any. While our hearts are warm with love to God and man, we shall feel an interest in your welfare. We have labored for you when there were few who cared for your souls. Our missionaries are buried on the rice, and cotton, and sugar plantations, who went preaching the gospel to your fathers and to you while slaves."[54]

The emphasis on continuity with Methodist theology and polity was clearly evident in the deliberations and accomplishments of the conference: an independent colored denomination with its own distinct nomenclature, revised Methodist *Discipline*, church polity, and episcopal leadership. What is striking is neither the novelty nor

---

[53]The eight annual conferences were comprised of six former Confederate states and one border state: Memphis Conference (1867); Kentucky Conference (1868); Mississippi Conference (1869); Alabama Conference (1869); Georgia Conference (1869); Arkansas Conference (1870); East Texas Conference (1870); South Carolina Conference (1870).

[54]*Nashville Christian Advocate*, 7 January 1871.

the radicalism of their mutual achievements, especially given the paternalistic presence and input of MECS representatives, but colored Methodists' adoption of the southern Methodist version of the spirituality of the church precisely at the apex of the Radical Reconstruction. When colored Methodists agreed to "let our churches be plain and decent, and with free seats, as far as practical; "they shall in no wise be used for political purposes,"[55] they came close to committing themselves to a policy of political neutrality at precisely the time other African-American churches were filling the void of political leadership among African Americans in the South.[56]

Was this policy merely an expedient concession by colored Methodists to MECS paternalism to guarantee to them the transfer of church property promised at the 1870 MECS General Conference in Memphis? Did they somehow envision this policy as a practical, interim strategy until a more progressive one could be effected? Or did they honestly believe that this policy was both theologically sound and politically appropriate for the times? Holsey apparently agreed with the latter option when he wrote in 1891, "Social religious equality, as well as any other kind of social equality, was utterly impracticable and undesirable, and coveted by neither class of persons composing a common churchship.... Christianity is what he (the

---

[55]*General Conference Minutes, 1870* (MECS).

[56]Lucius Holsey argued that in an effort to maintain a "pure and simple" version of Christianity, colored Methodists "always stood aloof from politics, not as individuals, but as officials representing an official organization for a certain and specific purpose" (quoted in Lakey, *The Rise of "Colored Methodism,"* 97). Two notable exceptions to this policy were L. J. [Little John] Scurlock of Memphis and I. H. Anderson of Georgia, both delegates at the 1870 General Conference. Scurlock was originally elected book agent and assistant editor of the *Christian Index* but resigned these positions in 1873 to serve as a member of the Mississippi state legislature. Prior to the 1870 conference, Anderson, the chair of the Committee on Church Organization, had been a member of the Georgia Constitutional Convention that rewrote the state constitution; see Lakey, *The History of the CME Church*, 198. In his directory of African-American lawmakers during Reconstruction, Eric Foner identifies Anderson as an AME minister and leading political organizer in the Macon area and does not specify Scurlock's denominational affiliation. He does note that Scurlock was killed by the Klan in 1872, which contradicts Lakey's biographical data (*Freedom's Lawmakers* [New York: Oxford University Press, 1993] 7, 191).

Negro) needs, pure and simple."[57] While no definitive answers can be given to these questions, an analysis of the religious and political views of the first generation of colored Methodists suggests that their paternalistic ties with southern Methodists and their social location as newly freed people helped to stifle their political activism.[58]

By 1870, when colored Methodist delegates had gathered in December 1870 to organize the CME Church, the Radical Reconstruction of the South was well underway. By December 1870, Congress had enacted three constitutional amendments: the thirteenth abolished slavery (1865); the fourteenth declared African Americans as U.S. citizens and accorded them equal protection under the law; and the fifteenth guaranteed African-American males the right to vote. By December 1870, all of the former Confederate states had been readmitted to the Union on the basis of their compliance to a series of Congressional Reconstruction Acts, which included the abolition of slavery and the enfranchisement of African-American males by constitutional state conventions. As a result of these national, state, and local initiatives, African-American males across the South, and across the nation, were politically enfranchised and empowered.[59]

---

[57]Quoted in Lakey, *The Rise of "Colored Methodism,"* 91–92. Bishop Charles Henry Phillips, who wrote the first official history of the CMEC, confirmed Holsey's description of the CMEC's apolitical stance (*From the Farm to the Bishopric: An Autobiography* [Nashville: Parthenon Press, 1932] 171).

[58]This is not to infer that colored Methodists were either devoid of a social consciousness or uninvolved in political activities altogether; denominational policy circumscribed partisan political activity involving clergy and church property but not necessarily that of individual members. The degree to which this distinction was blurred by colored Methodists in local communities across the South is difficult to substantiate, but given the exigencies of the time, it is plausible that lay members also adhered to this distinction.

[59]For a general treatment of the "Radical Reconstruction," see John Hope Franklin, *Reconstruction after the Civil War,* 2d ed. (Chicago: University of Chicago Press, 1994); Eric Foner, *Reconstruction: America's Unfinished Revolution* (New York: Harper & Row, 1988); Leon F. Litwack, *Been in the Storm So Long: The Aftermath of Slavery* (New York: Vintage Books, 1980); for information on African-American leaders during Reconstruction, see Howard N. Rabinowitz, ed., *Southern Black Leaders of the Reconstruction Era* (Urbana: University of Illinois Press, 1982) and Foner, *Freedom's Lawmakers.*

Historian Eric Foner has described African-American participation in Reconstruction politics as "the most radical development of the Reconstruction years, a massive experiment in interracial democracy without precedent in the history of this or any other country that abolished slavery in the nineteenth century."[60] But freedom had different shades of meanings for African-American freed people; not all freed people defined emancipation in political terms. While political empowerment through franchise and representation were highly valued by the masses of freed people, they also desired land ownership, economic improvement, and education.[61]

Colored Methodists were no exception, the overwhelming majority of whom were mostly illiterate, landless farm workers with few tangible assets. Their political aspirations were circumscribed by their social location in the New South as free laborers and by their ties to paternalistic structures intent on keeping them subservient and powerless. For example, of the early CME leaders during the church's formative years—William Miles, Richard Vanderhorst, Joseph Beebe, Lucius Holsey, and Isaac Lane—all five were born slaves and had been converted and called to preach under the auspices of the southern Methodist Church; all were self-educated and, except for Miles's brief residence in Ohio, chose to remain in the South. As historian Reginald Hildebrand notes:

> They had not been runaways or harborers. They did not flee to Union lines or wear the Union uniform. They did not become agents of the Freedmen's Bureau, delegates to state constitutional conventions, or members of state legislatures. None of them were the scions of prominent black families. Save for their being preachers, they had none of the

---

[60] Foner, *Reconstruction*, xxv.

[61] Historian August Meier rightly warns against the tendency to characterize the Reconstruction thinking of the African-American leaders or the masses as devoted almost entirely to civil rights and political activity; see Meier's *Negro Thought in America, 1800–1915* (Ann Arbor: University of Michigan Press, 1963).

characteristics generally associated with black leadership during Reconstruction.[62]

While their deep sense of place in the South certainly circumscribed their social and political visions of freedom, it also contributed to an ecumenical vision that ironically included white southern Methodists in the uplift of African Americans in the South, even if it meant racial separation and social inequality.[63] Thus, willing to accommodate to the "racial etiquette" of the South, colored Methodists and white Methodists channeled their collective resources into educating colored ministers and members, spreading the gospel, and establishing new congregations. In 1873 the CME Church launched its inaugural Missionary Board to focus on church expansion. And despite several aborted attempts to establish schools in Louisville, Kentucky, and Sardis, Mississippi, the church successfully operated several schools in the 1880s: CME High School in Jackson, Tennessee (1883); Paine Institute in Augusta, Georgia (1883); Haygood Seminary in Washington, Arkansas (ca. 1887); and Beebe Institute in New Orleans.[64]

It was the MECS's mission to educate colored ministers and people that bore the most fruit from this collaboration, and Paine Institute (later Paine College) represents the apotheosis of this collaboration. With the collapse of political reconstruction and the return of white hegemony in the 1870s, southern Methodists were more disposed to support educational efforts for African Americans. In an 1869 editorial in the *Nashville Christian Advocate*, Bishop Holsey appealed to white Methodists to support Paine Institute as the continuation of the work of slave missions. He later described the role of colored Methodists in this mission as threefold: "servants, citizens

---

[62]Hilderbrand, *The Times Were Strange and Stirring*, 20.

[63]Compare this view to the accommodationist philosophy articulated by Booker T. Washington in his 1895 "Address Delivered at the Opening of the Cotton States' Exposition in Atlanta, Georgia," reprinted in *The Negro Orators and Their Orations*, ed. Carter G. Woodson (New York: Russell and Russell, 1925) 580–83.

[64]For the development of early CME schools, see Lakey, *The History of the CME Church*, 338–39.

and Church-children." "With this three-fold cable," he explained, "we are strongly bound together and united in a manner that cannot be analyzed or fully understood by a stranger.... It seems natural that we should follow you, and make ourselves a duplicate of you as far as we are able."[65]

The decision of colored Methodists to eschew political activism in the New South had some important religious and social implications in the late nineteenth and early twentieth centuries. First, their decision to focus on educational uplift rather than politics limited their critique of racist ideology and of racial segregation within the MECS and southern society at large. Moreover, by seeking to merely duplicate the educational models of the MECS, as Holsey implored, colored Methodists were perpetuating a system still predicated on racial inferiority and segregation. Second, colored Methodist accommodationism also limited the church's involvement in either local and regional politics or social movements for racial justice. Third, colored Methodist accommodationism aggravated the already strained ecumenical ties with other African-American Methodist denominations and congregations. Colored Methodists' rejection of overtures by the AMEZ Church for organic union in 1872 fanned the flames of interdenominational competition and conflict over church property and members.

Nonetheless, there were some hopeful portents of a broader ecumenical vision that were emerging as African-American Methodists engaged each other in pan-Methodist conferences outside of the South. Beginning in 1878, the CME Church dispatched fraternal delegates to other Methodist general conferences of black and white denominations. In 1881 Bishop Holsey represented the church at the Ecumenical Conference in London, and a CME delegation attended the 1884 Centennial of American Methodism at Lovely Lane Church in Baltimore, Maryland.

---

[65]Quoted in Glenn T. Eskew, "Black Elitism and the Failure of Paternalism in Postbellum Georgia: The Case of Bishop Lucius Henry Holsey," *Journal of Southern History* 58/4 (November 1992): 469.

These wider ecumenical contacts with other Methodists, nationally and internationally, helped to heighten CME racial and social consciousness. With the collapse of the Radical Reconstruction in the South, colored Methodists began to reassess their stances on religion and politics. Though they never questioned their firm commitment to the racial uplift of their people, as their critics accused, neither political accommodation nor deference to the MECS had accomplished the desired goals of racial uplift and interracial harmony. In fact, these goals had become virtually irreconcilable—and with dire consequences, as "Veritas," a pseudonymous contributor to the *Christian Index*, pointed out in the following jeremiad:

> Can two distinct races live in this country, and be forever separate, each pursuing its own line of thought, and action, and never encroach each other? Can the South by its virtual disfranchisement of thousands of colored voters, continue to obtain additional power in the councils of the nation, without a violent protest from the liberty-loving, law-abiding sections of the country?... The Colored man owes the American people nothing; to speak of a debt of gratitude, because our ancestors were rescued from the barbarism of Africa, is an insult to the manhood of the colored man. We had better borne the ills of savage life than to have been taught the duties and rights of civilized manhood, and then be denied the privilege of their enjoyment.[66]

This more strident tone was uncharacteristic of the accommodating rhetoric of first-generation colored Methodists. Rather, it was more suggestive of a rising generation of "New Negroes" in the South. By 1896 even Bishop Holsey's social views shifted from racial accommodationism to separatism because of his disenchantment with "bourbon Democracy," his opposition to the convict lease system,

---

[66]"The Negro Problem in Church and State," *Christian Index*, 3 December 1887.

and his support of prohibition.[67] Racial prejudice in the South, lamented Holsey, made it "impossible for the two separate and distinct races to live together in the same territory in harmonious relations, each demanding equal political rights and equal citizenship."[68] Holsey's separatist stance, however, remained a minority viewpoint among colored Methodists and did not signal a significant shift in colored Methodist social consciousness or activism.

---

[67]Glenn T. Eskew, "Black Elitism and the Failure of Paternalism in Postbellum Georgia," 658.

[68]Quoted in ibid., 658.

CHAPTER 3

The "Paine College Ideal": CME Responses to Racial Injustice, 1900–1954

Given the dire prognosis announced at its birth by both southern and northern Methodists, the growth of the CME Church in the first half of the twentieth century was remarkable. In 1906 the CME Church reported a membership of 172,996 in twenty-four states, the majority still concentrated in the South. By 1945 the church, aided by the Great Migration of African Africans during the two world wars and the Depression, would expand to eighteen states.[1] Through the dogged determination and visionary foresight of first-generation leaders like William Miles, Isaac Lane, and Lucius Holsey, the young church managed to thrive in an environment mined with racial and denomi-

---

[1] U.S. Department of Commerce, Bureau of the Census, *Religious Bodies: 1906, Part II, Separate Denominations: History, Description, and Statistics* (Washington, DC: Government Printing Office, 1910) 479–84. The 1906 census data also reported the following increases from the 1890 report: 622 organizations, 43,613 communicants, and $1.3 million in the value of church property (480). Moreover, prior to the Great Migration, the church slowly began to grow beyond the bounds of the eight southern states included at the founding 1870 conference; new churches had been added in Pennsylvania, Maryland, the District of Columbia, Ohio, Indiana, Illinois, Missouri, Kansas, Oklahoma, New Mexico, and Arizona; see also Othal H. Lakey, *The History of the CME Church* (Memphis: CME Publishing House, 1985) 345–50; Milton C. Sernett, *Bound for the Promised Land: African-American Religion and the Great Migration* (Durham NC: Duke University Press, 1997) appendix, 252.

national tensions. The second generation of colored Methodists would confront these tensions with no less determination and optimism than their predecessors.

This chapter examines how the CME Church responded to the problem of racial injustice during the Jim Crow era in their public discourse, mission programs, and ecumenical relations. Although CME leaders often expressed support for Booker T. Washington's accommodationist philosophy and strategies for racial progress, they developed their own distinctive approach as colored Methodists. Best embodied in the "Paine College Ideal," this approach included an emphasis on educational uplift, ecumenism, and Civil Rights activism, and was most visibly represented in the life and ministry of Channing Tobias. As CMEs increasingly weaned themselves from the paternalism of the MECS, they formed new alliances with ecumenical bodies like the Fraternal Council of Negro Churches and pursued organic merger with other African-American Methodist bodies.

Charles Phillips and Mattie Coleman in many ways were representative of this rising generation of CME leaders in the early twentieth century. Both were born during the final years of slavery in the Deep South and benefited from the fruitful labors of southern and northern Methodists to educate freed people. Phillips, the first college-educated minister in the CME Church, graduated from Central Tennessee College (1880) and Meharry Medical College (1882), schools founded by the MEC in Nashville, Tennessee. Coleman, a native of Clarksville, Tennessee, also graduated from Central Tennessee College and Meharry Medical College (1906). These two colored doctors initially took divergent paths, only to converge again in the interests of the CME Church. Both were instrumental in enlarging their denomination's vision beyond the geographical scope of the South and the restrictive, accommodationist policies of first-generation colored Methodists.[2]

---

[2]Unlike the majority of CME Churches in the first three decades of the century, Phillips and Coleman were members of a smaller, elite class of middle-class professionals that historian Willard B. Gatewood has labeled "aristocrats of color" (*Aristocrats of Color: The Black Elite, 1880–1920* [Bloomington: Indiana University Press, 1990]). The major distinction between Phillips and Coleman from

Charles Phillips had a long and varied career in the CME Church as a teacher, pastor, editor, church historian, and bishop, beginning in 1878 when he was licensed to preach in Barnesville, Georgia. After a rather disappointing semester at Atlanta University, Phillips transferred to Central Tennessee College with a ten-dollar scholarship from a white benefactor from New York whose name Phillips had found in a newspaper.[3] While matriculating in Nashville, Phillips honed his ministerial skills, serving a circuit of churches in nearby Gallatin. After completing medical college, he returned to Central Tennessee College for his Master of Arts and Doctor of Divinity degrees. Phillips' formative years at MEC schools in Nashville prepared him for later ecumenical dialogue and relations with other African-American Methodists. Among these fellow Methodists was his college roommate, the Reverend I. B. Scott, who later served as editor of the *Southwestern Christian Advocate* and the first elected missionary bishop to Africa in the MEC (1904).[4]

In the summer of 1882, Phillips taught school and practiced medicine in Tullahoma, Tennessee, but he never regarded medicine as his primary vocation. After a brief stint in the public school system in Clarksville, Tennessee, in 1882, Phillips was appointed principal of Jackson High School, a colored Methodist school organized in Union City, Tennessee.

Phillips' career as an educator ended when he was directed by Bishop Miles to devote full time to itinerant ministry. Recognizing Phillips' potential for leadership in the church, the venerable senior bishop appointed the twenty-seven-year-old Phillips to Collins Chapel CME Church in Memphis, the largest appointment in Tennessee. This appointment strategically placed Phillips within the vanguard of progressive, new leadership within the CME Church and the wider African-American community in the South.

---

the majority of the "black elite" in this study is their affiliation with the southern, rural-based, majority working-class constituency of the CME Church.

[3]Charles H. Phillips, *From the Farm to the Bishopric: An Autobiography* (Nashville: Parthenon Press, 1932) 45.

[4]Ibid., 57.

But this rising vanguard of African-American leadership in the CME Church was not solely restricted to male leaders like Phillips. The case of Mattie Coleman demonstrates that colored Methodist women, like their female counterparts in other African-American denominations, played a major role in mobilizing and organizing African-American communities for collective action in the South. Conspicuously silent and invisible in the early history of the CME Church, except as dutiful mothers, wives, and daughters, colored Methodist women's activism at local and regional levels helped to transform CME social consciousness in the twentieth century.[5] In 1918, when the CME General Conference voted unanimously to permit women to organize a "Woman's Connectional Council," colored Methodist women culminated almost fifty years of struggle to organize their own connectional organization. Led by professional, middle-class women like Mattie Coleman and Helena Cobb, an educator from Georgia, these women sought to carve a wider sphere of activity for women in church and society.[6] What the bishops regarded in their 1918 episcopal address as an "open door and vaster opportunities for the exercise of [women's] varied gifts and talents," chiefly in raising money for church missions, CME women saw a stepping stone toward equal rights as members and fuller inclusion into the church's ministry (i.e., ordination as ministers).[7]

In September of that year, forty-one women delegates met at Capers Memorial Church in Nashville for their organizational

---

[5]Much of the early history of women in the CME Church remains undocumented in the official records and histories of the denomination. One of the primary reasons for this omission, says Lakey, "is [that] women were denied leadership and had no official role to play. They were members of the church, sat on the 'women's' side of the church...sang, prayed, shouted, and raised money" (*The History of the CME Church*, 270).

[6]For a fuller treatment of the organization of the Woman's Missionary Society of the CME Church, see L. D. McAfee, *History of the Women's Missionary Society* (Jackson TN: Publishing House of the CME Church, 1934); Lakey, *The History of the CME Church*, 303–305; Othal H. Lakey and Betty Beene Stephens, *God in My Mama's House: The Women's Movement in the CME Church* (Memphis: CME Publishing House, 1994).

[7]Quoted in Bishop Charles Henry Phillips, *History of the Colored Methodist Episcopal Church* (Jackson TN: Publishing House of the CME Church, 1898) 554.

meeting, choosing Dr. Mattie Coleman as their president. A medical examiner who was married to a CME pastor in Clarksville, Coleman rehearsed the long struggle leading to this moment and heralded it as the onset of the "Age of Women."[8] At the 1924 General Conference, Coleman would lead a delegation to petition for full voting rights for women in the church. After the women marched, sang, and spoke, the conference voted 231 to 27 for women's suffrage.[9]

CMEs AND THE "RACIAL ETIQUETTE" OF JIM CROW

At the same time colored Methodist women were discovering their voice and sphere within the CME Church, more malignant forces outside the church were threatening the lives and well-being of all African Americans. The elaborate construction, codification, and enforcement of a system of racial segregation—known as Jim Crow—served notice to colored Methodists that their triple identity as colored, Methodist, and American would not spare them from the day-to-day indignities and horrors of living under this oppressive system. Accustomed to living in the house of bondage as slaves and under the twilight of freedom as freed people, how would colored Methodists adjust now to a social system designed to ensure their total subordination? In other words, how would a new generation of colored Methodists adjust to what sociologist and CME minister Bertram

---

[8]See McAfee, *History of the Women's Missionary Society.* Ironically, none of the CME bishops were present at the meeting, although all the bishops, general officers, and presiding elders were invited. Furthermore, the General Conference stipulated that one of the bishops serve as "patriarch" to the new organization, leading Lakey and Stephens to speculate that the bishops did not overwhelmingly endorse the meeting; Lakey and Stephens, *God in My Mama's House,* 137–38. In addition to the bishops' lukewarm support, the effectiveness of the society was hampered by confusion over its relation to the church's General Mission Board and the MECS Woman's Missionary Council.

[9]The women also received strong, unambiguous support from the bishops in their episcopal address, which included a subsection, titled "Liberate the Women of the [CME] Church," appealing to the enfranchisement of American women in 1920 as a basis for granting equal rights to women in the CME Church; *Journal of the General Conference, 1926,* 33; Lakey and Stephens, *God in My Mama's House,* 142; Lakey, *The History of the CME Church,* 417–18.

Doyle called the "etiquette of race relations" in the South.[10] Would they return to the safer forms of social accommodation and political neutrality of the Reconstruction era? Or would they risk loss of status, property, and life to challenge an oppressive system? Or would they affect a compromise solution that would allow them to maintain some semblance of human dignity while publicly capitulating to the Jim Crow system? And, if so, at what cost would they compromise?

The option of social and political accommodation adopted in the church's earliest years had proven a safe but controversial strategy during the turbulent transition from Reconstruction to the Jim Crow era. Aside from the stinging approbations of northern critics, not many CME churches had been burned; relatively few CME members had been lynched for their church affiliation, and hardly any CME ministers had been driven from their homes for political activity.[11] Furthermore, these strategies received a new hearing in the 1890s with the ascendancy of Booker T. Washington to national prominence as the widely acclaimed leader of African Americans in the South. Washington's epoch-making 1895 Atlanta Exposition address at the Cotton States and International Exposition propelled Washington, the founder and principal of Tuskegee Institute in Alabama, into the national limelight for his promotion of African-American economic development, industrial education, and social

---

[10]Bertram Doyle defines "racial etiquette" as "the forms required by custom and tradition to be observed in contacts and relations of the two races during…the ceremonial side of race relations; the behavior that is expected and accepted when white and colored persons meet or associate" (*The Etiquette of Race Relations: A Study in Social Control* [New York: Schocken Books, 1971] 11). As a form of social control, the purpose of this etiquette was threefold: (1) to prescribe correct behavior in the maintenance of African-American subordination, (2) to minimize friction between the races by prescribing certain patterns of behavior, and (3) to clearly assert white superiority and African-American inferiority. Doyle, a southerner from the black belt in Alabama, earned a PhD in sociology at the University of Chicago, where he studied race theory with Robert E. Park. In 1950, he was elected a CME bishop after teaching at several historically black colleges in the South.

[11]This claim is based on a survey of denominational literature during the Jim Crow era, which reveals that while CME churches and leaders were not specifically targeted for racial violence and reprisals per se, they were acutely conscious of the pervasive and often random nature of these attacks on African Americans.

accommodation, at the expense of political and social equality with white southerners.[12]

Acknowledging his role as a spokesman for the race, Washington informed his largely white audience of his desire to "convey...the sentiment of the masses of my race."[13] Among other things this sentiment included a veiled apology for African-American participation in the failed Reconstruction experiment, with African Americans mostly to blame, according to Washington: "Ignorant and inexperienced, it is not strange that in the first years of our new life we began at the top instead of the bottom; that a seat in Congress or the state legislature was more sought than real estate or industrial skill; that political convention or stump speaking had more attraction than starting a dairy farm or truck garden."[14] It was at the bottom of the economic ladder of the New South that African Americans needed to "cast down [their] buckets" in "agriculture, mechanics, in commerce, in domestic service, and in the professions."[15] Using the same metaphor, Washington implored southern business leaders to "cast down your buckets" among the "eight million Negroes...who have, without strikes and labor wars, tilled your fields, cleared your forests, built your railroads and cities...and helped make possible this magnificent representation of the progress of the South."[16]

---

[12]On the role of Booker T. Washington, see especially Booker T. Washington with W. E. B. Du Bois, *The Negro in the South: His Economic Progress in Relation to His Moral and Religious Development* (Philadelphia, 1903);; Louis R. Harlan, *Booker T. Washington: The Making of a Black Leader, 1856–1901* (New York: Oxford University Press, 1972) and *Booker T. Washington: The Wizard of Tuskegee* (New York: Oxford University Press, 1983); August Meier, *Negro Thought in America, 1880–1915* (Ann Arbor: University of Michigan Press, 1963); Raymond W. Smock, ed., *Booker T. Washington in Perspective* (Jackson: University Press of Mississippi, 1988); John Hope Franklin and Alfred A. Moss, Jr., *From Slavery to Freedom*, 7th ed. (New York: McGraw-Hill, 1994) 270–77; Emma Lou Thornbrough, comp., *Booker T. Washington* (Englewood Cliffs NJ: Prentice-Hall, 1969).

[13]Booker T. Washington, "Atlanta Exposition Speech," in *Lift Every Voice: African-American Oratory, 1787–1900*, ed. Philip S. Foner and Robert James Branham (Tuscaloosa: University of Alabama Press, 1998) 802.

[14]Ibid., 802–803.

[15]Ibid., 803.

[16]Ibid.

It was Washington's sentiments on mutual accord between the races through social and political accommodation that struck a responsive chord with colored Methodist leaders, vindicating a social philosophy and "racial etiquette" they had practiced for over a quarter of a century. When Washington pronounced that "[i]n all things that are purely social we can be as separate as the fingers, yet one as the hand in all things essential to mutual progress,"[17] he had aptly described the "racial etiquette" that already existed between the CME Church and the MECS. Like Washington, colored Methodists stressed the close familial bonds between the races, which enabled them to understand and relate to one another. Moreover, in his vehement opposition to emigration from the South as a viable protest strategy, Washington appealed to colored Methodists' sense of place in the South. While other regions were targeted as mission fields for church expansion, most CME leaders, with the notable exception of Bishop Holsey, neither advocated nor supported proposals for emigration.[18]

As the twentieth century progressed—with racial segregation becoming more entrenched and racial violence escalating throughout

---

[17]Ibid., 804.

[18]In a speech delivered on 18 August 1899, Lucius Holsey voiced his mounting frustration with race relations in the South and outlined a plan for racial separatism, identifying Oklahoma and New Mexico as possible sites for an African-American state; "Will It Be Possible for the Negro to Attain, in this Country, Unto the American Type of Civilization?" in *Twentieth-Century Negro Literature*, ed. D. W. Culp (Miami: Mnemosyne Publishing Co., 1969). Holsey's separatist ideology was consistent with other nineteenth-century black nationalists, including fellow Georgian and AME bishop Henry McNeal Turner; see Glenn T. Eskew, "Black Elitism and the Failure of Paternalism in Postbellum Georgia: The Case of Bishop Lucius Henry Holsey," *Journal of Southern History* 58/4 (November 1992): 663. For interpretations of black nationalism, see Wilson J. Moses, *The Golden Age of Black Nationalism*; 1850-1925. *Classical Black Nationalism, 1850–1925* (New York: Oxford University Press, 1988) and *Classical Black Nationalism: From the American Revolution to Marcus Garvey* (New York: New York University Press, 1996); Sterling Stuckey, ed., *The Ideological Origins of Black Nationalism* (Boston: Beacon Press, 1976); E. U. Essien-Udom, *Black Nationalism: A Search for an Identity in America* (Chicago: University of Chicago Press, 1972); Floyd Miller, *The Search for a Black Nationalism: Black Colonization and Emigration, 1787–1863* (Urbana: University of Illinois Press, 1975).

the South—Holsey's advocacy of emigration and racial separatism provided an alternative strategy to colored Methodist accommodationism. Already housed in segregated congregations, uprooting to another region appeared to be a safer alternative to political agitation or self-defense. Furthermore, CMEs, like other former slaves, had a precedent for tactfully asserting their autonomy and protecting their well-being against the abuses of southern white paternalism. Still, as thousands of their southern neighbors would increasingly join a procession of African-American migrants out of the South, protesting with their feet, the overwhelming majority of colored Methodists remained solidly rooted in the South.[19]

Ruling out political agitation and emigrationism, CMEs now devised their own distinctive way of effecting change in the Jim Crow South, a middle way that allowed them to affirm their sense of place in the South, their unique history as colored Methodists, and their inalienable rights as free citizens of the United States. With these moorings firmly planted, CMEs responded to Jim Crow racism in the first half of the twentieth century with an interrelated, three-pronged approach: educational uplift, ecumenism, and Civil Rights activism. This three-fold approach marked a progressive yet precarious step forward for a church that was weaned on the "racial etiquette" of the New South.

EDUCATIONAL UPLIFT AND THE "PAINE COLLEGE IDEAL"

From its inception in 1870, the CME Church has deemed education as a high priority. Having been denied access to formal education, the first generation of colored Methodists flocked to make-shift classrooms across the South to learn the "three Rs"—reading, writing, and arithmetic. By the first decade of the twentieth century, several

---

[19]On African-American sense of place in the South, see Jimmie Lewis Franklin, "Black Southerners, Shared Experience, and Place: A Reflection," *Journal of Southern History* 60/1 (February 1994): 3–18. Franklin discusses the attachment to the land, agrarian values, and material culture as shared experiences between African-American and white southerners, to which I would add the shared religious experience of evangelical Protestantism.

of the primary and secondary schools established by the CMEC were converted to normal schools, colleges, and seminaries, including Lane College in Jackson, Tennessee; Paine Institute in Augusta, Georgia; Haygood Seminary in Washington, Arkansas; Mississippi Theological and Industrial College in Holly Springs, Mississippi; and Miles College in Booker City, Alabama. Operating with low budgets and sparse resources, these schools struggled to survived in the Jim Crow era, when funding for African-American schools was not a priority. That the CME Church was able to operate a disproportionate number of colleges, compared to other African-American denominations, was in part a measure of its fervent commitment to education and also a testament to the continuing support it received from the MECS.

In a 1923 report on cooperation between the CME Church and the MECS,[20] W. A. Bell, a CME educator and layman, published the following summary of financial appropriations to CME schools from various MECS boards and departments from 1918 to 1932:

Contributions to Paine College	$1,252,644.00
Contributions to Lane College	$132,000.95
Contributions to other CME schools	$414,587.38[21]

The sizable amount of aid channeled to Paine underscored the place of this institution in the MECS's ongoing mission to and relation with their former colored charges. But the initiative for such a school began in 1882 when the CMEC authorized Bishop Holsey to attend the MECS General Conference to request assistance for building schools for colored teachers and preachers. The conference responded by appointing the Reverend James Evans, along with three white trustees, to work with a committee of CMEs, consisting of Holsey, J. S. Harper, and R. A. Maxey. Together they chartered Paine Institute in Augusta, named after MECS senior bishop Robert Paine. The

---

[20]W. A. Bell, ed., *Missions and Cooperation of the Methodist Episcopal Church, South with the Colored Methodist Episcopal Church* (Nashville: Board of Missions, MECS, 1923).

[21]Ibid., 91–92.

school officially opened in October 1883 with Dr. Morgan Calloway, former vice-president of Emory College in Atlanta, as the school's first president. Enrolling only five pupils in the first class, the institute initially consisted of a grammar school and a normal department, with a college or "higher normal" department being added in 1892. The entire administration and staff were white, but by the next decade the faculty and trustee board became more interracial.[22] With the financial and administrative support tightly controlled by paternalistic MECS officials, the racial etiquette of the New South was perpetuated to a new generation of colored Methodists.

The "Paine College Ideal," advocated by Bishops Pierce and Holsey for colored education in the South, was viewed by some critics as merely an "extension of the plantation mission ideology of paternalism," writes historian Glenn Askew.[23] For Holsey and other CME leaders, however, the "Paine College Ideal" represented a practical model for racial comity and cooperation with southern whites for the mutual benefit of both races. While this model would be severely tested in the twentieth century by the increasing insurgency of African Americans in the South, the "Paine College Ideal" had a lasting effect on a generation of CME leaders on the eve of the modern Civil Rights movement of the 1950s and 1960s.

One of the earliest colored Methodist exemplars of the "Paine College Ideal" was John Wesley Gilbert, a member of the school's first graduating class and its first African-American faculty member.[24] After leaving Paine, Gilbert, a CME minister from Hephzibah, Georgia, attended Brown University, where he received a scholarship

---

[22]Ibid., 49–61; for the early history of Paine College, see also William L. Graham, "Patterns of Intergroup Relations in the Cooperative Establishment, Control, and Administration of Paine College (Georgia) by Southern Negro and White People: A study of Intergroup Process" (PhD diss., New York University, 1955).

[23]Eskew, "Black Elitism and the Failure of Paternalism in Postbellum Georgia," 649.

[24]For a brief portrait of Gilbert's encapsulation of the "Paine College Ideal" as a student and professor at Paine, see J. C. Colclough, *The Spirit of John Wesley Gilbert* (Nashville: Cokesbury Press, 1925).

to study languages at the American School of Classics in Athens, Greece. A promising scholar and gifted linguist, Gilbert returned to Augusta in 1888 to teach Greek at Paine College.

In 1911 Gilbert's linguistic and ministerial gifts were further tapped when he was appointed the denomination's first commissioned missionary to Africa, working closely with Bishop Walter Lambuth of the MECS.[25] The MECS's newly organized Board of African Missions then commissioned the pair for an exploratory visit to the Belgian Congo in Central Africa. On 14 October 1914, after spending two years preparing for their Congo mission, Lambuth and Gilbert set sail to the Congo from Belgium. They returned to the United States in the spring of 1912 after a grueling seven-month tour of the Congo, having planted a promising mission outpost in the village of Wembo Niami in the Atetela region. The next year, the MECS officially launched its Congo Mission at the annual meeting of the Board of Missions, with Gilbert and his wife later appointed as missionary candidates.[26]

Unfortunately, the Gilberts were unable to return to the Congo with Lambuth's party in November 1913 to open the Congo Mission. Despite Gilbert's persistent appeals for a cooperative mission in the Congo with the MECS and the incorporation of Africa under a CME episcopacy, other pressing domestic priorities—like education and church expansion—dictated that African missions be placed on a back burner for future consideration.[27] Despite the dashed hope of establishing a cooperative Congo mission, Gilbert's faith in the "Paine College Ideal" of racial cooperation between colored and white

---

[25]Lambuth had earlier visited the 1910 General Conference in Augusta, where he addressed the conference, suggesting a cooperative mission venture in Africa. The conference adopted resolutions to form a committee to investigate the plan. Gilbert, in attendance at the conference, had earlier that year volunteered to serve as a missionary to Africa. Sylvia Jacobs, "African Mission and the African-American Christian Churches," in *Encyclopedia of African-American Religions*, ed. Larry Murphy, J. Gordon Melton, and Gary L. Ward (New York: Garland Publishing, 1993) 14–16.

[26]Ibid.

[27]Ibid., 17. In 1918, Gilbert was elected the first editor of Sunday school materials in the CME Church.

Methodists in the South remained undiminished, and his example would provide a legacy for those who followed him.

Among the impressionable young Paine students inspired by Gilbert's idealism and example was Channing Tobias (1882–1961), who would emerge as one of the nation's most influential "race leaders" in the 1940s and 1950s. Like Gilbert, Tobias was a native Georgian and a minister nurtured in the CME Church and educated at Paine College, not far from his birthplace in Augusta. In an autobiographical portrait published in *Thirteen Americans: Their Spiritual Autobiographies,*[28] Tobias described the impact that his youth in racially segregated Augusta had on his views on race relations, noting that Augusta had what "was commonly known as a good relationship between the races, but of course what was all within the framework of segregation.... The fact that I was born and grew up in such a city, accounts in part for the lack of bitterness with which I have been able to approach consideration of racial relationships."[29]

From the racially segregated world of Augusta and Paine College, Tobias's journey toward racial harmony would take him to Drew University for seminary education. Joining thousands of other African-American migrants, Tobias was exposed to a vortex of social, intellectual, and religious currents that would influence his views on race relations in the United States, as well as anticolonial struggles abroad. For example, his seminary studies at Drew University exposed him to new currents in theological liberalism, such as the social gospel movement, and to voluntary Christian movements like the student volunteer movement and the Young Men's Christian Association, all of which directly impacted the emergent ecumenical movement in the United States and abroad.[30]

---

[28]Louis Finklestein, ed., *Thirteen Americans: Their Spiritual Autobiographies* (New York: Institute for Religious and Social Studies, 1953).

[29]Ibid., 179; for a fuller biographical treatment, see Rayford Logan, "Channing H. Tobias," in *The Dictionary of American Negro Biography*, ed. Rayford Logan and Michael R. Winston (New York: W. W. Norton, 1982) 593–95.

[30]For general treatments of Protestant transitions to theological modernism in the nineteenth and twentieth centuries, see Kenneth Cauthen, *The Impact of American Religious Liberalism* (New York: Harper & Row, 1962); William R. Hutchinson, *The*

Tobias quickly immersed himself in this flux of Christian activism, serving from 1911 to 1946 as an international and then senior secretary for Negro work of the YMCA and from 1946 to 1953 as the first African-American director of the Phelps-Stokes Fund in New York. On the eve of the 1955 Montgomery bus boycott, Tobias served as chairman of the board of the National Association for the Advancement of Colored People (NAACP), the nation's oldest and largest Civil Rights organization. Recognized by *Ebony* magazine in 1959 as the "senior statesman of Negro America," Tobias remained throughout his career a consistent critic of Jim Crow segregation, both in the YMCA and in U.S. society. Speaking at the 1944 Christian Youth Conference of North America, Tobias issued this challenge to the 800 delegates: "Personally realize that any discrimination against an individual based solely on race, color, or creed is un-American and un-Christian; insist that the Church with which you are identified remove all written or common law restrictions for membership solely based on race, color or national origin."[31]

Anticipating personalist themes that Martin Luther King Jr. would articulate in his own critique of racism, Tobias made this statement in a 1926 speech to the World Conference of YMCAs in

---

Modernist Impulse in American Protestantism (New York: Oxford University Press, 1976); Martin E. Marty, *The Irony of It All, 1893–1919*, vol. 1 of *Modern American Religion* (Chicago: University of Chicago Press, 1986); Ralph E. Luker, *The Social Gospel in Black and White: American Racial Reform, 1885–1912* (Chapel Hill: University of North Carolina Press, 1991); Donald K. Gorrell, *The Age of Social Responsibility: The Social Gospel in the Progressive Era* (Macon GA: Mercer University Press, 1988); William R. Hutchinson, ed., *Between the Times: The Travail of the Protestant Establishment in America, 1900–1960* (Cambridge MA: Harvard University Press, 1989). For studies of this transition within American Methodism, see Robert E. Chiles, *Theological Transition in American Methodism, 1790–1935* (Lanham MD: University Press of America, 1984); Paul S. Schilling, *Methodism and Society in Theological Perspective* (Nashville: Abingdon Press, 1960); William McGuire King, "Denominational Modernization and Religious Identity: The Case of the Methodist Episcopal Church," in *Perspectives on American Methodism*, ed. Russell E. Richey, Kenneth E. Rowe, and Jean Miller Schmidt (Nashville: Abingdon Press, 1993) 343–55.

[31]Quoted in the *Christian Index*, 30 July 1944, 2.

Helsinki, Finland: "I am unalterably opposed to segregation based on race, creed, or color.... First, it cheapens human personality and leads to crimes against those affected by it.... Second, segregation is un-American in spirit and practice.... Third, and most important of all, I object to racial segregation, because it is an insult to the Creator."[32]

In a likely allusion to his own formative experiences in the CME Church and Paine College, Tobias identified himself "with the Negro who will not bow or bend obsequiously before other people in order to gain something for himself, who will not lie about conditions, who is willing to cooperate, but only in terms of mutual respect. This is the group with which all who are interested in true democracy will have to deal."[33]

Although Tobias's views clearly retained the emphasis on racial cooperation embodied in the "Paine College Ideal," the militancy of the "New Negro" was also emerging, one that uncompromisingly condemned racist systems and institutions as evils to be confronted. The old etiquette that dictated racial relations between blacks and whites in both the Old and New South had become outmoded. It had been unmasked for what it really was: an ideology of white supremacy and black subordination. Thus, a new etiquette had to be constructed on the basis of social equality, equal rights, and mutual respect.

---

[32]Quoted in Nina Mjagki, *Light in the Darkness: African Americans and the YMCA, 1852–1946* (Lexington: University of Kentucky Press, 1994) 120–21. Compare Tobias's critique with two other contemporaries in Georgia, President Benjamin E. Mays and Professor George D. Kelsey at Morehouse College in Atlanta, both of whom were PhD ethicists; see George D. Kelsey, *Racism and the Christian Understanding of Man* (New York: Charles Scribner's Sons, 1965); Benjamin E. Mays, *Born to Rebel* (New York: Charles Scribner's Sons, 1971). It is likely that Tobias encountered personalist themes at Drew through the teachings of systematic theologian Olin A. Curtis, who emphasized racial solidarity in his theology; see, for example, his *Christian Faith* (New York: Eaton and Manis, 1905). However, Boston Personalism as a philosophical school of thought emphasizing personality as ultimate reality was developed more formally by Curtis's successors at Boston University, beginning with philosopher Borden Parker Bowne and theologian Albert Knudson; see Rufus Burrow Jr. (*Personalism: A Critical Introduction* [St. Louis: Chalice Press, 1999]) for an interpretive history of Personalism that includes African-American personalists.

[33]Quoted in Mjagkij, *Light in the Darkness*, 120–21.

Tobias's progressive views on race relations were influenced further by his involvement with anticolonial organizations in the North like the International Council on African Affairs (ICAA), organized in New York City in 1923 by Max Yergan and Paul Robeson.[34] These radical leaders helped Tobias link anticolonial struggles in Africa and India with the Civil Rights struggle of African Americans in the United States. As a member of the U.S. delegation to the 1937 World Conference of YMCAs in India, Tobias, along with Benjamin Mays, met with Mahatma Gandhi to discuss strategies for empowering oppressed minorities. Tobias rejected Gandhi's call for absolute pacifism and favored independence leader Jawaharlal Nehru's more aggressive stance against British imperialism. Commenting on the global implications of World War II, Tobias offered this critique of imperialism and colonialism: "We are concerned that this war bring an end to imperialism and colonial exploitation. We believe that political and economic democracy must displace the present system of exploitation in Africa, the West Indies, India, and all other colonial areas."[35] Furthermore, Tobias's 1946 appointment by President Harry Truman to the Committee on Civil Rights served as another important context for connecting anticolonialism with Civil Rights activism.[36]

Throughout his long career as Civil Rights leader and social agency director, Tobias remained active in the CME Church as a minister and ecumenical leader.[37] It would be Tobias, along with

---

[34]See Penny M. Von Eschen, *Race Against Empire: Black American and Anticolonialism, 1937–1957* (Ithaca NY: Cornell University Press, 1997) 17–21.

[35]Quoted in *The Dictionary of American Negro Biography*, 594, originally from an interview with Henry Beckett in *Closeup* (20 September 1945).

[36]The report, for example, recognizes the expanding ethnic and racial diversity of the U.S. population through the growth of African-American, Hispanic, and Asian minority groups and sees the denial of civil rights to these groups as an impediment to the promotion of global democracy; see *To Secure These Rights: The Report of the President's Committee on Civil Rights* (New York: Simon & Schuster, 1947) 13–17, 146–48.

[37]In addition to his denominational involvement, Tobias represented the CME Church as a member of the Federal Council of Church's (FCC) Executive Committee and Advisory Board; see *Christian Index* (March 1941), 3.

another Civil Rights activist and minister, the Reverend Henry Bunton of Memphis, who would offer a resolution to the 1954 CME General Conference requesting that the church's name be changed from "Colored" to "Christian" Methodist Episcopal Church to reflect the changing reality in the church's racial and social consciousness.

EXPANDING CIRCLES OF CME ECUMENISM

The spirit of racial cooperation embodied in the "Paine College Ideal" was closely related to the CME Church's expanded vision of ecumenism in the twentieth century. Myopic views of its relationship with the parent MECS gradually gave way to more inclusive understandings of the organic relation to other churches, particularly other African Methodist denominations. Still, the ingrained patterns of the older racial etiquette were difficult to erase altogether as CMEs continued to encounter the MECS as unequal stepchildren. The bitter legacy of southern white racism and paternalism, this unequal relationship was especially apparent in the relationship between white and colored Methodist women in the South.

By the twentieth century, both white and colored Methodist women were organized in a network of local and regional societies committed to a variety of reform and benevolent activities (for example, education, temperance, moral reform, and missions). For colored Methodist women, who had more limited options for educational and professional opportunities, the uplift of the race through education became a dominant mission concern. "The CME Church operated from the perception that the schoolhouse and the church were inseparable," says historian Othal Lakey, "that as the schoolhouse and church house were almost invariably located near each other...they were virtually one and the same."[38] Consequently, the earliest CME schools were organized by local congregations in mostly rural communities and later by annual conferences mobilizing resources from a wider constituency, including the MECS. By 1910, the CME Church operated twelve high schools and four colleges,

---

[38]Lakey, *The History of the CME Church*, 438.

enrolling more than 2,000 students across the South. Colored Methodist women swelled the ranks of these fledgling schools not only as eager students but also as founders, administrators, teachers, and supporters. In 1882, Jennie Lane, daughter of Bishop Lane, became the first principal of the CME high school in Jackson, Tennessee (later Lane College). In 1906, Helena Cobb, a leading advocate for women's rights in the CME Church, opened the Helena B. Cobb Institute for Girls in Barnesville, Georgia. Founded on the model of Booker T. Washington's industrial school at Tuskegee, Cobb's school sought to provide a broad range of religious, moral, and domestic training for colored girls.[39]

If education provided one sphere of activism for colored Methodist women, relief and temperance work opened other channels. Historian Kathleen Berkeley's case study of colored women's activism in Memphis sheds light on the origins, motivations, and leadership of African-American women's benevolent societies.[40] With a keen eye to dimensions of race, class, and gender in Memphis, Berkeley demonstrates how African-American women contributed to the institutional infrastructures of their communities (e.g., churches, benevolent societies, presses, political parties). She suggests these "women were often at the vanguard in founding and sustain[ing] autonomous organizations designed specifically to improve social conditions."[41] Furthermore, she maintains that the origins of autonomous African-American women's organizations can be traced to the division of sexual labor during slavery, where slave women were primarily cast as caretakers of black and white families. With the retreat of federal services and protection after the war, working-class women like the Daughters of Zion of the Zion Chapel AMEZ Church

---

[39]Ibid., 465.

[40]Kathleen C. Berkeley, "'Colored Ladies Also Contributed': Black Women's Activities from Benevolence to Social Welfare, 1866–1896," in *The Web of Southern Relations: Women, Family, and Education*, ed. Walter Fraser Jr., R. Frank Saunders Jr., and Jon L. Wakelyn (Athens: University of Georgia Press, 1985) 181–203.

[41]Ibid., 184.

helped to fill this vacuum by organizing their own relief and self-help programs.[42]

Granting the autonomy that colored Methodist women asserted in filling the social vacuum after emancipation, they were nonetheless constrained by the racial etiquette of the New South and the paternalistic ties to the MECS. As historian Mary Frederickson perceptively observes, joint interracial reform by CME and MECS women "consistently took place in ways that let white women preserve the power they derived from their race and class."[43] Her analysis of their respective demographic profiles, organizational structures, programmatic goals, and publicly endorsed issues paints a portrait of a complex relationship involving mutuality and antagonism. For example, white Methodist reformers generally came from middle- to upper-middle-class families, with the majority having never worked outside the home. Colored Methodist women, on the other hand, generally came from working classes and rural farming communities, the vast majority of whom were employed outside the home as domestic workers, teachers, and other professionals.[44]

Perhaps the most significant divergence between white and colored Methodist missionary women was their approach to public reform. As white women began to shift their focus in the twentieth century from "the prevention of social problems to a more active political program designed to achieve social change,"[45] CME women adopted a more guarded approach—a comprehensive strategy under

---

[42]Ibid., 188.

[43]Mary E. Frederickson, "'Each One Is Dependent on the Other': Southern Churchwomen, Racial Reform, and the Progress of Transformation, 1880–1940," in *Visible Women: New Essays on American Activism*, ed. Nancy A. Hewitt and Suzanne Lebsock (Urbana: University of Illinois Press, 1993) 298.

[44]Ibid., 303–308. On African-American professional women during the Jim Crow era, see Stephanie J. Shaw, *What a Woman Ought to Be and Do: Black Professional Women Workers during the Jim Crow Era* (Chicago: University of Chicago Press, 1996); Cynthia Neverdon-Morton, *Afro-American Women of the South and the Advancement of the Race, 1895–1925* (Knoxville: University of Tennessee Press, 1989); Jacqueline Jones, *Labor of Love, Labor of Sorrow: Black Women, Work, and the Family from Slavery to the Present* (New York: Basic Books, 1985).

[45]Shaw, *What a Woman Ought to Be and Do*, 307.

the rubric of "christianizing" their people. "Christianizing" referred to a blanket of moral and social concerns that included educational uplift, economic development, voting, and citizenship rights. The key difference between the two groups was that colored women protected themselves and their families by cloaking their progressive goals and agendas, thus cultivating what Frederickson calls an "indirect form of speaking out" that allowed them to subtly critique racist and sexist structures.

This mode of indirect speaking was not limited to colored Methodist women, but represented the modus operandi by which the CME Church formally and informally interacted with their white MECS counterparts. W. A. Bell's 1933 report on the cooperation between the two churches sheds light on ecumenical relations between colored and white pastors at the local level.[46] In a questionnaire distributed to 500 pastors, college professors, social workers, and recommended individuals, representing 472 southern communities and 1,069 churches, Bell surveyed the state of ecumenical relations between the churches. On the question of personal acquaintance with members of another race, 50 percent of both races responded favorably while 42 percent indicated no acquaintance.[47] But when CMEs were asked about their awareness of relations between the two churches, only 43 percent responded yes while 47 percent said no, a clear indication of the social distance between the two churches.[48]

White pastors were equally aware of—and even tacitly condoned—this social distance. When asked about their attitudes toward cooperation with CME churches and pastors, only 16 percent of white ministers described themselves as either "active" or "responsive"; 21.8 percent described their attitudes as "brotherly" or "friendly"; 25.6 percent indicated they had no opportunity for cooperation or were undecided about it; and 36.6 percent were noncommittal or ambiguous in their responses.[49]

---

[46]Bell, "Missions and Co-operation of the Methodist Episcopal Church, South
[47]Ibid., 119.
[48]Ibid.
[49]Ibid., 120.

Overall, Bell found the responses deeply disappointing, lamenting that "transmuting 'favorable attitude' into concrete service" has probably for many not been so easy or the opportunities not so great and impelling."[50] One of Bell's unnamed investigators was more direct: "To be frank the [white] pastor has done little. He has simply gone along with kindly spirit and where the colored people have asked nothing, he has given nothing. When sought on a particular thing he has cooperated by advice and a friendly word, but nothing very much beyond this."[51]

Although there was no unanimity among the CME leaders quoted in the study, most favored more cooperation in education and missions. Dr. D. F. Lane, president of Lane College, stoutly defended the need for continuing cooperation, gently chided white Methodists for a lack of resolve, and indirectly challenged the prevailing racial etiquette:

> I do not mean a relation of patrimony; but a relation of sympathetic helpfulness in such a way each one can maintain his own self-respect and his own personal honor.... If the M.E. Church, South is too timid to speak its mind and convictions, we shall not be helped, and if our Church is not courageous in its convictions, the whole program of helpfulness is destroyed.... The influence of such an organization [Commission on Cooperation and Counsel] would reach far beyond the limits and confines of our respective churches; it would soon become recognized as a national or international "clearing house for the solution of many of our interracial problems."[52]

While Lane did not specify the nature of these "interracial problems" plaguing white and colored Methodists, he did entertain the hope that the creation of a regional, interracial commission could

---

[50]Ibid., 123.
[51]Ibid.
[52]Quoted in ibid., 159.

help effect "a newly arranged social order," one in which "[t]he practice of economic and social justice would naturally lead to a repudiation of a policy too prevalent in our country of exploiting the defenseless and ignorant, whether white or colored."[53]

The failure to create an interracial commission of southern Methodists to address "social and economic justice," as envisioned by Lane and Bell, did not prevent CMEs from seeking other progressive alliances with ecumenical bodies in the 1930s and 1940s. Among the major outlets for this heightened CME activism and ecumenism were CME participation in the Fraternal Council of Negro Churches (FCNC) and renewed relations with other African-American denominations. Founded in 1934 in response to an appeal by AME bishop Reverdy Ransom for collective action by African-American denominations, the FCNC was the fruit of a long struggle to organize a national, ecumenical organization of African-American clergy.

An early example of CME involvement in this effort came in 1927 when CME minister C. L. Russell organized the short-lived National Interdenominational Ministers' Alliance.[54] On 5 January 1934 CME delegates joined representatives from the AMEC, AMEZC, National Baptist Convention, USA, Inc., and the National Baptist Convention of America at the Mount Carmel Baptist Church in Washington, DC, to form a "Voluntary Committee on the Federation of Negro Religious Denominations in the United States of America."[55] Eschewing doctrinal consensus and organic merger as its

---

[53]Ibid., 159.

[54]Mary R. Sawyer, *Black Ecumenism: Implementing the Demands of Justice* (Valley Forge PA: Trinity Press International, 1994) 16. On the history and role of Reverdy Ransom in the Fraternal Council of Negro Churches, see Calvin S. Morris, *Reverdy C. Ransom: Black Advocate of the Social Gospel* (Lanham MD: University Press of America, 1990); Sawyer, *Black Ecumenism*, 15–34.

[55]Sawyer, *Black Ecumenism*, 18–19. On 4 and 5 August 1934, the Fraternal Council of Negro Churches in America was formally organized in Chicago, with Ransom as its first president. Representatives from several other churches had now joined the FCC: the Union American Episcopal Church, along with delegates from the MEC, the Congregational Church, and the Community Center Churches, 18 . Although in 1935 the name was officially changed "The Negro Fraternal Council of Churches in America" to signify openness to African Americans affiliated with

primary goals, the FCNC proposed "that the Negro religious denominations shall cooperate on all questions touching the spiritual, moral, social, political, economic and industrial welfare of our people."[56] With this mandate the council divided its work into twelve specific areas and committees: evangelism and worship, education, health and housing, race relations, industrial and economic relations, urban life, agricultural and rural life, family life, recreation and amusements, publication and publicity, Africa and peace, labor and business. Many of these areas reflected the plight of African-American migrants in northern urban areas and thus represented new ground for the CME Church.

CME participation in the Fraternal Council was especially visible and active in the Midwest under the leadership of Bishop James Bray (1870–1944), whose district included Illinois and Missouri.[57] Born in Carnesville, Georgia, Bray devoted his life to education. After graduating from Atlanta University in 1893, Bray taught in public schools, serving a term as president of the Georgia State Teacher's Association. From 1903 to 1912 he served as president of two CME Colleges (Lane and Miles) before being elected in 1914 as General Secretary of Education for the CME Church. With his election to the presidency of the Fraternal Council in 1942, Bray immersed himself in the task of ecumenical activism during the war years. Joining the battle to fight racial discrimination on two fronts, he called upon Christians in the United States to "join a movement to repeal the Poll Tax and hindrances to the full expression of citizenship of any group; support the President's Order 8802, for fair employment

---

predominantly white denominations, it was incorporated in 1945 as the "National Fraternal Council of Churches, USA."

[56]Quoted in Sawyer, *Black Ecumenism*, 18.

[57]However, this is not to insinuate that other CME ministers and bishops did not participate in the council prior to Bray's tenure as president 1942–1943. For example, in a heated letter to The Christian Index in 1944, Bishop Randall A. Carter reminded the editor that it was he (Carter) who responded to Bishop Ransom's 1934 invitation to attend the organizational conference in Chicago when other CME bishops, including Bray, declined the invitation; see Bishop R. A. Carter, "Just to Set the Record Straight," *Christian Index*, 6 July 1944, 4.

practice of all capable persons without regard to color or creed."[58] He charged individuals refusing to employ persons on the basis of color rather than merit of being "just as dangerous as Axis Spies."[59] On 15 June 1943, Bray led a commission to the White House to confer with President Roosevelt about the council's concerns. Bray reiterated these concerns the next year in a speech before the Republican National Committee, stressing the council and hence the African-American church's representative and political role among African-American citizens:

> The Fraternal Council of Negro Churches in America, representing eleven denominations, 40,000 churches and more than six million members and adherents...presents here some basic issues to the Executive Committee that they may receive consideration in the party's platform for the approaching election.
>
> This organization, touching every level of society and comprehending all ages and classes, feels responsibility to speak for its millions' earnest desires.
>
> The Negro Church and churches are not political institutions as such, but intelligent self-interest of the church itself demands its concerns in government and citizenry of the people, economically, socially, industrially, politically, educationally as well as spiritually. Moreover there is no organization that gets closer to the heartbeat of the people, understands their tempers, their longings, their purposes, their inner thinking, than the Church, and this is particularly true of the Negro Church.[60]

As a prime example of African-American religious insurgency from the mid-1930s to the early 1950s, the council represents a

---

[58]"An Address of the Fraternal Council of Negro Churches in America," *Christian Index*, 21 January 1943, 4.

[59]Ibid.

[60]*Christian Index*, 29 June 1944, 5.

significant counter-example to historian Gayraud Wilmore's "deradicalization thesis."[61] Wilmore regards the death of AME bishop Henry McNeal Turner in 1915 as a turning point in the history of "black religious radicalism" in the United States. With the loss of a radical black nationalist of Turner's stature and the virulent racism of the Jim Crow era and the influx of African-American migrants from the South, many African-American churches and clergy retreated from struggles for racial justice and equality by adopting the progressive accommodationism of Booker T. Washington (who also died in 1915) and by channeling their energies into denominational growth and maintenance. Instead of maintaining the momentum of the first Reconstruction through social and political agitation, the African-American mainstream churches (Methodist, Baptist, Presbyterian, Congregational, and Episcopal) retreated into the enclaves of moralism and revivalism. Only with the emergence of Martin Luther King Jr. and the Civil Rights movement of the 1950s and 1960s do we see a revival of black religious nationalism among these churches.

Wilmore, however, acknowledges some notable exceptions to his thesis, particularly the urban institutional churches, such as Ransom's Institutional AME Church in Atlanta, H. H. Proctor's First Congregational Church in Atlanta, and Adam Clayton Powell's Abyssinian Baptist Church in Harlem.[62] Outside of Ransom's broad-

---

[61]See chapter 7, "The Deradicalization of the Black Church," in Gayraud S. Wilmore, *Black Religion and Black Radicalism: An Interpretation of the Religious History of Afro-American People*, 2d rev. ed. (Maryknoll NY: Orbis Books, 1983).

[62]Wilmore, *Black Religion and Black Radicalism*, 190. While I agree with Wilmore on an ideological shift on the part of mainstream African-American churches on social and political activism, I disagree with him on the following three matters: (1) his timing of this shift, (2) his analysis of the causes and the extent of this shift, and (3) the significance of his exceptions to this shift. Wilmore's thesis not only obscures individual and collective efforts by a host of African-American religious activists (e.g., Ida B. Wells-Barnett, Reverdy Ransom, Benjamin E. Mays), but also downplays the forces militating against African-American religious activism in the South (e.g., racial violence and out-migration). Moreover, Wilmore does not account sufficiently for the increasing diversification of African-American religions as a factor of "deradicalization"; instead, he interprets diversification as a cause of deradicalization. For example, Marcus Garvey's Universal Negro

based ministry in Chicago, Wilmore says little about the FCNC's efforts or interracial alliances committed to combating racial injustice at home and abroad.

The CME Church in the 1940s and 1950s thus represents an ironic twist to Wilmore's "deradicalization thesis." From its inception in 1870 the CME Church could never be characterized as radical in its social, political, or theological orientations; even in the 1940s it remained faithful to it roots as a southern, evangelical, Protestant church fervently committed to the spread of the gospel and the uplift of the race. What had changed since the first Reconstruction of the 1870s was the evolution of CME social and political consciousness in response to Jim Crow segregation in the South and elsewhere. Mired in a system of economic exploitation of sharecropping and peonage, racial terror and violence, and de jure segregation and discrimination, CMEs could no longer passively sit on the sidelines.

Though deeply rooted in and committed to the South, CMEs joined a throng of African Americans in migrating out of the South to the Midwest, North, and West, not primarily for the purpose of spreading the gospel or extending the bounds of the church but to search for full freedom and equal opportunity as American citizens.[63]

Improvement Association (UNIA) and Alexander McGuire's African Orthodox Church can be, in one sense, a continuation of Bishop Turner's black nationalism and, in another sense, a more radical alternative to the NAACP's integrationism. In sum, Wilmore's "deradicalization thesis" is too sweeping a thesis to accurately characterize the complex stances of African-American churches and leaders; there are simply too many incongruities and exceptions to this thesis, of which the CME Church's involvement in the National Fraternal Council of Negro Churches is only one.

[63]For the impact of the Black Migration on the CME Church, see Lakey (*The History of the CME Church*, 488–95), who concludes that although the majority of its membership remained concentrated in the South, the CME Church by 1960 had largely become "an urban denomination as its largest and most prestigious churches were located in the cities, and its style of worship and polity were influenced by the values of the rising Black middle class" (491). This phenomenon reflects the migration patterns of southern African Americans from rural areas to urban centers in the South and North, resulting in a sharp decrease of rural church membership. On the impact of the Black Migration on African-American churches and religious life, see Sernett, *Bound for the Promised Land*; Hans A. Baer and Merrill Singer, *African-American Religion in the Twentieth Century* (Knoxville: University of Tennessee

Unlike the founding fathers of the CME church, who labored diligently to find an appellation that would aptly describe the nature of colored Methodism in 1870, CMEs in the twentieth century, under a new breed of leadership, placed much more attention on unpacking the meaning of the last part of its denominational name, that is, what it meant to be a member of the Colored Methodist Episcopal Church in the United States of America. Consequently, while other African-American churches may have been undergoing a process of "deradicalization," as Wilmore asserts, the CME Church was undergoing its first phase of radicalization.

If CME participation in the Fraternal Council of Negro Churches represented one sign of the church's evolution of social and racial consciousness, then the enlargement of its ecumenical relations with other African-American Methodist bodies was another tangible sign. In fact, these ecumenical relationships with other African-American Methodists predate and presage CME openness to the Negro Fraternal Council and other ecumenical initiatives (e.g., the Federal [National] Council of Churches and the World Council of Churches).[64] As early as May 1864, the AME and AMEZ churches had engaged in merger conversations when representatives from the two denominations met

---

Press, 1992) 44–55; E. Franklin Frazier, *The Negro Church in America* (New York: Schocken Books, 1964) 47–67; Harold Dean Trulear, "The Role of the Church in Black Migration: Some Preliminary Observations," *Journal of the Afro-American Historical and Genealogical Society* 8 (Summer 1987): 51–56. For historical and demographical treatments of the Black Migration, see Joe William Trotter, *The Black Migration in Historical Perspective* (Urbana: University of Illinois Press, 1985); Daniel M. Campbell and Rex R. Johnson, *Black Migration in America: A Social Demographical History* (Durham NC: Duke University Press, 1981); Florette Henri, *Black Migration: Movement North, 1900–1920* (Garden City NJ: Anchor/Doubleday Books, 1976); Jack T. Kirby, "The Southern Exodus: 1900–1960," *Journal of Southern History* 49/4 (November 1983): 585–600.

[64]For historical treatments of these initiatives and attempts at merger, see Dennis C. Dickerson, "Black Ecumenism: Efforts to Establish a United Methodist Episcopal Church, 1918–1932," *Church History* 52 (December 1983): 479–91; Roy W. Trueblood, "Union Negotiation between Black Methodists in America," *Methodist History* 8/3 (July 1970): 18–29; Mary R. Sawyer, "Efforts at Black Church Merger," *Journal of the Interdenominational Theological Seminary* 8/2 (Spring 1986): 305–16.

at Bethel AMEC in Philadelphia; a "platform" of consolidation was created to be sent to the annual conferences for adoption. The plan received favorable response in the AMEZ annual conferences and was officially ratified by the 1868 AMEZ General Conference. The plan was derailed in 1892 when the AME General Conference rejected it, but the issue of union remained a live issue at the 1872, 1876, and 1880 AMEZ general conferences.[65]

Full merger talks between the AME and AMEZ churches resumed in 1885 under the initiative of AMEZ bishop William Walls, who saw the growth of the CME Church in the South as an area of mutual concern. A joint committee met at two meetings that year, producing fourteen articles of agreement and the name "First United Methodist Episcopal Church." Disagreements over the issues of episcopacy and the name would deadlock discussions until 1892 in Harrisburg, Pennsylvania, when AMEZs proposed the creation of a new Commission on Organic Union and a revised plan of union. Once again the plan floundered on the issue of a proposed name—"The African Zion Methodist Episcopal Church."[66]

Disillusioned, the AMEZ Church would not engage in another merger effort until 1900, this time with the CME Church. Ironically, the initiative for merger came from a CME fraternal delegate to the 1900 AMEZ General Conference. Following established protocol, a joint committee of commissioners from both churches met in October 1900 in Washington, DC, to prepare "Articles of Agreement" for consideration by each church's general conference. The momentum of the plan, however, was disrupted in 1904 when the AME Church proposed a new plan with the AMEZ Church, calling for a joint hymnal and catechism. By 1908 CMEs had also been drawn into the proposal, resulting in an historic meeting in Washington, DC, of the bishops from all three churches and the creation of the Tri-Federation Council of Bishops.

By its third meeting in Birmingham, Alabama, in April 1918, the Tri-Federation Council had appointed denominational commissioners

---

[65]See Sawyer, "Efforts at Black Church Merger," 305–17.
[66]Ibid., 306–307.

to create a plan for organic merger—The Birmingham Plan of Organic Union—to be considered by the general conferences before being ratified by the annual conferences. Accounts vary as to the reasons why the historic Birmingham Plan collapsed, but they generally conclude that the CME Church was the primary dissenter. Leading the charge against organic merger was Bishop C. H. Phillips, who now acted as a pivotal transitional figure between the colored Methodism of the postbellum era and Christian Methodism of the Civil Rights era.[67]

Prior to his election as bishop, Phillips strongly favored organic union with the AMEZ Church, trumpeting its cause in editorials and speeches. In a speech delivered at the October 1896 centennial of the AMEZ Church on "The Relation of the Colored Methodist Episcopal Church to the African Methodist Episcopal Church Zion," Phillips sought to minimize the long-standing antipathy between the two denominations.

> Excepting a few petty jealousies that exist between churches as much as between individuals, our relations have always been cordial; and, so far as I know, there has never been a laxity of our religious feelings sufficient, nor an apathy of our cordial relations calculated to produce estrangement.
>
> For a long time the [CME Church] has been cultivating the warmest feelings for Zion. If there has been little talk of organic union, that is due to the fact that we have been endeavoring to develop and extend our Methodism; to build our schools; and otherwise strengthen our stakes.[68]

Phillips confessed his pro-merger sentiments "may seem strange to many," but he was satisfied that "[union] would be to the glory of God to unite the people and put an end to the controversy that has

---

[67]Phillips was elected a bishop in 1902, after serving eight years as editor of the *Christian Index*; at the age of forty he became the youngest person to be elected a CME bishop.

[68]Quoted in Phillips, *From the Farm to the Bishopric*, 141.

existed between us."[69] Phillips' conversion, and that of the CME Church, can be partly explained by his immersion in the world of Methodist ecumenism. As a leading pastor, editor of the *Christian Index*, and bishop, Phillips represented the CME Church at ecumenical events, including five Methodist ecumenical conferences in Washington, DC (1891), London (1901, 1921), Toronto (1910), and Atlanta (1931), and as a fraternal delegate to AME and AMEZ general conferences.[70] This exposure to the ecumenical scene—its global vision, theological underpinnings, interracial composition— helped Phillips to develop his own perspectives on the promise and problems inherent in merger negotiations.

After his election to the episcopacy, Phillips' optimism for organic merger with the African Methodist denominations began to wane, in apparent opposition to the sentiment of the denominational mainstream. Phillips vigorously opposed the 1918 "Birmingham Plan" of union drafted by the nine commissioners representing the CME, AME, and AMEZ churches, even though the plan was approved 304 to 48 by the delegates of the 1918 CME General Conference, before being sent to the annual conferences for ratification. After the conference, Phillips published a pamphlet titled "Fourteen Points against Organic Union, on the Birmingham Plan," which he widely distributed to CMEs across the country. As a committed loyalist to the "church of Miles," Phillips' primary objections to the plan were the following: It was hastily prepared in one day, neither providing a comprehensive program nor a constitutional basis for union;[71] it did

---

[69]Ibid., 142.

[70]References to CME fraternal delegates attending MECS conferences appear less frequently in the twentieth century. Phillips's participation at the Second Ecumenical Conference in Washington, DC, included a speech on temperance, "The Legal Prohibition of the Saloon," in which he made no reference to the race problem in the United States but highlighted the "development of progressive civilization" as one of the benefits of legal prohibition "because it is compatible with rational liberty and all the claims of justice; and because it would guarantee greater positive advances in social culture" (*From the Farm to the Bishopric*, 91–93). At the 1911 Ecumenical Conference, Phillips was elected a secretary, a first for a "colored delegate."

[71]*From the Farm to the Bishopeic*, 609.

not "safeguard or protect" the smaller denomination (i.e., the CME Church) from being assimilated into the larger ones;[72] and it was illegitimately foisted on the CME Church by its bishops without the input and approval of the General Conference.[73] Furthermore, Phillips questioned whether union would be in the best interest of the CME Church, especially considering its remarkable growth and expansion:

> The Colored Methodist Episcopal Church has made a most phenomenal development since her organization; and according to numbers and progressive ideas, has outclassed her big sisters. She has hoisted her banner on the lakes of the North and the gulf of the South.... [S]he broke down the Mason and Dixon line which confined her to the South; bosommed [sic] her children who cried for her embrace from sea to sea; and made her two big sisters throw off some apathy and lethargy in church work, and move forward at a more rapid pace in things spiritual and material.[74]

Phillips' anti-merger polemic was instrumental in defeating the ratification of the plan by CMEs, effectively halting deliberations on organic union for almost five decades.[75] When the dust settled, the three churches not only resumed cordial relations with each other, but cooperated as equal partners in the Fraternal Council of Negro Churches, an even more inclusive ecumenical body of African-American denominations and clergy. In the long run, the process of ecumenical dialogue, though often messy and painful, proved to be a beneficial experience for CMEs on the eve of the Civil Rights movement.

First, immersion into the waters of ecumenism helped CMEs clarify their unique identity while affirming commonality with other

---

[72]Ibid., 612–13.
[73]Ibid., 621–22.
[74]Ibid., 620.
[75]Sawyer, "Efforts at Black Church Merger," 309. The AME and AMEZ churches continued to try to revive the "Birmingham Plan" in 1926 and 1932 with only mixed results.

Methodist bodies, particularly the AME and AMEZ churches with which they had been estranged. Relationships and alliances forged in ecumenical dialogue with AMEs and AMEZs, moreover, served to heighten CME social and political consciousness in the South, giving them other interlocutors than the MECS, which by 1939 had reunited with the MEC to become the Methodist Church. By the end of World War II a new generation of CME leaders was emerging; they had consumed the sour grapes of Jim Crow in the South during two world wars and their teeth were set on edge against racial injustice. By the early 1950s it was clear that neither the reformist policy of the "Paine College Ideal" nor the effort to forge ecumenical ties with white and African-American Methodists had been successful in creating a racially just and harmonious social order. With the advent of Dr. Martin Luther King Jr. and the modern Civil Rights movement in the 1950s, different strategies and alliances were called for by a third generation of CMEs no longer constrained by the "racial etiquette" of the New South.

CHAPTER 4

The CME Church and the Birth of the Civil Rights Movement, 1954–1960

Scholars differ on the precipitating causes of the Civil Rights movement of the 1950s and 1960s. Some see the historic 1954 Supreme Court decision that outlawed racial segregation in public schools as the event that energized African-American insurgency and placed Civil Rights on the nation's agenda.[1] Others are more prone to see the Supreme Court's decision as the culmination of decades of struggle to dismantle the 1896 *Plessy v. Ferguson* Supreme Court decision, which enshrined the doctrine of "separate but equal" into law

---

[1]For a full treatment of the *Brown v. Board of Education* decision and the crucial role of the NAACP Legal Defense and Educational Fund, see Richard Kluger, *Simple Justice: The History of Brown v. Board of Education and Black America's Struggle for Equality* (New York: Vintage Books, 1975). For critical appraisals of the role of the NAACP in the *Brown v. Board of Education* decision and the Civil Rights movement, see Charles Flint Kellogg, *NAACP: A History of The National Association for the Advancement of Colored People* (Baltimore: John Hopkins University Press, 1967); Mark V. Tushnett, *The NAACP's Legal Strategy against Segregated Education, 1925–1950* (Chapel Hill: University of North Carolina Press, 1987); Elliot Rudwick and August Meier, "Integration vs. Separatism: The NAACP and CORE Face Challenge from Within," in *Along the Color Line: Explorations in the Black Experience*, ed. by August Meier and Elliot Rudwick (Urbana: University of Illinois Press, 1976) 238–64.

and custom.[2] Still others point to the spontaneous action of Rosa Parks on 1 December 1955, when she refused to give up her bus seat to a white passenger. This singularly courageous act ignited the Montgomery bus boycott and catapulted Martin Luther King Jr. to national and international prominence.[3]

Common to all these perspectives is the realization that by the mid-1950s the struggle for racial equality in the United States had reached a critical juncture, with African-American restiveness and insurgency becoming more pronounced. A number of internal and external factors contributed to this turning point in Civil Rights activism. At the forefront was the heightened expectation of social change created by the NAACP's legal strategy to attack Jim Crow laws in state and federal courts. Though this strategy proved painfully slow and financially costly, a team of interracial lawyers, headed by Charles Hamilton Houston, dean of Howard University Law School, and his protege, Thurgood Marshall, won some important desegregation cases on the road to the 1954 *Brown v. Board of Education* decision.[4]

---

[2]For perspectives of this approach stressing continuities with post-World War II precedents, see Harvard Sitkoff, *The Struggle for Black Equality:1954-1980*, (New York: Hill and Wang, 1981); David R. Goldfield, *Black, White, and Southern: Race Relations and Southern Culture 1940 to the Present* (Baton Rouge: Louisiana State University Press, 1990); Manning Marable highlights the role of black nationalist leaders and organizations in developing alternative theories and programs to the integrationist ones of the NAACP (*Race, Reform, and Rebellion: The Second Reconstruction in Black America, 1945–1990*, 2d ed. [Jackson: University Press of Mississippi, 1991]).

[3]For studies that emphasize the movement as a social irruption precipitated by indigenous leaders and communities—generally church-based and clergy-led—which gave rise to the SCLC, see especially Aldon D. Morris, *The Origins of the Civil Rights Movement: Black Communities Organizing for Change* (New York: Free Press, 1984); Adam Fairclough, *To Redeem the Soul of America: The Southern Christian Leadership Conference and Martin Luther King, Jr.* (Athens: University of Georgia Press, 1987).

[4]On the pioneering role of Charles Hamilton Houston and Howard University Law School in developing the NAACP's legal strategy, see Genna Rae McNeil, *Groundwork: Charles Hamilton Houston and the Struggle for Civil Rights* (Philadelphia: Temple University Press, 1983); Rayford W. Logan, *Howard*

While the NAACP was by far the largest and most visible organization in the Civil Rights struggle, it was hardly the only one. Its work was supported and supplemented by dozens of other local, regional, and national organizations of varying ideological stances that shared a commitment to racial equality. To the far left of the spectrum was a small contingent of communist or socialist-inspired groups like the Communist Party of the United States (CPUSA), A. Philip Randolph's March on Washington Movement (MOWM), and black nationalist groups like the Nation of Islam, the African Blood Brotherhood, and the Moorish Science Temple, who advocated racial separatism.[5]

Closer to the middle of the ideological spectrum were organizations strongly committed to ideals of racial inclusivity and integration but divided on the means of achieving these ends (e.g., economic boycotts, political action, judicial redress, moral suasion). Included in this broad category were the historic African-American denominations and churches that constituted the membership of the Fraternal Council of Negro Churches, as well as local civic, voting, and social service associations scattered across the postwar South.[6]

University: The First Hundred Years, 1867–1967 (New York: New York University Press, 1969); Kluger, *Simple Justice.*

[5]For a discussion of black nationalist ideology and organizations prior to the Civil Rights movement, see Marable, *Race, Reform, and Rebellion*, 40–60; William L. Van Deburg, ed., *Modern Black Nationalism from Marcus to Louis Farrakhan* (Philadelphia: Temple University Press, 1997); John T. McCartney, *Black Power Ideologies: An Essay in African-American Political Thought* (Philadelphia: Temple University Press, 1992) 74–90.

[6]For characterizations of the historic, mainline African-American denominations as integrationist, see E. Franklin Frazier, *The Negro Church in America* (New York: Schocken Books, 1964) 72–80; Peter J. Paris, *The Social Teaching of Black Churches*, (Philadelphia: Fortress Press) 75–80; Hans A. Baer and Merrill Singer, *African-American Religion in the Twentieth Century* (Knoxville: University of Tennessee Press, 1992) 58–59, 65–110; see Hart M. Nelsen and Anne K. Nelsen (*Black Church in the Sixties* [Lexington: University of Kentucky Press, 1975]), who debunk the claim that either religious orthodoxy or racial accommodationalism inhibited black church involvement in the Civil Rights movement.

These organizations were the outgrowth of postwar African-American migration and urbanization patterns across the nation. In 1940, 68 percent of African Americans still resided in the South, but the growth rate of African-American population had slowed to 1 percent, the lowest in the nation. Between 1940 and 1950, the African-American populations of Atlanta and Memphis increased by 704 and 2,281, respectively, while the African-American population of Birmingham decreased by 2,880.[7] A major redistribution of the African-American population, begun during the Great Migration, was underway, with three major streams: from the south Atlantic states to the midwest and east north central states; from the mid-south states to the midwest or east north central states; and from the trans-Mississippi South to Los Angeles and San Francisco.[8] Like previous migratory patterns, the migrations could be interpreted as spontaneous and planned protest to the structural inequities that kept African Americans trapped at the bottom of the socioeconomic ladder, despite the postwar prosperity and progress enjoyed by other Americans.

Regardless of where they migrated, African-Americans found themselves largely confined to segregated neighborhoods in urban areas, where they were forced to carve out a tenuous sphere of economic, political, and social autonomy. While certain associations (businesses, churches, social organizations) clearly benefited from racial segregation in the South, none of them escaped the pernicious effects of an order that systematically denied them civil rights, political participation, and equal access to government services. No more was this disparity more evident than in the area of public education. In almost every measurable standard the education of African Americans in the South lagged behind that of white southerners: literacy rate, drop-out rate, public funding, teacher training and salaries, etc. By 1940, for example, only 64 percent of

---

[7]Cited in Daniel M. Campbell and Rex. R. Johnson, *Black Migration in America: A Social Demographical History* (Durham NC: Duke University Press, 1981) 117.

[8]Ibid., 118.

African-American students of school age were attending school, as compared to 71.6 percent of white students; the median schooling completed by African Americans was 5.7 percent compared to 8.7 percent for whites.[9]

Despite private and federal initiatives to improve educational opportunities for African Americans in the South, education for the masses of African Americans remained separate and unequal. Thus, on 17 May 1954, when the Supreme Court declared, "We conclude that in the field of public education, the doctrine of 'separate but equal' has no place. Separate educational facilities are inherently unequal,"[10] it signaled a hopeful message to African Americans and their allies across the nation: Jim Crow could be successfully wounded, but it would take a more concerted effort to destroy it completely. In the wake of the Supreme Court decision and the massive resistance it incited in the South, African-American euphoria soon gave way to chastened optimism.

This chapter discusses CME responses to the *Brown v. Board of Education* decision, beginning with a proposal to change its denomination name from "Colored" to "Christian" Methodist Episcopal Church at its 1954 General Conference. An issue of much debate, the name change can be understood as a reflection of the denomination's evolving commitment to racial inclusivity and ecumenical commitment, as initially embodied in the "Paine College Ideal." Although the proposal to change the name was not a direct result of the Supreme Court's decision to outlaw segregation, the two events became linked as significant turning points for the CME Church. Together they propelled the CME Church into deeper levels

---

[9]Thomas Minter and Alfred Prettyman, "Education," vol. 2 of *Encyclopedia of African-American Culture and History* (New York: Simon & Schuster Macmillan, 1996) 858. For the state of African-American education in the postwar era, prior to the *Brown v. Board of Education* decision, see Henry Allen Bulluck, *A History of Negro Education in the South from 1619 to the Present* (New York: Praeger, 1967) and "The Schooling of Black Americans," in *A Common Destiny: Blacks and American Society*, ed. by Gerald D. Jaynes and Robin M. Williams (Washington DC: National Academy Press, 1989) 329–90.

[10] Albert P. Blaustien and Robert L. Zangrando, eds., *Civil Rights and African Americans* (Evanston IL: Northwestern University Press, 1968) 437.

of Civil Rights activism and ecumenism, especially in response to the 1955–1956 Montgomery, Alabama, bus boycott under the leadership of Martin Luther King Jr. This chapter also examines the immersion of two CME leaders in the earliest phases of the Civil Rights movement: the Reverend Henry Bunton in Memphis, Tennessee, and Professor Charles Gomillion in Tuskegee, Alabama.

1954—A TURNING POINT FOR THE CME CHURCH

On 17 May 1954, the Colored Methodist Episcopal Church met on the final day of its twenty-third General Conference at the Mt. Olive Cathedral CME Church in Memphis, a cavernous structure that formerly housed the all-white First Baptist Church.

The conference had already proven to be momentous, if not contentious. The election of bishops generated even more intrigue than usual as the College of Bishops included a special addendum in their episcopal address. They requested that two of their senior colleagues, James Hamlett and Henry Porter, not be retired because of age, in direct opposition to the mandatory age retirement law passed at the previous General Conference. Their health, both physical and mental, was good, the bishops argued, and these venerable fathers represented an important link between the church's past and future. Without much debate, the conference voted almost two to one to retain the two bishops for an additional four years.[11] Little did the church realize that it was about to be engulfed in a social revolution that would require not only the energy and vision of these two transitional leaders, but also of a new generation of leaders.

Even if the 1954 General Conference did not fully anticipate the imminent social eruptions of the 1954 Supreme Court decision and the 1955 Montgomery bus boycott, it was not totally surprised. For several years preceding the conference the church had been wrestling with a proposal to change the racial designation in its name to reflect these new social realities. Consequently, one of the major issues confronting the General Conference was that of changing the

---

[11]*Journal of the General Conference 1954*, 129–30; see Othal H. Lakey, *The History of the CME Church* (Memphis: CME Publishing House, 1985) 542–43.

denominational name, an issue involving hotly contested constitutional, theological, and social matters, all of which had been debated for four years in church meetings and articles in the *Christian Index*. Advocates of the name change believed that excising "Colored" and replacing it with a more inclusive name was a progressive sign of the church's commitment to racial inclusivity and Christian ecumenism. Advocates like Henry Bunton saw the retention of the name "Colored" as morally and theologically indefensible, comparing it to the shameful display of Jim Crow signs in the South.[12]

In a strongly worded editorial titled, "'Colored' a Hate Sign' Yes!" Bunton laid out his arguments for a name change. He began with a biblical and theological analysis of the word "church," suggesting that although the New Testament word for church originally meant a localized town meeting or gathering, it had wider implications, because even in these local meetings care was taken to represent all interests and people residing in that locale. From this interpretation, Bunton defined the church as "the entire body of human servants of God, irrespective of race, color, or place of abode. The Church is the depository of divine truth; to preserve...a pure theist faith and practice of holy and worthy service, and to keep alive the truth of a universal empire."[13]

If one accepts this definition of the church, Bunton reasoned, then "we must face the fact that there cannot be a 'Colored Church.'" In a tactful demur to traditionalist objections, Bunton appealed to the notion of progressive development: "When one suggests the idea of replacing the word 'Colored' with 'Christ' it is not to discredit the work of the fathers; it is to honor the fathers proving that we can not build on the foundation laid by them but can see the necessity of pulling baby clothes off an adult institution."[14] Bunton concluded his editorial with a compelling analogy that appealed to the day-to-day experiences of many of his readers. Bunton charged it was embarrassing enough to see "colored" signs on cafes, bus seats,

---

[12]*Christian Index*, 5 February 1954, 4, 13.
[13]Ibid.
[14]Ibid., 14.

drinking fountains, and toilets, but to see them on churches was immoral. He implored the CME Church to remove the "Jim Crow signs off our churches" by replacing the name "Colored" with "Christ": "For years I have contended against white supremacy.... But we must remember if we insist on 'colored' just as the white people have insisted, either directly or by implication, on 'white' we are attempting to substitute black supremacy for white supremacy. There is not a fundamental difference between the two. Give me 'Christ Methodist Church!'"[15]

Not all CMEs agreed with Bunton's "Jim Crow" analogy and arguments. For example, P. L. Hardin, a lay leader from Indianapolis, dismissed Bunton's arguments as propaganda. In defense of the founders' choice of the name "Colored" in 1870, Hardin countered, they chose it "voluntarily and without any thought of segregation," since Jim Crow laws did not emerge until 1891 in Tennessee.[16] In a veiled reference to the NAACP, Hardin charged that the resolution to change the church's name was initiated by "sinister forces and civic organizations" outside of the church. Without mentioning Channing Tobias by name, Hardin refereed to "[o]ne of the leaders of our church...who is an officer on a civic organization" as using "high powered methods" to persuade the conference that the change from "Colored" to "Christian" was a fight against segregation.[17] Like Bunton, Hardin conceded that racial segregation was an evil, but argued that it would not be abolished through legislative or judicial action—"only by the Spirit of the Master." Although Hardin invoked the notion of the separation of religion and politics embodied in the "spirituality of the church" ideology of first-generation CMEs, his ten objections were more constitutional than spiritual in nature, pertaining more to property rights and incorporation laws.[18] Nevertheless, Hardin's invoking of the "spirituality of the church" suggests the doctrine's tenacious hold on the social views of the

---

[15]Ibid.
[16]*Christian Index*, 1 July 1954, 8.
[17]Ibid.
[18]Ibid.

church and proved to be an undercurrent in the conference debate
between CME traditionalists and progressivists.

DENOMINATIONAL NAME CHANGE AT 1954 GENERAL CONFERENCE

As anticipated, the issue of changing the church's name became the
dominant issue of the 1954 conference. In the quadrennial address,
delivered by Senior Bishop Bertram Doyle, the College of Bishops
made two references to a possible name change, thus setting the stage
for debate. First, in a section discussing the current state of race
relations in the country, the bishops expressed the hope that
"Negroes may stand on their feet, first; as Americans; and last, if at
all, as Negroes." Such an occasion, they suggested, might signal the
desire to "seek new names for ourselves, names…that would remove
some of the stigma that adheres to the political subordination,
economic depression, social ostracism, and personal disfavor. It is not
written that the terms 'colored' and 'Negro' may not yet become as
respectable as 'Christian' and Methodist."[19]

A second and more explicit reference to changing the name came
at the conclusion of the address in one of nine recommendations the
College of Bishops made to the General Conference. The bishops
plainly recommended that the conference consider changing the name
to reflect present conditions and progress toward racial integration:
"It will neither be a departure from the temper, or trend, of the times
if this General Conference will give consideration to a change in the
name of the Colored Methodist Episcopal Church."[20] Thus the stage
was set for the formal presentation of the resolution to change the
church's name.

That day came on 5 May 1954 when a committee of eight clergy
and lay delegates, led by Channing Tobias of the New England
Conference, presented the following resolution to the General
Conference:

---

[19]*Journal of the General Conference 1954*, 59.
[20]Ibid., 90.

A RESOLUTION TO TAKE THE RACIAL DESIGNATION
FROM THE NAME OF THE [CME] CHURCH

We believe the true Church of Jesus Christ is a fellowship of all believers who own him as Lord and Master and worship him in spirit and truth, and that no exclusion of any follower from participation in the work of his kingdom on account of race, color or national origin is justifiable.

We therefore in the ever increasing number of Christian denominations that are adopting the principle and practice of inclusiveness in membership, and membership participation without racial and color discrimination.

We are aware of the inconsistency of having racial designation in the name of our Church. Therefore, without implying any lack of loyalty to or respect for the founding fathers, we recommend that in harmony with the times, and in accordance with the recommendation in the message of the Bishops to the General Conference, proper steps be taken to change the name of our church from Colored Methodist Episcopal Church to Christian Methodist Episcopal Church, or some other suitable name that retains the initials, but does not carry a racial designation.[21]

In addition to Channing, other signers of the resolution were W. L. Graham (central Georgia); Mrs. W. F. Harris (east Georgia); Henry Bunton (Kansas–Missouri); N. S. Curry (California); E. W. Taggart (Birmingham); Aaron Brown (south Georgia); and J. B. Bullock (Dallas-Fort Worth). The committee's composition is noteworthy for several reasons. First, as a result of both mission outreach and African-American migration, every region of the nation was represented. The committee reflected the geographical dispersion of the church at mid-century, from its strong base in the South (Georgia, Alabama) to the North (New England), to the Midwest (Kansas–Missouri), to the West (Dallas-Fort Worth, California). This

---

[21]*Journal of the General Conference, 1954*, 129–30.

geographical diversity, however, almost obscures the second characteristic of the committee: the majority, if not all, of its members were born and reared in the South. Third, at least two members of the committee, Channing and Graham, were educated at Paine College, where they were influenced by the "Paine College Ideal" of racial and ecumenical cooperation.[22] Fourth, a follow-up on these delegates reveals that more than half of them—Tobias, Curry, Graham, Bunton, Harris—would go on to serve in denominational positions where they would directly and indirectly shape the church's stances on Civil Rights and ecumenism.[23]

As expected the committee's resolution sparked considerable debate on the conference floor. A motion to adopt the resolution passed, but as Lakey points out, the original motion called for the approval of the resolution and not the actual name changes itself. On 17 May 1954, the same day the Supreme Court handed down its historic decision, the General Conference of the CME Church approved a motion to change its name from "Colored" to "Christian" Methodist Episcopal Church.[24] The conference hastily scrambled to

---

[22]Like Tobias, Graham became an articulate exponent of the "Paine College Ideal," both as an educator at Paine College and a lay leader in the CME Church. Graham outlined his views on racial and denominational cooperation in a PhD dissertation at New York University and in several articles, in which he used Paine College as a case study on the evolution of racial integration through mutual and cooperative enterprises between southern blacks and whites; see William L. Graham, "Patterns of Intergroup Relations in the Cooperative Establishment, Control, and Administration of Paine College (Georgia) by Southern Negro and White People A Study of Intergroup Process" (PhD diss., New York University, 1955); "An Historic Instance of the Mutual Involvement of the Southern Negro," *Journal of Educational Sociology* (28 October 1954): 83–87; "A Way of Racial Integration," *Christian Index*, 14 April 1955, 5, 13–15.

[23]For example, Harris, the lone female member of the committee, would later serve as president of the Woman's Connectional Council (1955–1963); Graham would serve as General Secretary of the Board of Lay Activities; Curry and Bunton would be elected bishops at the 1958 General Conference.

[24]Lakey, *The History of the CME Church*, 539–41. Denominational and scholarly accounts vary considerably in pinpointing when the actual name change occurred: Was it in May 1954 when the General Conference approved the motion to change the name? Or was it on 19 June 1956 when the College of Bishops announced that the name change had been ratified by the majority of annual conferences as

draft a resolution commending the Supreme Court for its courageous decision:

> The Twenty Third General Conference of the Colored Methodist Episcopal Church now in session at Mt. Olive Cathedral, Memphis, Tennessee, has just been apprized by an Associated Press Release that the Supreme Court of the United States has reached its long awaited decision on cases contesting the constitutionality of segregation in the public schools. And the decision was unanimously upheld by the Justice of the Courts [sic].
>
> Throughout the whole course of its history, the [CMEC] has stood for and religiously advocated the principles of brotherhood and fellowship, and has advocated under this fellowship equal treatment for all citizens of the United States.
>
> It has been our considered judgement that a nation advocating universal democracy and Christian fellowship could not afford to have any laws, or customs with the force of laws operating to deny any citizen of the nation equal rights set forth by the constitution.

---

stipulated by the church's Judicial Council? According to Lakey's chronology (*The History of the CME Church*, 685, n.8), the motion passed at the 1954 General Conference was vetoed by the College of Bishops on constitutional grounds and was referred to the Judicial Council. Lakey found no corroborating evidence to indicate that the Judicial Council deliberated on the matter and interpreted the 17 May 1954 vote at the General Conference as the official and legally necessary action to effect the name change. Any subsequent procedures were "ex post facto attempts to correct the record." Reports in the *Christian Index*, however, dispute Lakey's interpretation. The *Index* reported not only the Judicial Council's deliberations and decision to send the resolution to the annual conferences for ratification, but also the announcement by the College of Bishops on 19 June 1956 of the majority vote in favor of the name change; see "Judicial Court Rules Changing Denominational Constitutional," 1954, *Christian Index*, 26 August 1954, 7, 15. In a meeting on 28 July 1954 at Mt. Olive Cathedral in Memphis, the nine justices unanimously affirmed and upheld the bishops' veto and recommendation that the name change be ratified by the majority of annual conferences.

We therefore, commend the Supreme Court of the United States for its heroic and just decision regarding the matter and we urge all people to accept this decision as a fair and just one; and that we unite in an effort to secure for all people alike the fullest and richest blessing under what we regard as the most epochal and significant decision rendered by our Supreme Court since the day of Reconstruction.[25]

For progressive church leaders like Tobias and Bunton, the fortuitous timing of these two decisions was more than coincidental: it was the fruit of a long battle against racial segregation and discrimination. The two decisions would remain historically linked and etched in the memories of CMEs, marking significant turning points in the history of the CME Church and the freedom struggle for all African Americans. More than a cosmetic change to the denominational face, the name change represented the denomination's deepest commitment to the ideal of racial inclusivity. Though the church had long been committed to this ideal, its actualization had been hampered by two obstacles: the entrenchment of racial segregation in the South, and the captivity of CMEs by the southern, evangelical conception of the "spirituality of the church." Both obstacles had been challenged in the postwar era as the CME Church became increasingly immersed in Civil Rights activism and ecumenism. Consequently, by the 1950s the denomination had developed a new consensus and optimism that the racial problem could be successfully confronted through a combined effort of religious, social, and political action. The name change, then, embodied the church's emerging consciousness about its identity as an inclusive body and agent of racial reconciliation.[26]

---

[25] 1954 General Conference Minutes.

[26] Elements of this consensus and optimism can be discerned clearly in the bishop's address and the resolution for the name change. Both documents refer to favorable times and trends for race relations, with the resolution pointing specifically to "an ever increasing number of Christian denominations that are adopting the principle and practice of inclusiveness in membership" ("The Episcopal Address," *Journal of the General Conference 1954*, 59; "Resolution to

Even though the 1954 Supreme Court and General Conference's decisions were quickly stalled by constitutional challenges, CMEs euphorically hailed them as epochal events. E. P. Murchison, editor of the *Christian Index*,[27] joined other CMEs in seeing the name change as a blow against racial segregation. He reprinted an excerpt from the resolution and described its passage and immediate reception by CMEs and other Christian bodies, including the World Council of Churches. "Changing our name," he wrote, "received more attention than any other act of the general conference."[28] He proudly recapped how the World Council of Churches had recently used the CME name change as an "illustration of the churches [sic] attitude against segregation throughout the world." In light of this world-wide recognition, Murchison offered the following challenge to opponents of the resolution:

> Changing the name of our church is definitely a fight against segregation.... We hope those who conscientiously oppose the changing of the term "Colored" to "Christian for other reasons will now reconsider their point in light of world-wide publicity, focus of attention, and condemnation prematurely given our church in the fight against segregation. To defeat the legislation...would be more than embarrassing, it would be tragic.[29]

Six years later Murchison's successor as editor, N. S. Curry, recalled the dual events of 17 May 1954 as a holy day comparable to the exodus of the Hebrews.[30]

Take the Racial Designation from the Name of the C.M.E. Church," *Journal of the General Conference 1954*, 129–30).

[27]During the Civil Rights movement (1954–1968) the *Christian Index* functioned as the main forum for information and commentary for the CME Church, with a succession of three activist-editors advocating support for the movement: E[lias] P. Murchison, N[orris] S. Curry, and M. C. Merriweather.

[28]*Christian Index*, 26 August 1954, 3.

[29]Ibid., 3.

[30]"May 17 A Day to Remember: Will You?" *Christian Index*, 3. 26 August 1954

Yet like the biblical exodus, emancipation from bondage in Egypt did not translate into immediate occupation of the Promised Land. Although the Supreme Court declared the doctrine of "separate but equal" unconstitutional and ordered the desegregation of public schools, the schools did not suddenly become integrated. Likewise, although the CME Church discarded "Colored" from its name to signify a more inclusive identity, the racial inclusivity it desired did not materialize overnight. Within a very short time, Christian Methodists learned with other African Americans that entry into the promised land of equality would demand even greater struggle on their part.

In the wake of massive southern resistance to the *Brown v. Board of Education* decision, N. S. Curry accused southern politicians of blocking efforts to implement desegregation.[31] By invoking the principle of "states' rights," these politicians had reduced the decision to "a propaganda sheet with which to stir the fires of racism for political gain," wrote Curry. "They are Un-American and might well be investigated for their conduct." Although Curry pointed out these injustices, he offered no specific proposals or strategies to counter this resistance. Instead, he appealed to the noblest principles of American democracy as embodied in the Declaration of Independence and the U.S. Constitution. "These legal instruments," he said, "objectify our noblest spirit and highest principles; they, together with our religious heritage, are all for which we ought to live and

---

[31]"Politicians and the Supreme Court Decision," *Christian Index*, 30 September 1954, 4. Massive resistance to the *Brown v. Board of Education* decision in the South included political action by local, state, and federal legislators; litigation to reverse or block implementation; the organization of white citizens councils and other white supremacist organizations to rally mass protest; and the use of violence and intimidation to thwart implementation. For general treatments of the entire region, see Numan V. Bartley, *The Rise of Massive Resistance: Race and Politics in the South during the 1950s.* (Baton Rouge: Louisiana State University Press, 1969); Kluger, *Simple Justice*; *The Citizens' Council: Organized Resistance to the Second Reconstruction, 1954–1964* (Urbana IL: University of Illinois Press, 1994).

die."[32] In contrast to the race-baiting rhetoric of demagogues like Senator Theodore Bilbo of Mississippi, Curry's critique seemed moderate and restrained. CME activism, however, was not limited to occasional editorials and episcopal statements in the *Index*. After 1954, CME activism broadened in scope to include more visible participation in local Civil Rights struggles and organizations.

CMES AND THE NAACP

Perhaps the most visible expression of this heightened level of CME activism as a result of its resounding triumph in the 1954 *Brown v. Board of Education* decision was the denomination's renewed commitment to the NAACP. The CME Church had long supported the NAACP and its legal strategies;[33] several bishops and clerics had served on its national board and others as officers and members of local chapters. But with or without the endorsement of the College of Bishops, church-wide support of the NAACP, especially in the South, was scattered and tepid because of the risks entailed. However, after 1954, CME support for the NAACP increased, influenced by a three-

---

[32]N. S. Curry, "Politicians and the Supreme Court Decision," *Christian Index*, 30 September 1954, 4. Curry's appeal to democratic principles as a means of political redress is consistent with what Peter Paris has described as the "black Christian tradition" principle, which is rooted in the "biblical doctrine of the parenthood of God and the kinship of all peoples" (10) and institutionalized in the independent black churches in their struggle against racial injustice (*The Social Teachings of the Black Churches* [Philadelphia: Fortress Press, 1985] 10–14). While I do not deny this principle was normative for earlier CMEs, I am aware that it was often consciously and unconsciously veiled to deflect white retaliation and was subjugated to the southern evangelical norm of the separation of religion and politics.

[33]In 1948, for example, the *Christian Index* ([7 October 1948], 7–8) published an abridged version of "Defending Your Rights" from the NAACP Handbook, of which pastors were urged to read from their pulpits and post on their bulletin boards. The excerpt identified which states were complying with federal laws and proposed specific steps to follow if people were denied or arrested for seeking accommodations.

pronged strategy for implementing the *Brown v. Board of Education* decision: legislative action, political pressure, and public action.[34]

Among the methods the NAACP used to rally church support was a regular column in church periodicals called "Surveying Social Action," written by the Reverend Edward Odoms, national church secretary of the NAACP. These brief columns focused broadly on the church's role in society, keeping churches informed of the latest developments in Civil Rights laws and policies. For example, in one of Odoms' first columns in the *Christian Index*, he addressed the issue of integration in the church, a concept that "must be accepted in theory and principle if we are to be consistent in our hope for a more inclusive brotherhood as well as a constantly developing democracy."[35] Odoms pointed to the progress made in the integration of education, sports, housing, and industry as positive examples for the church to emulate, lamenting "it would be a pity if the 'House of God' should remain the last bulwark of segregation."[36] Odoms, though, was careful to clarify what he meant by integration: "First it does not mean the assimilation of Negro churches into white ones; integration is a 'two-way street' that respects the 'distinctive' religious experience of all parties; they have spiritual and cultural values that can enrich the larger community."[37] With this important clarification in mind, Odoms encouraged African-American congregations to vigorously "evangelize among whites." Likewise, Odoms exhorted white churches to become more socially active in their local neighborhoods and to integrate their churches at the "levels of leadership and the pew."[38]

A second way the CME Church demonstrated its renewed support of the NAACP was through financial support. At its May 1961

---

[34]This strategy was devised at a 4 June 1955 meeting of state representatives in the District of Columbia to counteract the legal and political resistance to the implementation of the *Brown v. Board of Education* decision; see *Crisis* magazine (June–July 1955): 337–40, 381.

[35]"Church Integration," *Christian Index*, 29 October 1954, 6.

[36]Ibid.

[37]Ibid.

[38]Ibid.

meeting in Atlanta, the College of Bishops launched a church-wide fundraising drive for the NAACP, designating July as "Freedom Month." "The struggle for freedom is much more than a financial or legal matter," declared the bishops. "Struggle leads to success when we support instruments of freedom with love, service, and finances. Our legal support for freedom is effectively at work for us in the NAACP."[39] Each bishop was responsible for mobilizing support and raising funds within his episcopal district, a portion of which was donated to a lifetime NAACP membership for the bishop.

Third, in addition to giving the NAACP wider visibility and increased financial support, CME clergy and lay members offered leadership and service to the NAACP at all levels. For example, Channing Tobias served as president of the Board of Directors from 1953 to 1960, while several bishops served as national board members.[40] Several local CME pastors accepted the challenge of heading local NAACP chapters, including the Reverend David Cunningham in Memphis.[41]

However, it was in the South where the NAACP became the opprobrium of die-hard segregationists and the target of racial violence and legal restrictions. Here CME and NAACP activists would encounter other allies in the struggle, advocating a different philosophy and strategy than the NAACP's three-prong approach. These alternatives included the nonviolent philosophy and strategies of Dr. Martin Luther King Jr. and the Southern Christian Leadership Conference (SCLC), the Congress of Racial Equality (CORE), and the Student Nonviolent Coordinating Committee (SNCC). For CMEs in the South, the conflagration of competing philosophies, strategies,

---

[39]"CMEC Endorses Program to Financially Support NAACP," *Christian Index*, 13 July 1961, 3.

[40]On Tobias's tenure as NAACP board president, see O. Joyce Smith, "Channing H. Tobias: An Educational Change Agent in Race Relations, 1940–1960" (PhD diss., Loyola University of Chicago; William L. Graham, "A Commemoratory Statement of Dr. C. H. Tobias, 1882–1961," *Christian Index* 1962, 8.

[41]*Christian Index*, 22 June 1961, 4. In 1961, Cunningham was commended by the NAACP for helping to increase membership in the Memphis chapter from 400 to 6,000 during his three-year tenure.

and organizational ties was nowhere more evident than in the city of Memphis, the site of the 1954 General Conference.

By 1954, Memphis had become the unofficial headquarters for the CME Church. The city boasted several large congregations and denominational offices, including Mt. Olive Cathedral, Collins Chapel CMEC, Collins Chapel Hospital, and the offices and residences of several bishops and general officers.[42] Moreover, Memphis's strategic location on the Mississippi River literally and figuratively allowed it to function as the unofficial "capital" of three states—Tennessee, Mississippi, and Arkansas.[43]

Life in Memphis and the Mississippi Delta was hardly idyllic. Founded in 1819, the city's first African-American settlers were largely free and worked as laborers and artisans in an antislavery environment, where they enjoyed voting and citizenship rights. The fortunes of the African-American community in Memphis changed drastically, however, as Memphis became a major port city for the slave trade. In 1834 a new state constitution opened the way to African-American disenfranchisement and the growth of slavery in Memphis. Slavery ended in Memphis in 1862 when the Union army laid siege to the city and occupied it for the duration of the war, setting up a large freedmen's camp that attracted thousands of former slaves throughout the region.[44]

---

[42]In 1968, Memphis was officially designated the headquarters for the CME Church when the publishing house moved from Jackson, Tennessee, to a new facility that also housed other denominational offices. The denominational seminary, Phillips School of Theology, had already moved to Atlanta in 1958, joining a consortium of theological schools from six denominations to form the Interdenominational Theological Center (ITC); see Lakey, *The History of the CME Church*, 566, 592–93.

[43]Henry C. Bunton, *A Dreamer of Dreams: An Autobiography* (Memphis: CME Publishing House, 1998) 68.

[44]On the history of African Americans in the antebellum and Reconstruction eras, see Ida B. Wells-Barnett, *Crusade for Justice: The Autobiography of Ida B. Wells*, ed. Alfreda M. Duster (Chicago: University of Chicago Press 1970); Bobby Lee Lovett, "The Negro in Tennessee, 1861–1866: A Socio-Military History of the Civil War Era" (PhD diss., University of Arkansas, 1978); Lester C. Lamon, *Blacks in Tennessee, 1791–1970* (Knoxville: University of Tennessee Press, 1981); Joseph H.

This large influx of African Americans in Memphis and other urban areas in the South adversely affected race relations in the postwar era. In 1866, mounting tensions between African Americans and struggling white immigrants over jobs in Memphis culminated in a race riot that ravaged the African-American community. The plight of African Americans in Memphis tenuously improved with the passage of Civil Rights laws during the Radical Reconstruction, led by the Republican-dominated Congress. In coalition with Irish and Italian immigrants, African Americans were elected to seats on the Memphis city council and school board and appointed to other municipal positions. This short-lived experiment in a multiracial democracy collapsed with the legal establishment of Jim Crow in Tennessee. From that time no African American would hold elective office until the Civil Rights movement in the 1960s.

In the long interim, civil, political, and property rights eroded for African Americans in Memphis, forcing many to migrate in search of better opportunities. For those who remained, segregated life in Memphis evolved into a thriving and semi-autonomous African-American community centered around Beale Street, a commercial center lined with theaters, salons, small businesses, real estate agencies, law offices, and other professional services. From 1928 to 1948, African-American political life was dominated by the political machine of Mayor Edward "Boss" Crump, a Democrat whose machine dominated Memphis politics well beyond his terms as mayor. An avowed segregationist, Crump was able to forge an alliance with African Americans that provided his political machine with a dependable voting bloc in exchange for services to the African-American community. Only in the 1950s did an independent African-American party emerge, the Shelby County Democratic Party, to challenge the segregationist stance and policies of the Crump machine.[45]

Cartwright, *The Triumph of Jim Crow: Tennessee Race Relations in the 1880s* (Knoxville: University of Tennessee Press, 1976).

[45]For social and political developments within the African-American community in Memphis during the Jim Crow era, see Lester C. Lamon, *Black Tennesseans, 1900–1930* (Knoxville: University of Tennessee Press, 1977) and

In 1954, about the same time Martin Luther King Jr. arrived in Montgomery, Alabama, as the new pastor of Dexter Avenue Baptist Church, Henry Bunton arrived in Memphis. The forty-one-year-old Bunton had just completed his seminary studies and a brief stint with CME Board of Christian Education.[46] Although Bunton was twenty-six years older than King, they shared several commonalities. Both were born and raised in the South, Bunton in rural Alabama to a sharecropping family and King in urban Atlanta to a middle-class family. They both received their seminary education at theologically liberal schools in the North.[47] Both left promising career opportunities in the North to return to the segregated South, and both

---

Blacks in Tennessee; David M. Tucker, *Lieutenant Lee of Beale Street* (Nashville: Vanderbilt University Press, 1971) , *Black Pastors and Leaders: The Memphis Clergy, 1819–1972* (Memphis: Memphis State University Press, 1975), and *Memphis Since Crump: Bossism, Black, and Civic Reformers, 1948–1968* (Knoxville: University of Tennessee Press, 1980);

[46]Bunton initially transferred to Memphis to work as director of leadership training and as a writer for Sunday school literature with the CME Board of Christian Education; however, after a year, he was appointed as pastor of Mt. Olive Cathedral, his largest appointment to date; Bunton, *A Dreamer of Dreams*, 68. On King's theological studies at Crozer Theological Seminary and Boston University, see "The Crozer Years," in vol. 1 of *The Papers of Martin Luther King Jr.*, Called to Serve, Vol. 1 ed. Clayborne Carson (Berkeley: University of California Press, 1992) 161–441; "Boston University," in vol. 2 of *The Papers of Martin Luther King Jr.*, ed. Clayborne Carson (Berkeley: University of California Press, 1994) 59–284; John J. Ansbro, *Martin Luther King Jr.: The Making of a Mind* (Maryknoll NY: Orbis Books, 1982). On King's ministry at Dexter Avenue Baptist Church in Montgomery, see Martin Luther King Jr., *Stride Toward Freedom* (New York: Harper & Row, 1958).

[47]Because of his impoverished background in rural Alabama, Bunton's early education was often interrupted by the demands of sharecropping; at age twenty-two, married with two children, he returned to Miles College in Birmingham to complete high school. He completed two years of college at Miles before dropping out to serve as a full-time pastor, eventually receiving his bachelor's degree at Florida Agricultural & Mechanical College in Tallahassee, Florida, in 1941. After another five-year interim, during which he served as a chaplain in World War II, Bunton enrolled as a non-degree-seeking student at Perkins School of Theology in Dallas (which did not accept African-American applicants) before completing seminary at Iliff School of Theology in Denver (1951); see Bunton, *A Dreamer of Dreams*, 19–27, 50.

regarded themselves primarily as pastors rather than Civil Rights leaders.[48]

Besides their age difference, there were striking differences in the two leaders as well. First, Bunton, unlike King, did not descend from a long line of preachers, making his ascent to denominational visibility and prominence a much longer and more arduous ordeal. Second, belonging to a hierarchical denomination like the CME Church, Bunton had to operate under more institutional constraints than King did in the more localized autonomy of the Baptist churches. Bunton's compliance with denominational superiors and structures played a much larger factor in his rise up the denominational ladder than did King's in the National Baptist Convention. Despite these differences, Bunton and King were on a trajectory that thrust them into the

---

[48]But their conceptions of ministry included the church's involvement in and ministry to the community; for a comparative perspective on their early views on social ministry, see, for example, Henry C. Bunton, "The Church and the Community" (Henry C. Bunton Papers, Schomburg Center for Research in Black Culture, New York) in which he criticizes African-American churches for failing to provide effective social, health, and educational services to their communities. However, Bunton's proposal for rectifying this problem does not explicitly address civil rights or political activism as viable options for African-American churches; he merely asserts, without elaboration, that "Negro churches should cooperate with all agencies designed to train for definite participation in the affairs of citizenship" (35). For a fuller elaboration of Bunton's views on social ministry at the zenith of the civil rights movement, see his collection of sermon meditations: Henry C. Bunton, *The Challenge to Become Involved* (published by author, 1966). Beginning his ministry at Dexter Avenue Baptist Church in Montgomery, King based his views on community ministry on the premise "that the gospel of Jesus is a social as much as a personal gospel seeking to save the whole man." In his "Recommendations to the Dexter Avenue Baptist Church for the Fiscal Year 1954–1955" (in vol. 2 of *The Papers of Martin Luther King Jr.*, 287–94), King recommended the establishment of the Social and Political Action Committee for the "purpose of keeping the congregation informed concerning the social, political and economic situation," as well as to remind members of the "importance of the NAACP" and the necessity of voter registration (290). Interestingly, several of the officers and members of the proposed committee—Mrs. Mary Burks (chair), Mrs. Jo Ann Robinson (co-chair), and Rufus Lewis—would play active roles as leaders of the Montgomery Bus Boycott and the Montgomery Improvement Association (MIA); see Jo Ann Gibson Robinson, *The Montgomery Bus Boycott and the Women Who Started It: The Memoir of Jo Ann Gibson Robinson*, ed. David J. Garrow (Knoxville: University of Tennessee Press, 1987).

vortex of the Civil Rights movement of the 1950s and 1960s—the "second Reconstruction" in the African-American struggle for freedom and equality. At the center of this social revolution was a church-based movement of scattered southern African-American communities led by a cadre of educated, progressive lay and clergy and activists, of which Bunton in Memphis and Charles Gomillion in Tuskegee, Alabama, were early CME representatives.

THE MONTGOMERY BUS BOYCOTT AND THE EMERGENCE OF MARTIN LUTHER KING JR.

On 1 December 1955, the singular but heroic act of a seamstress in Montgomery, Alabama, ushered in a new phase of the African-American freedom struggle. By refusing to give up her bus seat to a white passenger, thereby defying the city's segregated seating ordinance on city buses, Rosa Parks set into motion a series of events that culminated in a 381-day boycott by the African-American community and the ultimate defeat of segregated bus ordinances.[49]

There was hardly anything novel about African Americans organizing bus boycotts in the South to protest segregated seating and unfair treatment; these boycotts had been practiced with limited success since the turn of the century.[50] In fact, two years earlier

---

[49]On the unfolding of the Montgomery Bus Boycott, see the following eyewitness accounts: Robinson, *The Montgomery Bus Boycott and the Women Who Started It*; King, *Stride toward Freedom*; vol. 3 of *The Papers of Martin Luther King Jr.: Birth of a New Age*, ed. Clayborne Carson (Berkeley: University of California Press, 1997*)*; Rosa Parks, *Rosa Parks: My Story* (New York: Dial Books, 1992). For primary sources, see Stewart Burns, ed., *Daybreak of Freedom: The Montgomery Bus Boycott* (Chapel Hill: University of North Carolina Press, 1997); for interpretive treatments, see the essays by Thomas J. Gilliam, Dominic J. Capeci Jr., Steven Miller, J. Mills Thornton III, and David J. Garrow in *The Walking City: The Montgomery Bus Boycott, 1955–1956*, ed. David J. Garrow (Brooklyn: Carlson Publishing, 1989); Taylor Branch, *Parting the Waters: America in the King Years, 1955–1963* (New York: Touchstone Books, 1988).

[50]See August Meier and Elliot Rudwick, "The Origins of Nonviolent Direct Action in Afro-American Protest: A Note on Historical Discontinuities," in *Along the Color Line: Explorations in the Black Experience*, ed. August Meier and Elliot Rudwick (Urbana: University of Illinois Press, 1976) 307–404; Richard M.

King's family friend and Baptist colleague, the Reverend T. J. Jemison, led a bus boycott in Shreveport, Louisiana, and supplied King with advice on organizing a carpool.[51]

Several factors, however, converged to make the Montgomery bus boycott unique in galvanizing African-American resistance to Jim Crow laws in and beyond Montgomery. First, the bus boycott effectively mobilized a unified community under one umbrella organization, the Montgomery Improvement Association (MIA), to protest racial injustice, thus transcending traditional class, religious, and ideological barriers.[52] Second, this united front allowed the MIA to escalate its initial demands for better treatment within the segregated bus system to a frontal assault on the unconstitutionality of the segregated bus system in Montgomery, thus opening a breech to directly challenge segregation laws in other areas. Third, the recruitment of the largely untested King as the MIA's president and spokesman provided the African-American community with an articulate leader who possessed the extraordinary ability to combine thoughtful social analysis with prophetic fervor and stirring pulpit eloquence. King's pedigree as a socially-active Baptist preacher, his formative years at Morehouse College under the tutelage of mentors like Benjamin Mays, Samuel Williams, and George Kelsey, and his graduate education at liberal schools all prepared him for the challenges of communal leadership and social ministry.[53] Fourth,

---

Dalfiume, "The Forgotten Years of the Negro Revolution," *Journal of American History* 55/1 (June 1968): 90–105.

[51]On the connections between the Baton Rouge and Montgomery bus boycotts, see Morris, *The Origins of the Civil Rights Movement*, 17–25, 58; Adam Fairclough, *Race and Democracy: The Civil Rights Struggle in Louisiana, 1915–1972* (Athens: University of Georgia Press, 1995) 159–62.

[52]King, *Stride toward Freedom*; Morris, *The Origins of the Civil Rights Movement*, 42–63.

[53]For discussions of King's cultural and intellectual roots within the African-American traditions (i.e., family, church, and schools), see chapters 2 and 3 of Lewis V. Baldwin, *There Is a Balm in Gilead: The Cultural Roots of Martin Luther King Jr.* (Minneapolis: Fortress Press, 1991); William D. Watley, *Roots of Resistance: The Nonviolent Ethic of Martin Luther King Jr.* (Valley Forge PA: Judson Press, 1985) 17–45; James H. Cone, *Martin and Malcolm and America: A Dream or a Nightmare* (Maryknoll NY: Orbis Books, 1991) 19–37.

because of King's predilection to a socially active and prophetic ministry, he was more receptive to incorporating more radical philosophies and strategies of resistance, namely, the use of the nonviolent direct-action philosophy and tactics of Mahatma Gandhi.[54] Fifth, the media attention focused on the boycott generated widespread support and attention, influencing other African-American communities to organize similar campaigns.

HENRY C. BUNTON AND THE MEMPHIS MOVEMENT

The city of Memphis was one of the southern communities that experienced major effects of the Montgomery bus boycott. Prior to the 1950s African-American clergy and churches in Memphis were not especially noted for their militancy on social issues. Only a handful of dissenting clergy, like the Reverend George Albert Lee of Beale Street Baptist Church and the Reverend Dwight Kyle of the AME Church, defied African-American accommodation by challenging the Crump machine.[55] The 1954 *Brown v. Board of Education* decision spurred a new sense of insurgency in the Memphis African-African community, especially the local NAACP chapter and African-American clergy. In 1954, Baptist minister Van Malone assumed leadership of the NAACP, whose membership had now swelled to more than 4,000.[56]

In 1955, CME clergy in the city organized the Ministers' Alliance of the CME Church, Memphis, with Bunton as its first president. Serving as political-action wing of the church, the purpose

---

[54]The influence of Gandhi's nonviolent philosophy and tactics on King and the Montgomery movement was mediated through Bayard Rustin and Glenn Smiley, activists with the Fellowship of Reconciliation, who were dispatched to Montgomery to persuade King to incorporate nonviolent theory and practices; see King, *Stride toward Freedom*, 85; Burns, ed., *Daybreak of Freedom*, 18–23, 161–72; Ansbro, *The Mind of Martin Luther King Jr.*, 132–46; Sudarshan Kapur, *Raising Up a Prophet: The African-American Encounter with Gandhi* (Boston: Beacon Press, 1992) 146, 155–56.

[55]See Tucker, *Black Pastors and Leaders*, 101–107; in 1948, Kyle, a member of the executive committee of the NAACP, ran unsuccessfully for Congress on the Progressive party ticket with integration as his main platform.

[56]Tucker, *Black Pastors and Leaders*, 106–107.

of the new organization was "to furnish leadership for the members and followers of the Colored [MEC] in and around Memphis, to make itself a clearing house for discussions of and action upon community matters that may rightly affect the people, provided that at no time shall the Ministers' Alliance function as a purely partisan political organization."[57] Meeting twice a month on Tuesdays, the CME Alliance organized its members into the following committees: executive, program, finance, public relations, social relation, civic, evangelistic, courtesy, and sick committees. The social relation and civic committees, in particular, reflect the church's increased involvement in local community affairs, notwithstanding its disclaimer that the alliance would not "function as a purely partisan political organization."[58] Even if the alliance was committed to a nonpartisan political stance, it did not hesitate to offer commendations and criticisms to area politicians. For example, in the aftermath of the murder of Emmett Till in Money, Mississippi, Bunton wrote this note to Governor Hugh White: "We have observed with satisfaction that the Press and the good people of Mississippi have taken a similar position for law and decency. Every person of Christian conscience in the Nation is looking with hope and confidence to you and the law enforcement agencies in the great State of Mississippi to see that the guilty parties are apprehended and that justice prevails."[59]

The emerging social and political consciousness of CMEs in the South, as expressed by the Ministers' Alliance in Memphis, was further enhanced by expanding ecumenical involvement with other African-American churches and associations. Encouraged by local African-American politicians and business leaders in Memphis, for instance, the alliance members linked with other local clergy and laity on 17 August 1955 at the Pentecostal Church of God in Christ to organize a political-action organization called the Ministers and

---

[57]Constitution of the Ministers' Alliance of the Colored Methodist Episcopal Church, Memphis, Tennessee (1955) (Henry C. Bunton Papers).

[58]Ibid.

[59]Letter from Bunton to Governor Hugh White, 6 September 1955 (Henry C. Bunton Papers).

Citizens League. To his surprise, Henry Bunton, president of the CME Ministers' Alliance and the newly appointed pastor of Mt. Olive Cathedral CME Church, was unanimously elected the league's first president.[60] Avowedly nonpartisan, the purpose of the organization was to "protect and promote the civic, political, religious and educational welfare of the citizens irrespective of race, creed or color." But unlike Bunton's CME alliance, the Ministers and Citizens League more aggressively pursued voting registration as a Civil Rights strategy. With Mt. Olive as headquarters for this drive, Bunton stressed to his own congregation the necessity of voting as a criterion for good citizenship. "If more of us register, it will mean more consideration," Bunton implored. "I feel a person can be a better Christian by being a better citizen, and that means registering to vote."[61] While the drive generated only moderate success in boosting the number of African-American voters in Memphis, adding only 5,000 new voters out of a potential pool of 39,000,[62] it marked a major turning point in the involvement of African-American churches in Memphis politics, particularly those affiliated with the former Colored Methodist Church. By linking Christian moral behavior with civic responsibility, Bunton mounted yet another challenge to the inherited doctrine of "the spirituality of the church" that had stymied the CME Church's social activism during the first Reconstruction. In the mid-1950s, Bunton and a cadre of other socially active CMEs were determined that the CME Church had to be involved in the second Reconstruction.

With the surge of African-American voters and political activism in the mid-1950s, it was just a matter of time before the African-American community would test its political clout by running a slate of candidates for political office. Consequently, in the 1959 municipal elections, a united front of church, civic, and business leaders

---

[60]Tucker, *Black Pastors and Leaders*, 110.

[61]Quoted in ibid., 110.

[62]Despite the increase in African-American voters, Reverend Roy Love lost a bid for a seat on the Memphis school board by 5,000 votes. However, African-American voters made the difference in electing several white candidates supportive of desegregation; see Tucker, *Black Pastors and Leaders*, 110–11.

supported a slate of four candidates: ministers Henry Bunton and Roy Love for board of education seats, attorney Benjamin Hooks (also a minister) for juvenile court judge, and attorney Russell Sugarmon for commissioner of public works.[63] Running on a ticket strongly supporting the desegregation of schools, Bunton and Love's platform included the following goals:

(1) to initiate immediate plans to comply with the 1954
    Supreme Court decision on segregation;
(2) to adopt objective standards in the hiring of teachers;
(3) to consolidate city and county school districts;
(4) to eliminate "frills" and incorporate fundamentals of
    education.[64]

Despite some minor breeches of unity by a few preachers, the majority of Memphis's 400 ministers supported the slate by contributing funds, attending mass rallies, hosting pre-election day prayer services, and urging members to vote. Although they succeeded in registering 5,000 new African-American voters, this unprecedented African-American turn-out was not enough to overcome the white majority vote, as all four candidates lost by rather substantial margins.[65] Nonetheless, the massive turn-out in support of a united slate of candidates not only revealed the potential political power of African Americans in Memphis, but also encouraged progressive leaders to press more vigorously for political representation and accountability.

For CMEs in Memphis, and for the denomination at large, Bunton's political activism had at least two important effects. First, by transgressing the accepted norm that clergy should steer clear of partisan politics, Bunton's candidacy helped pave the way for other CMEs, both clergy and laity, to run for municipal and government

---

[63]Tucker, *Black Pastors and Leaders*, 110–13.

[64]1959 Freedom Banquet program (14 August 1959) (Henry C. Bunton Papers).

[65]Tucker, *Black Pastors and Leaders*, 112–13; Bunton, 75–76.

offices, thus participating more fully in the political realm outside of the church. Prior to 1959, there is little record of CMEs running for municipal offices in the South.[66] While the number of CMEs running for office did not increase dramatically during the Civil Rights movement, Bunton's candidacy helped to pave the way for wider CME political participation by encouraging CMEs to vote and even pursue political office. By doing so, CMEs had taken another step toward challenging and reversing the inherited doctrine of the "spirituality of the church."

Second, by mobilizing an independent political coalition to represent African-American interests in Memphis, Bunton offered an example for CMEs to emulate in other local contexts. The Bunton-led Ministers and Citizens League and the Volunteer Coalition were locally based and supported, only indirectly tied to national political parties or Civil Rights organizations, including the highly influential NAACP. Although Bunton and Love ran on a ticket that strongly endorsed the NAACP desegregation stances, their campaigns were directed by neither the local chapter nor national office; consequently, they were free to adopt a variety of strategies to fit their local context, including those from King's SCLC and its affiliate chapters.

---

[66]However, this is not to suggest that CME ministers or lay persons never ran or campaigned for government offices in the South, only that the CME stance toward political engagement tended to militate against active involvement. Moreover, with the complete political domination of whites in the Jim Crow system, few African Americans of any religious affiliation were able to mount successful campaigns for office; the blatant use of such political stratagems as majority white primaries, poll taxes, registration tests, and violent intimidation effectively blocked African-American political representation and empowerment; see Steven F. Lawson, *Black Ballots* (New York: Columbia University Press, 1976).

PROFESSOR CHARLES GOMILLION AND
THE TUSKEGEE MOVEMENT

Another CME leader influenced by the 1955 Montgomery movement was Charles Gomillion, professor of sociology at Tuskegee Institute and president of the Tuskegee Civic Association (TCA).[67] Born in Edgefield County, South Carolina, Gomillion arrived in Tuskegee in 1928, the same year he graduated from Paine College. Initially assigned to teach ancient and medieval history in the high school department, Gomillion began teaching sociology after returning from a leave of absence in 1933, which he spent studying sociology at Fisk University. At Fisk, Gomillion honed his skills as a sociologist and "race leader" under the mentorship of Dr. Charles Johnson and Dr. Bertram Doyle.[68] Although Gomillion never fully adopted the accommodating philosophy of Booker T. Washington, his exposure to race-relations theory at Paine, the University of Chicago, and Fisk afforded him a more nuanced appreciation of Washington's philosophy and program.

When he returned to Tuskegee in the fall of 1934, Gomillion channeled his energies into teaching sociology and challenging the

---

[67]Outside of Robert J. Norrell's pioneering study of the Civil Rights movement in Tuskegee (*Reaping the Whirlwind: The Civil Rights Movement in Tuskegee* [New York: Vintage Books, 1986]), Gomillion's role in the broader movement has received only scant attention from civil rights and church historians. For example, there are only brief references to Gomillion in the *Christian Index*, which refer to him as a "CME layman" (3 December 1959; 1 February 1962, 11, 14; 24 December 1964, 3), and no references to him at all in Othal Lakey's discussion of CME leaders in the Civil Rights movement (*The History of the CME Church*, 578–84). There are two possible reasons for this oversight. First, unlike King and Bunton, Gomillion was not a preacher, but an educator; in fact, he was not active in a local church or denomination. Second, despite his twenty-five-year term as the undisputed race leader in Tuskegee (and Macon County), his gradualist approach to race relations in the 1940s and 1950s was largely superseded by the more aggressive, direct-action approaches in the 1960s, led particularly by student activists.

[68]Norrell, *Reaping the Whirlwind,* 34–35. Both Johnson and Doyle had completed their doctoral work in the sociology of race relations under the direction of Robert E. Park, who himself had ties with Booker T. Washington and the Tuskegee Institute.

white hegemony of the political system in Macon County that shut African Americans out of the electoral process as voters and elected officials. The chief mechanism for challenging this system was the TCA, originally founded in 1910 as the Tuskegee Men's Club, a civic organization of the Tuskegee Institute comprised of faculty and administrators devoted to improving public services. By 1941 Gomillion led the group in adopting a new name to reflect its expanded constituency and mission. Though still dominated by Tuskegee faculty the association included a wider spectrum of the African-American populace in Macon County, including several women's groups. The name "Civic" referred to Gomillion's strong commitment to the idea of "civic democracy," which he defined as "a way of life...in which all citizens have the opportunity to participate in societal affairs, and benefit from or enjoy public services, in keeping with their interests, abilities, and needs without the limitation or restriction based on race, color, creed, or national origin."[69]

On the practical level, a number of instruments were employed by the TCA to achieve Gomillion's idea of color-blind civic democracy in Macon County: economic boycotts, voter registration drives, and civil litigation. However, a law passed by the 1957 Alabama state legislature, outlining a plan to reconfigure the political boundaries of the city of Tuskegee and to exclude all-black sections from the vote, presented the TCA with its most severe test to the implementation of "civic democracy." Left unchallenged, the state legislature's plan to gerrymander Tuskegee would reduce the African-American voting population from 400 to a mere dozen, reversing the meager political gains African Americans had achieved in the previous two decades. On 25 June 1957, 3,000 people crowded in and around the Butler Chapel AMEZ Church, the same church where Booker T. Washington founded Tuskegee Institute in 1881, to discuss a plan of action to fight the bill. Gomillion informed the audience that the TCA had exhausted all avenues in meeting with local and state officials but to no avail. African Americans in Macon County had no

---

[69]Quoted in Norrell, *Reaping the Whirlwind*, 41.

effective representation in local government and this new bill threatened to evict them as voters.

Gomillion announced that TCA would lead a "selective buying" campaign as its first response. "We are going to buy goods and services from those who make no effort to hinder, from those who recognize us as first-class citizens," said Gomillion, intentionally avoiding the word "boycott."[70] Weekly mass meetings, like those held in Montgomery and other movement centers across the South, were held on Tuesday evenings throughout July and August to sustain the momentum of the campaign; Martin Luther King Jr. and Fred Shuttlesworth attended the 2 July meeting to address the demonstrators.

In August 1958 Gomillion and the TAC launched the next phase of protest by filing suit against Tuskegee mayor Phillip Lightfoot and the city of Tuskegee, charging that the gerrymander had denied Tuskegee blacks of their citizenship rights. On 15 November 1960 the U.S. Supreme Court, in *Gomillion v. Lightfoot (364 U.S. 399)*, ruled unanimously that racial gerrymandering had violated the Fifteenth Amendment rights of Tuskegee's African-American population.

CMEs and the Southern Christian Leadership Conference

As a result of his forceful leadership in the Tuskegee movement, Gomillion was invited to participate in the launching of a new regional Civil Rights organization, the SCLC. Founded in 1957 as a means of building upon the momentum of the Montgomery bus boycotts and other southern boycotts, the SCLC embodied the African-American church's institutional thrust for racial justice and equality in the South and beyond.[71] Adopting as its motto "To

---

[70]Ibid., 93–95.

[71]The initiative to organize a regional organization of civil rights leaders came from a circle of advisors from the North who supported the Montgomery movement, including Bayard Rustin, Ella Baker, and Stanley Levinson. Rustin, a protégé of A. Phillip Randolph and A. J. Muste, was the executive director of the War Resisters League (WRL) and former director of race relations of the FOR (Fellowship of Reconciliation), a Christian-based pacifist organization committed to racial justice.

Redeem the Soul of America," the nascent organization drew deeply from the prophetic roots of the African-American church tradition—its most progressive leadership, its moral fervor, its prophetic preaching, and, most importantly, the expressive spirituality and suppressed rage of African-American Christians.

While the Ministers and Citizens League of Memphis did not become an affiliate member of the SCLC, Bunton did represent Memphis at the organizational meeting as one of the city's most visible Civil Rights leaders. He was subsequently appointed to the SCLC board of directors and the executive board, joining Reverend Joseph Lowery of Mobile, Alabama, and Reverend James Lawson of Nashville, Tennessee, as the only Methodist members of the Baptist-dominated hierarchy of the SCLC. Bunton's tenure as a board director apparently did not include direct participation in SCLC campaigns in the 1960s in Augusta, Georgia (1961), Albany, Georgia (1962), Birmingham, Alabama (1963), Selma, Alabama (1965) and Memphis, Tennessee (1968). Possibly one reason for Bunton's detachment from SCLC campaigns was his increased responsibility in the denomination, especially upon his 1962 election to the episcopacy. Even prior to his election, Bunton wrote to King that he (Bunton) had "spread himself too thin," both in church and community work, and he alerted King that he would not be able to attend the 1960 SCLC convention in Shreveport, Louisiana.[72]

In 1942, Rustin helped the FOR give birth to the Congress of Racial Equality (CORE) in an effort to apply interracial civil disobedience to the anti-segregation struggle. Two earlier conferences in January and February of 1957 (in Atlanta and New Orleans) preceded the August 1957 conference in Montgomery, where the organization was formally constituted with a shortened new name, a constitution, a slate of officers and board of directors, and nonviolent direct-action as its selected strategy; on the organization of the SCLC, see especially Morris, *The Origins of the Civil Rights Movement*; Burns, ed., *Daybreak of Freedom*, 29–33; Fairclough, *To Redeem the Soul of America*; Thomas R. Peake, *Keeping the Dream Alive: A History of the Southern Christian Leadership Conference from King to the Nineteen Eighties* (New York: Peter Lang, 1987).

[72]Letter from Bunton to Martin Luther King Jr., 26 July 1960 (Henry C. Bunton Papers).

In some ways Bunton's limited involvement in crucial SCLC campaigns in the South appears highly ironic, even contradictory, to his earlier advocacy of personal and institutional involvement in the Civil Rights struggle. After being elected bishop, the highest elected office in the CME Church, did Bunton redirect his attention from Civil Rights activism to denominational maintenance? Evidence from his post-Memphis career suggests otherwise. While his involvement in the SCLC obviously declined, there was no abatement in his commitment to or advocacy of Civil Rights activism; his election to bishop merely gave him a broader base and more authority to advocate for both denominational and local church support for the movement. And with his appointment to the Seventh Episcopal District, which extended along the Atlantic seaboard from New England to South Carolina, Bunton preached his message of radical involvement to CMEs in the North and the South from his strategic headquarters in the nation's capital. It was a message that emphasized social activism and ecumenism as necessary to push the Civil Rights agenda forward.

The 1955–1956 Montgomery bus boycott led by Martin Luther King Jr. not only provided a new strategy for social change, but also infused new hope in the CME quest to build a fully integrated society and church. While denominational leaders responded to the unfolding events of the 1950s by drafting position statements and rallying church-wide support for the NAACP, local leaders like Henry Bunton in Memphis and Charles Gomillion in Tuskegee played key roles in organizing local protest movements clearly influenced by the Montgomery bus boycott. By the late 1950s the CME Church as a denomination publicly committed itself to the Civil Rights movement through its social witness and public proclamations. In May 1957 a throng of CME bishops, ministers, and laypeople joined 30,000 other marchers in the ecumenical Prayer Pilgrimage for Freedom held in Washington, DC, which was preceded by a denominational prayer at Lane Chapel CME Church.[73] At the 1958 General Conference the bishops declared in their episcopal address that the church needed to

---

[73]*Christian Index*, 30 May 1957, 3–4.

take a more active role in "creating a moral climate (through teaching, preaching, and practice) in which racial tensions and problems can emanate into cooperative efforts, practical solutions and understanding."[74] With such pronouncements and actions the recently christened "Christian" Methodist Episcopal Church had immersed itself in the treacherous waters of the Civil Rights movement. The turbulent decade of the 1960s would both test and refine the church's renewed commitment to racial justice and ecumenism.

---

[74] "The Episcopal Address," *Journal of the Twenty-fourth General Conference*, appendix 3.

CHAPTER 5

The Sacred Call to Activism:
CMEs and the Student Activism
of the 1960s

The year 1960 marked an upsurge in Civil Rights activism with the injection of youthful idealism and radicalism. Black and white students across the country were magnetically drawn to the swirl of activity taking place in the South. Perceptive observers within the CME Church could not help but notice this youthful insurgency. "Youth [are] awake," observed the Reverend C. D. Coleman, director of the church's Board of Christian Education and director of the 1960 National Youth Conference, which convened that July at Dusable High School in Chicago. Placing this awakening in a global context, Coleman added,

> Their awakening has set the world ablaze with an un-
> quenchable desire for human equality. This was demonstrated
> by the Freedom Fighters of Hungary. It is evidenced by the
> tide of Nationalism which floods Africa and the Far East. It is
> expressed in the peaceful demonstrations in the Southland, as
> they protest the pattern of segregation that blights our be-
> loved country. All these insurgents belong to the same move-

ment which is sweeping the world demanding full realization of liberty and justice.[1]

Bishop B. Julian Smith, whose episcopal district encompassed many of the hot spots in Tennessee, noted that youth were "growing impatient with the speed at which their adult leaders are bringing under control the forces that oppress the human spirit and threaten the very existence of civilization and human life on this planet."[2] Fortunately, he added, that impatience was largely nonviolent in nature "against what they consider to be man's inhumanity to man."

In their own carefully worded statement, "What This Conference Said to the World as a Group of Young People Concerning Human Relations," youth leaders echoed much of the burgeoning Civil Rights idealism of their elders. For example, they affirmed the theological underpinnings of the movement as "the Christian idea of the brotherhood of man, under the fatherhood of God in local, national and world economic and religious interaction. We believe that as young Americans and young Christians all men are brothers under God."[3] Similarly, they expressed their alarm at the "blighted areas of America in which citizens are denied their voting privileges and are faced with other acts of discrimination. We feel that all citizens should enjoy the abundance of American prosperity...including its community and the mutual advantages of its common economy."[4] In light of Christ's admonition to love one's neighbors, CME youth confessed that "to be silent in the face of injustice, need and exploitation would be denying [Christ]."[5] No doubt inspired by the student insurgency in Greensboro, North Carolina, and other southern cities, CME youth were likely also encouraged by recent statements and actions by their denominational leaders.

Four months prior to the National Youth Conference, the College of Bishops released a "Statement to the [CME Church]"

---

[1]*Christian Index*, 28 July 1960, 3–4.
[2]Ibid.
[3]*Christian Index*, 9–11.28 July 1960.
[4]Ibid.
[5]Ibid.

addressing a number of problem issues in the world and the country. On the domestic front, the bishops addressed the problems of racial violence, religious intolerance, urban renewal, labor tensions, and Civil Rights. In response to the bombing and desecration of churches in the South, the bishops charged, "We have suffered grievously from such practices as a minority group. Yet we register our unwavering condemnation.... We call upon our people to set their faces as hard as flint against all bombings, desecration and vandalism."[6] In the quest for Negro Civil Rights, however, the bishops stopped short of endorsing the direct-action strategies of the SCLC, CORE, or SNCC. Instead they called for a "stronger effort to broaden the scope of our present laws as well as to guarantee rights to a submerged minority" regarding the right to suffrage as the prime test of citizenship. "To deny, or restrict, the use of the ballot to any group results in second-class citizenship."[7] The bishops concluded that moral degeneration was at the root of the national and global problems highlighted in their statement: "Instances of graft and corruption, of decay in the centers of our government, of injustice and favoritism, [indicate]...that our moral fibre is weakening, our moral tone deteriorating." What was needed, they proclaimed, was "a moral rehabilitation within ourselves" in light of the Christian ethic.[8]

Although it is difficult to determine how many of the CME youth attending the 1960 conference heeded this call by joining the student movement, a minority did become active in movement centers across the South, particularly in Nashville, Atlanta, Birmingham, and Memphis. In addition to being major movement centers, each of these cities had a contingent of CME churches and African-American colleges from which to recruit young demonstrators. This chapter examines the distinct roles of three CME leaders who were drawn to the movement centers in Nashville and

---

[6]"A Statement to the [CME Church] by the College of Bishops," *Christian Index*, 4 August 1960, 5–7.
[7]Ibid.
[8]Ibid.

Atlanta: seminary professor Joseph Johnson Jr., SNCC activist Ruby Doris Smith, and Civil Rights attorney Donald Hollowell.

THE NASHVILLE STUDENT MOVEMENT

History has accorded the 1960 Greensboro, North Carolina, sit-in as the primary spark for the infusion of students in the Civil Rights movement.[9] The student movement in Nashville, however, was the source of the sit-in movement's early leadership and philosophy. Nashville's importance in the student movement of the 1960s can been seen in three major developments: the intensive training of students in the philosophy and tactics of non-violent resistance; the close relationship between students and existing leaders and organizations; and the subsequent role of Nashville student leaders in SNCC.[10]

Composed of students mostly from the city's African-American colleges (Fisk University, Tennessee A & I University, and American Baptist College), the Nashville student movement was closely related to the Nashville Christian Leadership Conference (NCLC). An affiliate of the SCLC, the NCLC was founded in 1958 under the leadership of the Reverend Kelly Miller Smith, pastor of First Baptist Capitol Hill and SCLC's first chaplain. Smith approached Martin Luther King Jr. about organizing an affiliate chapter in Nashville because he felt that the NAACP was "not equipped to do the whole job," even though it was the strongest Civil Rights organization in the

---

[9]On the origins of student sit-ins, see Martin Oppenheimer, "The Genesis of the Southern Student Movement: A Case Study in Contemporary Negro Protest" (PhD diss., University of Pennsylvania, 1963) ; on the Greensboro sit-ins, see especially William H. Chafe, *Civilities and Civil Rights: Greensboro, North Carolina, and the Black Struggle for Freedom* (New York: Oxford University Press, 1980); chapter 1 of Clayborne Carson, *In Struggle: SNCC and the Black Awakening of the 1960s* (Cambridge MA: Harvard University Press, 1981).

[10]On the Civil Rights movement in Nashville, see Kelly Miller Smith, *Pursuit of a Dream (The Nashville Story)* (Kelly Miller Smith Papers, Vanderbilt University); David E. Sumner, "The Local Press and the Nashville Student Movement, 1960" (PhD diss., University of Tennessee); Sandra A. Taylor, "The Nashville Sit-In Movement" (master's thesis, Fisk University, 1973); David Halberstam, *The Children* (New York: Random House, 1998).

city.[11] He sensed the need for a new organization that could involve the grass roots of the Negro community and that could function independently of other groups.

On 15 January 1958 Smith called a meeting of area ministers at Capers Memorial CME Church[12] to organize for SCLC's voter registration campaign, "Crusade for Voters." Despite King's warning to not create another Civil Rights organization in Nashville, the ministers voted to form a permanent organization, the NCLC, that would focus on voter registration and Christian social action. Smith was selected as president, along with Enoch Jones and Joseph Johnson Jr. as vice-presidents.[13] Johnson, the pastor of Capers Memorial CME Church, was completing his PhD in New Testament at Vanderbilt University, having been admitted in 1955 as the university's first African-American student.[14]

---

[11]Smith, *Pursuit of a Dream*, 2.

[12]Originally known as the "African Mission," Capers Memorial CME Church was founded in 1832 as one of the first churches organized exclusively for African Americans in Nashville. In 1852, the name of the church was changed to Capers in honor of William Capers, the nineteenth-century founder and promoter of slave missions in the Methodist Church; see Carmelia Gregory, "Leaders of Afro-American Nashville: Capers Memorial (CMEC)" (Nashville Conference on Afro-American Culture and History, 1987); Othal H. Lakey underscores the irony that on 1 January 1871, the first bishop of the CME Church, William Henry Miles, preached his first episcopal sermon at a "church of ex-slaves...at the center of the historic forces which brought the church into being" (*The History of the CME Church* [Memphis: CME Publishing House, 1985] 226–27).

[13]Smith, Pursuit of a Dream, 6–7.

[14]By the time of his acceptance to Vanderbilt and appointment to Capers, Johnson, a native of Louisiana, had already distinguished himself as a pastor-scholar in the CME Church. After graduating from Texas College in 1938, Johnson earned the Master of Theology (1943) and Doctor of Theology (1945) degrees at Iliff School of Theology. From 1943 to 1953, he served as the first president and professor of theology at Phillips School of Theology in Jackson, Tennessee, before moving to Nashville. After completing his studies at Vanderbilt, Johnson taught religion at Fisk University and continued to pastor at Capers Memorial CME Church. In 1960, Johnson's participation in the unfolding Nashville student movement was curtailed by his appointment as professor and director of religious services at the Interdenominational Theological Seminary in Atlanta; see *Christian Index*, 19 January 1967, 3.

In the fall of 1958 NCLC's goals shifted dramatically with the arrival of a young Methodist student named James Lawson Jr.[15] Born in Uniontown, Pennsylvania, and raised in Ohio, Lawson was the son of a Republican minister "who preached love but also wore a .38 on him as a precaution" from racial harassment. He graduated from Baldwin-Wallace College in Ohio, where he served as president of the National Conference of Methodist Youth. Influenced by the Christian pacifism of the Fellowship of Reconciliation (FOR), he served an eleven-month prison term for refusing induction into the Army during the Korean conflict. He was paroled in 1953 to teach at a mission in India. Upon returning to the United States, he enrolled at Oberlin School of Theology and transferred in 1958 to Vanderbilt University Divinity School. Before Lawson's arrival the NCLC had regarded itself as an affiliate of the SCLC but had not fully adopted SCLC's nonviolent philosophy or direct-action strategies. As a committed pacifist and regional director of FOR, Lawson quickly moved to convert the NCLC into a nonviolent organization. As newly appointed chair of the Projects Committee, Lawson conducted a series of workshops on nonviolent direct action at local churches in preparation for local demonstrations.[16]

These workshops attracted students from Nashville's black and white colleges and universities. By November 1959 Lawson and students were prepared to strike. On 28 November the students conducted test sit-ins at lunch counters at two downtown department stores and on 5 December conducted a second test sit-in, this time with little media coverage or public reaction. The holiday break interrupted the momentum of the Nashville sit-in movement, but it was rejuvenated by the outbreak of the 1 February 1960 sit-in

---

[15]This biographical profile of Lawson has been compiled from the following sources: Taylor Branch, *Parting the Waters: America in the King Years, 1954–63* (New York: Touchstone Books, 1988) 204–205; Halberstam, *The Children*, 11–50.

[16]On Lawson's role in the Nashville civil rights struggle, see Branch, *Parting the Waters*, 260–63; Halberstam, *The Children*, 121–234;

Greensboro, North Carolina, led by four students from North Carolina A & T University.[17]

In response to a call from Greensboro minister Douglas Moore, urging Nashville students to join the sit-in movement, Lawson consulted with area student leaders at Fisk University about resuming sit-ins in Nashville.[18] The Student Central Committee was organized, consisting of two representatives and an alternate from each of the participating schools. Meeting daily during the crisis, the student leaders rotated spokespersons for each demonstration and worked closely with Kelly Miller Smith and the NCLC. On 13 February, after a crash course in nonviolent direct action, 125 students from Fisk, Tennessee A & I, and American Baptist Theological Seminary commenced the first of four massive sit-ins at downtown stores during the month of February. "We took our seats in a very orderly, peaceful fashioned," recalled student leader John Lewis. "The students were dressed like they were on their way to church or going to a big social affair. They had their books, and we stayed there at the lunch counter, studying and preparing our homework, because we were denied service."[19] By the fourth sit-in demonstration on 27 February, tensions between local white citizens and student demonstrators reached a breaking point, as the first incidence of violence erupted

---

[17]On the spontaneous nature of the Greensboro sit-ins by four freshmen (Ezell Blair Jr., David Richmond, Joseph McNeil, and Franklin McCain) at North Carolina A & T, see the primary accounts of McCain (in *My Soul Is Rested: The Story of the Civil Rights Movement Remembered*, ed. Howell Raines [New York: Penguin Books, 1983] 75–82), who points to Gandhi rather than Martin Luther King Jr. as the dominant influence on their actions (79).

[18]According to Lawson, the Greensboro sit-in got underway before the Nashville movement commenced its public phase; it was a call from Moore in Durham, North Carolina, on 10 February that prompted Lawson to call a meeting of Nashville's student and adult leaders to discuss the resumption of sit-in demonstrations; *Nashville Tennessean*, 21 March 1960; Sumner, "The Local Press and the Nashville Student Movement," 27; Branch, *Parting the Waters*, 273; Linda T. Wynn, "The Dawning of a New Day: The Nashville Sit-Ins, February 13–May 10, 1960," *Tennessee Historical Quarterly* 50 (1991): 42–54.

[19]Quoted in Henry Hampton and Steve Fayer, eds., *Voices of Freedom: An Oral History of the Civil Rights Movement from the 1950s through the 1980s* (New York: Bantam Books, 1990) 57.

when a group of local white youth attacked the demonstrators, leading to the arrest of eighty students on charges of disorderly conduct. For Lewis and other students, being jailed for civil disobedience marked a turning point in their careers as Civil Rights activists. Said Lewis, "That was the first time that I was arrested. Growing up in the rural South, you learned it was not the thing to do. To go to jail was to being shame and disgrace on the family. But for me it was like being in a holy crusade, it became a badge of honor."[20]

Two days later when Nashville mayor Ben West appealed to 200 African-American ministers at First Baptist Capitol Hill to stop the demonstrations and to obey state statutes. Lawson accused the mayor of using the law to derail the demonstrations and vowed they would continue. Portrayed by local media as an "outside agitator" intent on violating the law, Lawson soon found himself pitted against both Mayor West and Vanderbilt chancellor Harvie Branscomb. When Lawson refused to halt the sit-ins, Branscomb and the Vanderbilt Board of Trustees gave him the choice of withdrawal or expulsion for violating a school policy that prohibited student participation in disorderly assemblies. Lawson's expulsion on 3 March incited a storm of controversy within the university and the community.[21] The sit-ins at lunch counters ended on 10 May, after a biracial committee of protest leaders (including Smith, Lawson, Diane Nash, and Rodney Powell) and downtown merchants negotiated a desegregation agreement. The Nashville movement as a whole, however, did not end

---

[20]Quoted in ibid., 58.

[21]While the Vanderbilt Student Senate supported Branscomb's decision to expel Lawson, other students protested by briefly picketing the administration building. On 10 March, 111 faculty members published a statement critical of the injustices that provoked the sit-ins but stopped short of openly condemning Branscomb's actions. However, on 20 March, a smaller contingent of faculty, led by nine professors and the dean of the Divinity School, along with four medical school professors, submitted their resignations. On the controversy at Vanderbilt University, see especially Paul K. Conkin, who notes that the 1960 Lawson episode gave Vanderbilt national notoriety as "one of the most reviled universities in the country" (*Gone with the Ivy: A Biography of Vanderbilt University* [Knoxville: University of Tennessee Press, 1985] 539); David E. Sumner, "The Publisher and the Preacher: Racial Conflict at Vanderbilt University," *Tennessee Historical Quarterly* 56 (Spring 1997): 34–43.

with the integration of lunch counters; it went on to target theaters, hotels, and restaurants for future demonstrations.

The success of the Nashville movement thrust several of its leaders into a broader arena of civil rights activism. Seizing upon the rising tide of student activism, Ella Baker, executive secretary of the SCLC, arranged a 16–18 April 1960 conference of sit-in leaders at Shaw University in Raleigh, North Carolina. The conference attracted more than 120 students from fifty-six colleges and high schools across the South, along with a dozen southern white students and observers from student and social reform organizations. Consisting of sixteen people, the Nashville delegation quickly emerged as leaders of the new umbrella organization—SNCC.[22] Atlanta student Julian Bond recalled that Lawson made a strong impact with his speech. Bond compared Lawson to a "bad younger brother pushing King to do more, to be more militant, to extend nonviolence—just to do more. I remember his as being a thunderous, militant speech with a more ambitious idea of what nonviolence could do than I had ever heard before."[23] Moreover, it was Lawson's firm belief in the religious underpinnings of nonviolent direct action that was reflected in SNCC's name and statement of purpose: "We affirm the philosophical or religious ideal of non- violence of our purpose, the presupposition of our faith, and manner of our action. Nonviolence as it grows up from Judaic-Christian traditions seeks a social order of justice permeated by love. Integration of human endeavor represents the crucial first step towards such a society."[24] Marion Barry of Fisk was elected SNNC's first chairman, edging out classmate Diane Nash, who in 1961 became the organization's director of direct action.

---

[22]The conference was underwritten by the SCLC and attended by King, who hoped to organize the students into a youth wing of the SCLC; on the pivotal role of Ella Baker in the organization of the SNCC, see Ella Baker, "Developing Community Leadership," in *Black Women in White America: A Documentary History*, ed. Gerda Lerner (New York: Vintage Books, 1973) 345–52; Carson, *In Struggle*, 19–26; Howard Zinn, *SNCC: The New Abolitionists* (Westport CT: Greenwood Press, 1964) 32–33; Joanne Grant, *Ella Baker: Freedom Bound* (New York: John Wiley & Sons 1998) 125–31.

[23]Quoted in Hampton and Fayer, eds., *Voices of Freedom*, 64.

[24]Quoted in Carson, *In Struggle*, 23.

American Baptist College students Bernard Lafayette, John Lewis, and James Bevel all became key staff members and field organizers for both SNCC and the SCLC.

JOSEPH A. JOHNSON JR., SCHOLAR-ACTIVIST

Joseph Johnson's departure for Atlanta in 1960 to teach at the Interdenominational Theological Seminary (ITC) preempted his taking a more active role as a CME leader in the Nashville movement, especially with his roles as a college professor and church pastor. However, the move to Atlanta thrust him into another hotbed of student activism—the hometown and operational base of Martin Luther King Jr. and the SCLC.[25] Moreover, the creation of ITC in 1957 provided Johnson with a rich ecumenical environment in which he could utilize his extraordinary gifts and extensive training for the wider church.[26] Thus, from 1960–1966, Johnson channeled his creative energies into teaching, administration, and ecumenical activities, rather than involving himself in either Atlanta's emerging student movement or the ongoing Civil Rights activism of the SCLC and the NAACP.[27] Unlike Lawson, his former Vanderbilt classmate,

---

[25]In 1960, King moved from Montgomery to Atlanta to co-pastor with his father Ebenezer Baptist Church and to devote more time to his responsibilities as president of the SCLC.

[26]In 1958, Phillips School of Theology moved from Jackson, Tennessee, to join a consortium of four seminaries within the Atlanta University Center that became the Interdenominational Theological Center (ITC). The other three schools were Gammon Theological Seminary (Methodist), Morehouse School of Religion (Baptist), and Turner Theological Seminary (AME). In 1970, two new denominational seminaries were added: Johnson C. Smith Theological School (Presbyterian USA) and Charles H. Mason Theological Seminary (Church of God in Christ); on the founding of ITC, Clarence A. Bacote, *The Story of Atlanta University* (Atlanta: Atlanta University Press, 1969).

[27]Johnson's involvement in ecumenical meetings dates back to 1950 when he represented the CME Church at the constituting convention of the National Council of Churches in Cleveland and the Eighth Ecumenical Methodist Conference in Oxford, England (1951). During his tenure at ITC, he attended the Tenth World Methodist Conference in Oslo, Norway (1961), and the Fourth World Conference on Faith and Order in Montreal, Canada (1963), where he delivered a sermon titled "The

Johnson never envisioned himself as a strategist or leader in the Civil Rights movement; he principally interpreted his role as that of a homilectician and theologian, seeking to articulate the meaning of the black religious experience.[28]

Returning to the seminary he had helped organize twenty-three years earlier in Jackson, Tennessee, Johnson turned to the task of constructing a firmer theological basis for CME ministry. In his 1947 inaugural address as the first dean and president of Phillips School of Theology,[29] Johnson declared, "The Negro minister has a great challenge and terrible responsibility. As a leader of his people and race, he must always lead the fight against discrimination and prejudice."[30] Phillips' mission was to prepare leaders to serve the "present age," said Johnson. These leaders would be guided by these four tasks: the assertion of the "sacredness of human personality"; the deliverance of the human spirit from the forces of "selfishness, hatred and fear"; the reshaping of institutional life to serve humanity;

Cost of Discipleship"; see *Christian Index*, 8 August 1963, 6 and 11; 5 October 1961, 7; 19 January 1967, 1, 3.

[28]For example, in a 1977 memo to the College of Bishops, titled "My Other Assignments" (Henry C. Bunton Papers, Schomburg Center for Research in Black Culture, New York), Johnson recounted a revelatory experience on 24 February 1976, in which Jesus Christ reminded Johnson of his "special commission and assignment" to (1) "preach the gospel, (2) to devote my talents to a writing ministry, (3) to care for the churches, and (4) to write about Him." Johnson's ultimate goal was to produce a new translation of the New Testament, based on the Greek text, and to write a four-volume systematic black Christian theology: *God of Our Weary Years*; *Jesus, the Liberator*; *Man, Broken and Redeemed*; and *The Structure of Christian Experience*. After his religious experience in 1976, Johnson published the following books and articles outlining his emerging black theology—*Proclamation Theology* (Shreveport LA: Fourth Episcopal District Press, 1977) and *Basic Christian Methodist Beliefs* (Shreveport LA: Fourth Episcopal District Press, 1978)—which built upon earlier works like *The Soul of the Black Preacher* (Philadelphia: United Church Press, 1971) and "Jesus Christ, the Liberator," in *Quest for a Black Theology*, ed. James J. Gardiner and J. Deotis Roberts Sr. (Philadelphia: United Church Press, 1971) 97–111.

[29]In 1954, Johnson resigned from Phillips to enroll as a full-time student at Vanderbilt University; four years later Phillips became a part of ITC in Atlanta.

[30]*Christian Index*, 27 March 1947, 13.

and the demonstration that fulfillment of life comes through serving the welfare of others.[31]

In August 1961, as students at the Atlanta University Center were engaged in their second year of demonstrations, Johnson attended the World Methodist Conference in Oslo, Norway. In his address to the conference, "Methodism in the Field of Social Service," Johnson traced Methodism's dual emphasis on personal and social transformation to John Wesley and the early Wesleyan movement

> The early Methodists attacked the liquor traffic. They attempted to bring into existence a classless society. They insisted on the stewardship of the plight of the poor. They insisted that the Christian was responsible for the political and social conditions which existed in society. They attempted to inaugurate prison reform and made vigorous attacks on slavery. It was axiomatic for the early Methodists that redeemed and saved men [sic] were the best instruments that God had for redeeming and saving a society.[32]

At least two ideas were implicit in Johnson's analysis of the social issues confronting Wesley's twentieth-century descendants. First, Johnson perpetuated the idea that the "problems of society are merely the reflection and manifestation of disintegration and moral collapse which occur[s] in individuals, one by one,"[33] with the corollary that the regeneration of society is effected through morally transformed individuals. Second, Johnson's analysis of historical and contemporary Wesleyan social ethics implied a subtle critique of world Methodism's failure to address the problem of racial injustice. After his election to the episcopacy in 1966, Johnson's writings gave sharper analysis of the church's role in social change and its complicity in racist structures, thus laying the groundwork for a black

---

[31]Ibid.

[32]"Dr. Joseph A. Johnson Speaks at World Methodist Conference," *Christian Index*, 5 October 1961.

[33]Ibid.

theology of liberation.[34] But as Johnson settled into his teaching and administrative duties at ITC, it would be Ruby Doris Smith Robinson, a student at nearby Spelman College, who perhaps best typified the rising tide of CME student activism in Atlanta and the wider South.

RUBY DORIS SMITH ROBINSON, STUDENT-ACTIVIST

Born in the segregated community of Summerhill to Reverend John and Alice Smith, Ruby Doris Smith Robinson was baptized into the movement in 1960 as a sophomore at Spelman College.[35] The second of seven children, Robinson was inspired by the Greensboro sit-ins and her elder sister, Mary Ann Smith. Robinson joined 200 students from the Atlanta University Center,[36] selected by the student steering committee to participate in the first wave of demonstrations against segregated facilities in downtown Atlanta. On 15 March 1960, the student-initiated Atlanta Committee of Appeal for Human Rights (ACAHR) conducted its first sit-in at the restaurant at the state

---

[34]See, for example, his "Jesus Christ, the Liberator" (97–111) and *Proclamation Theology* (Shreveport LA: Fourth Episcopal District Press, 1977), which sought to develop a black theological hermeneutic for preaching; for evaluations of Johnson's contributions to the early development of black theology, see Othal H. Lakey, "The Thought of Joseph Andrew Johnson Jr.," *Christian Index*, 25 August 1977, 4.

[35]Only within the last decade has Robinson begun to receive the scholarly attention of her male counterparts in SNCC; for an insightful treatment of Robinson's life and activism from a feminist perspective, see especially Cynthia Griggs Flemming, *Soon We Will Not Cry: The Liberation of Ruby Doris Smith* (Boston: Rowman & Littlefield, 1998) and "'More Than a Lady': Ruby Doris Smith Robinson and Black Women's Leadership in the Student Nonviolent Coordinating Committee," in *Hidden Histories of Women in the New South*, ed. Virginia Bernhard et al. (Columbia: University of Missouri Press, 1994) 204–23; Jacqueline Jones Royster, "A 'Heartbeat' for Liberation: The Reclamation of Ruby Doris Smith," *Sage: A Scholarly Journal on Black Women* (Student Supplement 1988): 64–65; Belinda Robnett, *How Long? How Long? African-American Women in the Struggle for Civil Rights* (New York: Oxford University Press, 1997) 103–11, 122, 174, 182–87.

[36]In 1960, the Atlanta University Center consisted of the following six historically African-American colleges and universities: Atlanta University, Clark College, Spelman College, Morehouse College, Morris Brown College, and ITC.

capitol building.[37] Growing up almost in the shadow of the capitol, Robinson vividly remembered her first sit-in protest: "And when the two hundred students were selected for the first demonstration, I was among them. I went through the food line in the restaurant at the State Capitol with six other students, but when we got to the cashier, she wouldn't take our money. She ran upstairs to get the Governor. The Lieutenant-Governor came down and told us to leave. We didn't, and we went to the county jail."[38]

The sit-ins escalated from the state capitol to downtown bus stations, businesses, and public facilities. As only a sophomore student, Robinson was not considered a leader in the Atlanta student movement. Robinson served on the executive committee but did not represent Atlanta at the founding meeting of SNCC in Raleigh, North Carolina. Rather, she was core member of the student committee whose level of commitment increased even as overall student participation began to wane by the summer. Along with a smaller contingent of summer volunteers, she continued to participate in demonstrations throughout the city, seeking to organize and generate support for an economic boycott of selected businesses and churches.[39]

It was her involvement in kneel-ins at white churches in Atlanta that opened her eyes to the level of racial segregation in Christian churches. When ushers blocked the door to the entrance of a white Methodist church, she admitted being shocked at their reaction, as well as the apparent indifference of the congregation.[40] However, this

---

[37]On the origins of the Atlanta student movement, see especially the essays by Jack L. Walker ("Sit-Ins in Atlanta: A Study in the Negro Revolt," 59–93) and Vincent D. Fort ("The Atlanta Sit-In Movement, 1960–1961: An Oral History," 113–87) in *Atlanta, Georgia, 1960–1961: Sit-Ins and Student Activism*, ed. David J. Garrow (Brooklyn: Carlson Publishing, 1989).

[38]Zinn, *SNCC: The New Abolitionists*, 17–18; Flemming, *Soon We Will Not Cry*, 52.

[39]Flemming, *Soon We Will Not Cry*, 51–58.

[40]Ibid., 56. Although Flemming begins her study with Robinson's funeral (14 October 1966) at Westside CME Church in Atlanta, she neither analyzes Robinson's roots in the CME Church nor her relationship with the church during her involvement in the movement. These are striking omissions, especially since

experience did not shake her faith in the church or the power of Christian idealism to confront racial injustice. Nevertheless, she expressed hope that the church would be the one arena where the race problem could be "thrashed out" and where a moral appeal to the consciences of Christians would eventually be persuasive. Consequently she saw her participation in the kneel-ins as part of the process of "awakening the hearts and minds of the people who turned us away."[41]

As Robinson's involvement in the Atlanta movement increased, the more she felt called to make a deeper commitment to the struggle. Perhaps the defining moment of her call came in the spring of 1961 when she decided to leave her junior year at Spelman to become a full-time Civil Rights activist with the ACAHR and SNCC, which was now headquartered in Atlanta. Through her attendance at several SNCC conferences and training sessions in Atlanta, Robinson met other regional leaders and organizers in SNCC, including Ella Baker, James Lawson, Diane Nash, and John Lewis. Not only did she extend her network of contacts beyond Atlanta, but she also expanded her knowledge of nonviolent theory and direct-action tactics through a variety of conference workshops and lectures.

One of the hot issues that surfaced at the October 1961 conference in Atlanta was the "jail-versus-bail" question. With the large number of students being jailed and released on bail, student leaders debated whether it would be more effective to refuse bail and overflow the jails, thereby straining local resources and putting more pressure on officials to negotiate settlements. With the matter unresolved, Robinson and her colleagues with the Atlanta student movement launched a series of demonstrations at Rich's Department Store.[42] As the negotiations among protest leaders, Mayor William Hartsfield, and city merchants dragged on throughout the fall of 1961,

---

Robinson was the daughter of a CME minister and a member of the CME Church, even serving as a delegate to the 1956 National Youth Conference in Memphis.

[41]Quoted in Flemming, *Soon We Will Not Cry*, 56.

[42]On King's involvement in the Atlanta demonstrations, see Walker, "Sit-Ins in Atlanta," 78–80, 84, 89–90; Branch, *Parting the Waters*, 286–87.

an intervening crisis in Rock Hill, South Carolina, caught Robinson's attention and summoned her involvement.

At the next meeting of SNCC in Atlanta the "jail-versus-bail" debate resumed, but the context had changed dramatically with the South Carolina crisis. A group of nine students from Friendship College in Rock Hill had actually implemented the "no-bail" strategy after being arrested for demonstrating at downtown stores. The nine were sentenced to serve out their full time by working on the York County chain gang.[43] SNNC's *Student Voice* expressed support of the Rock Hill student movement: "Their sitting shows their belief in the immorality of racial segregation and their choice to serve the sentence shows their unwillingness to participate in any system that perpetuates injustice."[44] To show its solidarity with the Rock Hill students, SNCC selected a delegation of experienced staffers to go to Rock Hill: Charles Jones, Diane Nash, Charles Sherrod, and Mary Ann Smith. However, a last-minute decision by Mary Ann to withdraw prompted Ruby Doris to volunteer for the mission, a decision that would prove to be a turning point in her career as a civil activist with SNCC. "I know that this sacrifice is small when compared with the cause which motivated me to do it," recalled Robinson. "I also realize that is the only way that one can express the philosophy of non-violence—the willingness to suffer...rather than to obey the evil of a system like segregation."[45]

The SNCC delegation harbored no illusions about what awaited them in Rock Hill; local police had anticipated their arrival and wasted little time in arresting them. The three men were assigned to thirty days of hard labor on the chain gang, while Robinson and Nash were confined to a cell with five other women. In between visiting with local community supporters and reading a steady stream of letters and books (including *The Ugly American*, *The Life of Mahatma Gandhi*, *The Exodus*, and the Bible), the two women spent long hours

---

[43]Carson, *In Struggle*, 32–33.
[44]*Student Voice*, 2 February 1961.
[45]Quoted in Flemming, *Soon We Will Not Cry*, 75.

conversing about the goals and strategies of the Civil Rights movement.[46]

Upon her release from the Rock Hill jail, Robinson returned to Atlanta, where she was greeted by a cheering crowd of family and students from Atlanta University.[47] However, there would be little respite for SNCC's battle-scarred women as they moved to the next stage of the struggle: the battle against segregation on interstate travel. Although James Farmer and CORE planned and initiated the 1961 freedom bus rides,[48] a courageous cadre of SNCC volunteers revived the rides when they were almost aborted in the Deep South.[49] Leaving Washington, DC, on 1 May, the interracial team of thirteen freedom riders traveled unmolested until they reached Rock Hill, South Carolina, where SNCC workers had only recently been released from jail. Here, the riders were attacked by a local mob but managed to escape with only minor injuries. From Atlanta, the group traveled west across the state line into Alabama. When they stopped in Anniston, a waiting mob slashed the Greyhound's tires and set the bus aflame with the riders still on board. An hour later another bus arrived

---

[46]Flemming, *Soon We Will Not Cry*, 75–76.

[47]"Spelman Co-ed Returns Home After 30 Days in South Carolina Jail," *Atlanta Inquirer*, 18 March 1961.

[48]The 1961 Freedom Rides were not the CORE's first attempt to challenge segregation in interstate travel in the South. In its 1947 "Journey of Reconciliation," CORE had sent an interracial team of sixteen activists on a two-week bus journey through Virginia and North Carolina to test a recent Supreme Court decision against segregation on interstate travel; see August Meier and Elliot Rudwick, "The First Freedom Ride," *Phylon* 30/3 (1969): 213–22; *Core: A Study in the Civil Rights Movement, 1942–1968* (Urbana: University of Illinois Press, 1975) 33–39. For accounts of the 1961 Freedom Rides, see Diane Nash, "Inside the Sit-Ins and Freedom Rides: A Testimony of a Southern Student," reprinted in vol. 3 of *We Shall Overcome: The Civil Rights Movement in the United States in the 1950s and 1960s*, ed. David J. Garrow (Brooklyn: Carlson Publishing, 1989); James Peck, *Freedom Ride* (New York: Simon & Schuster, 1962) ; McCain, *My Soul Is Rested*, 109–29; Hampton and Fayer, eds., *Voices of Freedom*, 73–96. For a detailed chronology of the rides, see Louis E. Lomax, "Freedom Rides," in *The Civil Rights Reader*, ed. Leon Friedman (New York: Walker & Company, 1962).

[49]For the role of SNCC activists in the Freedom Rides, see Carson, *In Struggle*, 32–44; Flemming, *Soon We Will Not Cry*, 72–87; Zinn, *SNCC: The New Abolitionists*, 40–61, from which the following account is derived.

to transport the freedom riders to Birmingham, where they were again met by a violent mob, this time without the protection of local law enforcement officials. The savage beating inflicted on the riders in Birmingham and the failure to secure a driver to complete the next leg of the journey effectively halted the freedom rides.

It was at this critical juncture that SNCC volunteered to resume the freedom rides. From her base in Nashville, Diane Nash recruited a group of students to journey to Birmingham for the purpose of resuming the rides. Arriving on the outskirts of Birmingham on 17 May, their bus was intercepted by local police and placed in "protective custody." After a sleepless night in jail, they were driven to the state line and dropped off along the side of the road. Shaken but undeterred, the Nashville delegation returned to Birmingham. Waiting for them at the Greyhound bus station was Robinson, who had feverishly raised funds for a flight to Birmingham.

With Robinson reunited with her former cellmate, Diane Nash, and other SNCC compatriots, the second phase of the freedom rides commenced. The second stage proved no less eventful and dangerous than the first. At their first stop in Montgomery on 20 May, the riders were viciously assaulted by a mob at the bus terminal. The next evening, as the riders attended a mass meeting at Ralph Abernathy's First Baptist Church, the church was besieged by a mob threatening to burn the church down. As sirens wailed outside and tear gas filled the air, the congregation inside assuaged their fears by praying, singing, and exhorting one another to keep faith. By dawn the next morning peace was restored in the city, and the freedom riders departed for the next leg of the journey—Jackson, Mississippi.

"If Alabama had been purgatory," warned James Farmer, "Mississippi would be hell."[50] To their surprise, though, the freedom riders did not find an angry mob awaiting them in Jackson; instead, they found the Jackson police ready to haul them off to jail. Sentenced to two months in jail, the freedom riders spent two weeks in the Hinds County jail before they were transferred to Parchman Penitentiary. In the filthy and overcrowded conditions of Parchman,

---

[50]Quoted in Flemming, *Soon We Will Not Cry*, 84.

the riders were subjected to harsher treatment, including strip searches, beatings, manual labor, and the confiscation of mattresses and other items.

According to some of her colleagues, Robinson not only left Parchman physically and emotionally scarred, but also with a changed perspective on the potential of nonviolence for social change. She acknowledged that many African Americans in the South did not consider nonviolence a realistic option over self-defense, a position she would adopt.[51] She spent the summer of 1961 working with the McComb Voter Education Project in Mississippi, urging citizens to register and teaching in a freedom school. Robinson returned to Atlanta as a youthful but experienced Civil Rights activist, but she also wanted to return to Spelman. "At the beginning of the second semester of the 1960–61 school year, I was torn between my desire to work wholeheartedly with the 'student' movement and my desire to complete my formal education," Robinson explained in her application.[52] With recommendations from Martin Luther King Jr. and others she was readmitted to Spelman College.

Even after being readmitted as a full-time student, Robinson continued to work with the Atlanta Committee on Appeal for Human Rights and SNCC. When James Forman was appointed as SNCC's first executive secretary in 1961 he tapped Robinson's administrative skills to help restructure the often chaotic organization. By 1963 Robinson formally joined SNCC's staff as Forman's administrative assistant. From 1963–1966 she served as SNCC's personnel director, southern student coordinator, bookkeeper, and administrator of the Sojourner Motor Fleet (a pool of about 100 cars for staff members in eight states). In 1966 she succeeded Forman as executive secretary, thus becoming SNCC's highest-ranking woman.[53]

---

[51]Flemming, *Soon We Will Not Cry*, 87–88.

[52]Quoted in ibid., 91.

[53]Royster, "A 'Heartbeat' for Liberation," 65; Smith's appointment came during a heated May 1966 meeting in Kingston Springs, Tennessee; the election of Stokley Carmichael as chairman and Cleveland Sellers as program secretary began the transformation of the SNCC into a black nationalist organization; see also Carson, *In Struggle*, 200–204; Flemming, *Soon We Will Not Cry*, 160–63; James

From 1963 to 1966, the newly married Robinson plunged headlong into the multiple roles of administrator, activist, student, wife, and mother. Although she suffered from a variety of medical problems, Robinson maintained a relentless schedule. With keen resourcefulness, she managed SNCC's participation in the 1964 Freedom Summer Project in Mississippi, coordinating the flow of student volunteers and resources to this massive voter registration project. In September 1964, she joined a SNCC delegation on a three-week tour to the newly independent country of Senegal in West Africa, where they conversed with President Sekou Toure about the global nature of the freedom struggle.[54]

Upon her return from Africa, Robinson participated in a series of highly intense meetings in an effort to determine SNCC's core ideology and future direction. The most volatile debate revolved around the following three issues: the necessity of including whites in the organization; the embrace of violence as a strategy for social change, thus renouncing SNCC's original commitment to nonviolence; and an ideological shift from the pursuit of racial integration to black nationalism/separatism.[55] Having already declared support for "self-defense" as an option for Civil Rights activists, Robinson even recommended that all staff members be trained in the martial arts and "gun firing." Further, it was reported that during her election as executive secretary at the 1966 Kingston meeting, she remained outside shooting targets.[56] Beyond self-defense, Robinson embraced other tenets of black nationalism, such as black economic development, cultural affirmation, and pan-African solidarity.

Although cancer was listed as the official cause of Robinson's death on 14 October 1967, some SNCC colleagues attributed it to other causes, including speculation that she may have been killed

---

Forman, *The Making of Black Revolutionaries,* 2d ed. (Washington DC: Open Hand Publishing, 1985) 447–56.

[54]Flemming, *Soon We Will Not Cry*, 145–48.

[55]On the ideological shift and ensuing debate within the SNNC, see chapters 12–15 of Carson, *In Struggle*; Forman, *The Making of Black Revolutionaries*, 433–60.

[56]Flemming, *Soon We Will Not Cry*, 158–59.

deliberately by the U.S. government. However, Kathleen Cleaver, a former SNCC coworker, said Robinson died from sheer exhaustion: "What killed Ruby Doris was the constant outpouring of work, work, work, work being married, having a child...the constant conflicts that she was subjected to because she was a woman.... She was destroyed by the movement."[57] Quite ironically, the same organization that some believed had worked Robinson to death eulogized her as the "heartbeat of SNCC, as well as one of its most dedicated administrators."[58] After her death, SNCC managed to survive a few years without this "heartbeat" before eventually collapsing.

It is difficult to assess Robinson's relationship with the CME Church during the final years of her life. Her funeral was held at her home church, West Mitchell CME Church in Atlanta, where her pastor, Reverend Earlie Hicks Jr., delivered the eulogy. However, no other denominational representatives either spoke or were listed as flower bearers or pallbearers.[59] Could it be that this courageous freedom fighter had outgrown the integrationist philosophy and tactics of elders in the church by embracing the philosophy of black power? Or did this female martyr of the movement die prematurely, before the CME Church could accept her as female leader in the movement and her more radical advocacy of self-defense and separatism?

DONALD L. HOLLOWELL, LAWYER-ACTIVIST

Unlike Ruby Doris Robinson, Atlanta attorney Donald Hollowell's contributions to the Civil Rights movement have received far more attention by both Civil Rights scholars and the CME Church.

---

[57]Quoted in Paula Giddings, *When and Where I Enter In: The Impact of Black Women on Race and Sex in America* (New York: William Morrow & Company, 1984) 315.

[58]Quoted in Royster, "A 'Heartbeat' for Liberation," 65.

[59]See the bulletin of Robinson's 14 October 1967 funeral in Flemming, *Soon We Will Not Cry*, whose work opens with a detailed account of the funeral in chapter 1. Among her SNCC colleagues present were James Forman, Julian Bond, John Lewis, Joyce Ladner, Dottie Zellner, and Cleveland Sellers; Martin Luther King Jr. and Ralph Abernathy were listed among the honorary pallbearers.

Robinson's early death, her embrace of black nationalism, her avoidance of the spotlight, and her gender all worked to marginalize her important contributions to the Civil Rights movement. Because of his long and distinguished legal career in Georgia, including many high-profile cases and clients, Hollowell has been labeled "Mr. Civil Rights" and the "hired legal gun of the movement" in Georgia.[60]

Born 19 January 1917 in Wichita, Kansas, to southern migrants Harrison and Ocenia Hollowell, "Don" Hollowell's future success in the legal profession was scarcely assured. In search of better job opportunities to support their family, Hollowell's industrious parents moved frequently, to Emporia, Eureka, and Leavenworth, Kansas, before eventually settling in California.[61] However, it was in Leavenworth that Hollowell was forced to make a critical decision concerning his own career options. In the summer of 1935, his father informed seventeen-year-old Don that he would have to drop out his senior year of high school to find a job. Stunned and angry, Hollowell enlisted in the Army, joining the 10th Cavalry in Leavenworth. His two years of noncombat service were enough to transform the rough-hewn teen into a disciplined young adult.[62]

From Leavenworth, Hollowell migrated south to attend Lane College in Jackson, Tennessee. Before being recalled to active duty in World War II in 1940, Hollowell distinguished himself as a well-rounded athlete, campus leader, and student.[63] Largely because of his religious commitment and speaking ability, Hollowell was selected to represent the CME Church at youth conferences across the nation and was identified as a promising candidate for ministry.

In 1946, Hollowell responded to the call to ministry, but it was the "sacred call to the legal profession" rather than to ordained ministry. His attendance at the 1946 Southern Negro Youth

---

[60]For the fullest treatment of Hollowell's life and career, see the admiring biography by Louise Hollowell and Martin C. Lehfeldt, *The Sacred Call: A Tribute to Donald L. Hollowell—Civil Rights Champion* (Winter Park FL: Four-G Publishers, 1997) 143–44; see also Lakey, *The History of the CME Church*, 583–84.

[61]Hollowell and Lehfeldt, *The Sacred Call*, 27–39.

[62]Ibid.

[63]Ibid., 40–47.

Conference at Allen University in Columbia, South Carolina, strongly influenced his decision to pursue a career in law.[64] As a returning World War II veteran who had experienced the brunt of segregation both at home and abroad, Hollowell's latent political consciousness was awakened by the conference's call to youth, workers, farmers, and veterans "who fought a war and dreamed a dream of free citizenship in a free South and a free world."[65] Joining hundreds of delegates from across the nation and world, he heard addresses from veteran activists Adam Clayton Powell Jr., Herbert Apthetker, W. E. B. Du Bois, and Paul Roberson.[66]

In 1947 his pursuit of the "sacred call" landed him at Loyola University Law School in Chicago. After completing law school in 1950, Hollowell and his wife, Louise, moved to her hometown of Atlanta, where he opened a fledgling law practice in the Auburn Avenue neighborhood, the center of Atlanta's segregated African-American community.[67] One of Hollowell's early cases, challenging segregation in state schools, brought him into close association with the lawyers from the NAACP's Legal Defense Fund, including Thurgood Marshall, Constance Baker, Robert Carter, Jack Greenberg, and others.[68] However, it was Hollowell's support of the Atlanta student movement in 1960 that formally marked his initiation into the Civil Rights movement.

Did Ruby Doris Robinson and Donald Hollowell know each other as lay members of the CME Church?[69] Or did they encounter each

---

[64]Ibid.

[65]Quoted in ibid., 85.

[66]Hollowell and Lehfeldt, *The Sacred Call*, 84–87.

[67]Ibid., 88–95.

[68]Ibid., 112–13; in the 1950s, the NAACP Legal Defense Fund targeted Georgia for an assault on its segregated university system. Horace Ward, a recent graduate from Morehouse College, was selected as the plaintiff, while Hollowell served as his chief counsel, along with senior Atlanta attorney A. T. Walden and other Legal Defense Fund attorneys. In 1957, a federal judge ruled that Ward's matriculation at Northwestern University Law School rendered his case moot and thereby dismissed the *Ward v. Board of Regents of Georgia* (1957) case.

[69]Hollowell was a member of Butler Street CME Church, where he served as a steward and Sunday school superintendent; he was also active on the district, annual, and general conference levels in the denomination.

other primarily as activists in Atlanta's unfolding Civil Rights movement? The latter seems more likely, given Robinson's growing alienation from the CME Church and the radicalization of her political views. Although neither leader referred to the other, their paths inevitably crossed during the 1960s, when both had established themselves as Civil Rights strategists and activists. For example, when Robinson joined the 200 students in the first demonstration organized by Atlanta University Center students, it was Hollowell whom the students sought out for legal counsel and representation.[70] With the backing of Atlanta's African-American leadership, Hollowell and other lawyers secured bail bonds for all the jailed students. Furthermore, Hollowell again represented students that October, when they resumed demonstrations at Rich's, this time joined by Martin Luther King Jr. When King refused to post bail, he was furtively transferred to a maximum-security prison in Reidsville, Georgia.[71] Despite the reservations of Martin Luther King Sr., Hollowell was called to serve as King's attorney.

In addition to Atlanta, Robinson and Hollowell were involved in the 1961–1962 Albany movement, the first combined direct-action campaign involving SNCC and the SCLC.[72] In the fall of 1961,

---

[70]Hollowell and Lehfeldt., 129–30, 141, n.2; however, there are conflicting accounts as to why the students selected Hollowell as their attorney, since he was relatively new to the city. Morehouse student Lonnie King remembered being directed to Hollowell by Samuel Williams, president of the Atlanta chapter of the NAACP, while his classmate Julian Bond said it was because Hollowell's fees were considerably lower than other well-known attorneys; see also the accounts of Bond and King *My Soul is Rested*, ed. Howell Raines New York (Penguin Books, 1983), 83–93.

[71]Holowell and Lehfeldt., 132–37; see also Branch, *Parting the Waters*, 358–62; Jack Walker ("Sit-Ins in Atlanta," 68–69) says that immediately after the first Atlanta sit-in, Hollowell and Walden left for New York to attend an NAACP conference focusing on the legal issues raised by the sit-ins.

[72]On the Albany campaign, see Hampton and Fayer, eds., *Voices of Freedom*, 97–114; Howard Zinn, *Albany: A Study in National Responsibilit* (Atlanta: Southern Regional Council, 1962) 123–46; John A. Ricks, "'De Lord' Descends and Is Crucified: Martin Luther King Jr. in Albany, Georgia," *Journal of Southwest Georgia History* (Fall 1984): 3–14; Carson, *In Struggle*, 56–65; Branch, *Parting the Waters*, 600–32.

Robinson joined eight SNCC colleagues on a bus ride from Atlanta to Albany to test Albany's compliance with the ICC's desegregation ruling. Sensing the impatience of Albany's students with the established leadership, SNCC field workers Charles Sherrod, Cordell Reagon, and Charles Jones organized the movement with the broad goal of dismantling segregation in the city.[73] In November of 1961 the movement had attracted hundreds of young volunteers from the local high school and Albany State College to test the new ICC ruling. "We told them that they would be the beginning, and we had people ready to go to the station right after they would be arrested," said Sherrod about the first students chosen. "Actually, some of us really didn't think they would be arrested because this was a federal mandate."[74] Seeking to avoid conflict with federal officials, Albany police instead arrested the students on local charges for failing to obey police orders to disperse.

As the movement gathered momentum, attracting national media attention and a flood of outside volunteers, police chief Laurie Pritchett continued to pack area jails with demonstrators. In December, in a tense situation exacerbated by further arrests and the failure of the Albany movement to win any concessions, local leaders called in Martin Luther King Jr. and the SCLC for assistance, a decision that rankled SNCC activists who resented King and the SCLC's usurpation of the movement they organized.[75] With his growing expertise and stature as a Civil Rights attorney in Georgia, Hollowell was recruited to serve as the SCLC's legal counsel.

---

[73]Only eighteen years old when he arrived in Albany, Sherrod had garnered organizational skills and nonviolent training from previous participation in the Nashville movement; see Carson, *In Struggle*, 56–58; Hampton and Fayer, eds., *Voices of Freedom*, 100–101.

[74] Hampton and Fayer, eds., *Voices of Freedom*, 100.

[75]King was initially invited by Dr. William Anderson, president of the Albany movement, to address a rally on Friday, 15 December at Shiloh Baptist Church; after negotiations broke down the next day, King led a prayer march to city hall, where he and 250 other demonstrators were arrested. On the tensions that surfaced between the SNCC and the SCLC in Albany, see Carson, *In Struggle*, 63; Adam Fairclough, *To Redeem the Soul of America: The Southern Christian Leadership Conference* (Athens: University of Georgia Press, 1987) 89–90, 103, 107.

Arriving in Albany, Hollowell was reunited with C. B. King, a close friend and legal colleague in Albany,[76] in an effort to negotiate with Chief Pritchett the release of jailed demonstrators and to devise a strategy for relieving the crowded and violent conditions in the jails. "I understood that the chief had a job he was doing, and I wanted him to exercise his job in as civil a way as possible," remarked Hollowell of his negotiations with Chief Pritchett. "When people have confidence in your common sense, you can get a lot done."[77] At SCLC's first mass meeting on 12 December, Hollowell introduced himself as one of the movement's attorneys and exhorted them to return the next morning with their "walking shoes." As the demonstrations proceeded, Hollowell and C. B. King met behind the scenes with city officials to wring out a desegregation settlement. Although city officials refused to sign a written agreement, they promised to desegregate the city's bus and train terminals and to negotiate further if the demonstrations stopped.[78] Consequently, the Albany movement agreed to a truce with city officials; Martin Luther King Jr. was released from jail and left the city. With King gone, city officials reneged on their promises, which was a crushing blow to King and the Albany movement.

The movement nonetheless sought to regroup by launching a new wave of demonstrations and arrests under the leadership of the SNCC activists; consequently, attorneys Hollowell and C. B. King

---

[76]The two had known each other for more than a decade; they had worked together in 1954 on a voting rights suit that led to the desegregation of polling places in Albany and, in 1961, represented a man charged with raping and killing an eight-year-old girl; see Hollowell and Lehfeldt, *The Sacred Call*, 156–58.

[77]Quoted in Hollowell and Lehfeldt, *The Sacred Call*, 163.

[78]Hollowell and Lehfeldt, *The Sacred Call*, 165; Aldon D. Morris, *The Origins of the Civil Rights Movement: Black Communities Organizing for Change* (New York: Free Press, 1984) 256; working behind the scenes as the chief negotiators for the Albany movement, Hollowell and C. B. King were able to secure only an oral agreement from city officials to return all bond money; to release all jailed demonstrators; to postpone all trials indefinitely, including the trials of Martin Luther King Jr. and Ralph Abernathy; to desegregate the bus stations immediately; and to establish a permanent biracial committee to oversee the process of desegregation. Within a few days, however, city officials reneged again on all points of the agreement.

stayed active in Albany during much of 1962. When Martin Luther King Jr. and Ralph Abernathy returned to Albany in July to receive sentencing for an earlier conviction, they chose to serve their forty-two-day sentence rather than to pay the fine. They were released after only three days in jail with the explanation that an anonymous person had paid their fines.[79] Plans for resuming demonstrations were halted on 20 July 1962, when a federal judge issued an injunction barring "Albany's Negroes from unlawful picketing, congregating or marching in the streets, and from any act designed to provoke breaches of the peace."[80] Wrongly believing that the federal government would intervene as an ally to the Albany movement, King decided to obey the injunction. This miscalculation proved catastrophic to the Albany campaign and to King's reputation as a Civil Rights leader.

The denouement of the "failed" Albany campaign came in August 1962 with King's arrest for leading a prayer meeting in front of city hall, prompting Hollowell to return to Albany to argue King's case (along with C. B. King, Constance Baker Motley, and Albert Kuntsler), using it to wrest some meaningful concession from city officials. King and Hollowell left Albany with no tangible concessions for Albany's African-American citizenry, but with some painful lessons for future campaigns.[81]

The following summer Hollowell returned again to southwest Georgia to join C. B. King, Constance Baker Motely, and Norman Amaker in challenging the segregated public school system in Doughtery County. This time they achieved a long-delayed victory. On 12 July 1963, a federal judge ruled that the Doughtery County

---

[79] Morris, *The Origins of the Civil Rights Movement*, 247.

[80] Quoted in ibid., 247.

[81] On the sobering lessons learned by movement leaders from the Albany campaign, see Slater King, "The Bloody Battleground of Albany," *Freedomways* 4/1 (1964): 93–101; "Our Main Battle in Albany," *Freedomways* 5/3 (1965): 417–23; Wyatt T. Walker, "Albany, Failure or First Step?" *New South* 18 (June 1963): 3–8; Martin Luther King Jr., *Why We Can't Wait* (New York: The New American Library, 1964) 43–45, 54, 71.

Board of Education was in violation of national law and ordered it to produce a desegregation plan within thirty days.[82]

The intersecting lives of Johnson, Robinson, and Hollowell in Atlanta represent the multiple responses of CMEs to the Civil Rights struggle during the 1960s. Although all three were initially drawn to the movement by the student insurgency of the early 1960s, each responded differently to his or her "sacred call" to racial justice. Johnson, the biblical scholar, professor, and preacher, channeled his protest activity to writing and speaking from his ecumenical base at ITC, where he would lay the groundwork for a theology of black freedom. Robinson, the middle-class college student at Spelman, rose from an idealistic volunteer in the Atlanta student movement to a high-ranking officer with SNCC during its transition from a Civil Rights organization to a black nationalist organization. Her tragic death in 1967 cut short a promising career, robbing both the movement and the CME Church of a persistent advocate for justice. Hollowell, who interpreted his vocation as lawyer as a sacred call to ministry, established the precedent for African-American lawyer-activists in the state of Georgia.

---

[82]Hollowell and Lehfedlt, *The Sacred Call*, 175–76.

CHAPTER 6

There Is a Balm in Birmingham: The CME Church and the Birmingham Movement, 1961–1964

In 1963 Martin Luther King Jr. and the SCLC targeted Birmingham, Alabama, as the site of their next campaign,[1] but only after several months of intense reflection on the Albany movement and the future direction of the movement. While King frankly acknowledged mistakes were made in Albany, he refused to concede that Albany was an unqualified failure. "Our movement had been checked in Albany

---

[1]For historical interpretations of the Birmingham movement, see David J. Garrow, ed., *Birmingham, Alabama, 1956–1963: The Black Struggle for Civil Rights* (Brooklyn: Carlson Publishing, 1989); David J. Garrow, *Bearing the Cross: Martin Luther King Jr. and the Southern Christian Leadership Conference* (New York: William Morrow & Company, 1986) 237–86; Glenn T. Eskew, *But for Birmingham: The Local and National Movements in the Civil Rights Struggle* (Chapel Hill: University of North Carolina Press, 1997); Edward S. LaMonte, *Politics and Welfare in Birmingham, 1900–1975* (Tuscaloosa: University Of Alabama Press, 1995); Adam Fairclough, *To Redeem the Soul of America: The Southern Christian Leadership Conference* (Athens: University of Georgia Press, 1987) 111–39; Aldon D. Morris, *The Origins of the Civil Rights Movement: Black Communities Organizing for Change* (New York: Free Press, 1984) 250–74; Taylor Branch, *Parting the Waters: America in the King Years, 1954–63* (New York: Touchstone Books, 1988) 688–812; Robert G. Corley, "In Search of Racial Harmony: Birmingham Business Leaders and Desegregation, 1950–1963," in *Southern Businessmen and Desegregation*, ed. Elizabeth Jacoway and David Colburn (Baton Rouge: Louisiana State University Press, 1982) 170–90.

but not defeated," said King.[2] "Though lunch counters remained segregated, thousands of Negroes were added to the voting-registration roll. In the gubernatorial elections that followed our summer there, a moderate candidate confronted a rabid segregationist."[3] In addition to the expanded African-American electorate, King touted the willingness of 5 percent of Albany's African-American population to go to jail as a resounding victory for nonviolent resistance. King was determined to build upon the successes of the Albany movement to save the movement from a loss of momentum and direction.

Birmingham, however, posed an enormous risk for the SCLC and movement as a whole; it was not only the largest industrial city in the South, but also had proudly earned its title as "the most segregated city in the nation." Seeking to avoid the tactical mistakes that plagued the Albany movement, the SCLC developed a more comprehensive and radical strategy for confronting segregation in Birmingham. The plan was secretly called "Project C"—"the 'C' for Birmingham's *Confrontation* with the fight for justice and morality in race relations."[4] At a three-day retreat in Dorchester, Georgia, in January 1963, SCLC staffers decided to target Birmingham's business

---

[2]Martin Luther King Jr., *Why We Can't Wait* (New York: The New American Library, 1964) 43.

[3]Ibid.

[4]Ibid., 54. While most historians have accepted King's origin and chronology of "Project C," described in King's *Why We Can't Wait*, Glenn Eskew recently has challenged this view in his detailed history of the Birmingham movement (*But for Birmingham*, 211–12, 376, n.42–44). He claims there is no reference to "Project C" in the SCLC Papers or King Papers housed at the King Center in Atlanta. However, he did locate a memo dated 23 January 1963, titled "A Tentative Schedule for Project—Birmingham," in box 1, file 7, Martin Luther King Jr. Papers, Atlanta. Moreover, the first available reference to a "Project C" came later in April 1963 in three separate memos from Wyatt Walker: "'Project C' Memo to King and Abernathy from WTW [Wyatt T. Walker]," "'Project C' General Format—Mass Meeting," and "'Project C' List of Volunteers." For treatments of "Project C" based on King's account, see Morris, *The Origins of the Civil Rights Movement*, 257–62; Branch, *Parting the Waters*, 688–91; William D. Watley, *Roots of Resistance: The Nonviolent Ethic of Martin Luther King Jr.* (Valley Forge PA: Judson Press, 1985) 73–74 and *Voices of Freedom: An Oral History of the Civil Rights Movement from the 1950s through the 1980s*, ed. Henry Hampton and Steven Fayer (New York: Bantam Books, 1990) 125–26.

community for protest. As in the earlier Montgomery campaign, the success of an economic boycott would depend greatly on mass support from Birmingham's African-American leadership and community.[5]

The SCLC already had close ties with Birmingham's Civil Rights leadership through its affiliate chapter, the Alabama Christian Movement for Human Rights (ACMHR). Organized in 1956 by Reverend Fred Shuttlesworth, the fiery pastor of Bethel Baptist Church, the ACMHR was primed to mount an assault on segregation.[6] Shuttlesworth had organized the church-based movement partly in response to Governor John Patterson's 1956 injunction against the NAACP, which effectively outlawed the organization in Alabama. As a member of the NAACP chapter in Birmingham, Shuttlesworth had often criticized the organization's alienation from the masses of African Americans. With the outlawing of the NAACP Shuttlesworth moved to organize a more grassroots movement. By 1959 the ACMHR claimed a regular membership of 900 to 1,200 people, the majority of whom were women (60 percent) and members of Baptist churches (90 percent).[7]

---

[5]King, *Why We Can't Wait*, 54–55.

[6]On the organization of the ACMHR, see Marjorie L. White, ed., *A Walk to Freedom: The Reverend Fred Shuttlesworth and the Alabama Christian Movement for Human Rights, 1956–1964* (Birmingham: Birmingham Historical Society, 1998) 2–9; Glenn T. Eskew, "The Alabama Christian Movement for Human Rights and the Birmingham Struggle for Civil Rights," in *Birmingham, Alabama, 1956–1963: The Black Struggle for Civil Rights*, 3–114; Wilson Fallin Jr., *The African-American Church in Birmingham, Alabama, 1815–1963: A Shelter in the Storm* (New York: Garland Publishing, 1997) 158–62. On the role of Shuttlesworth in the Birmingham movement, see Howell Raines, 154–61; Lewis Jones, "Fred Shuttlesworth, Indigenous Leader," in *Birmingham, Alabama, 1956–1963: The Black Struggle for Civil Rights*, 115–50; Andrew Michael Manis, "Religious Experience, Religious Authority, and Civil Rights Leadership: The Case of Birmingham's Fred Shuttlesworth," in vol. 5 of *Cultural Perspectives on the American South*, ed. Charles Reagan Wilson (New York: Gordon and Breach, 1986) 143–54.

[7]Glenn T. Eskew, "The Alabama Christian Movement for Human Rights and the Birmingham Struggle for Civil Rights. 1956–1963," Chapel Hill: University of North Carolina Press, 1997. 45–46. A membership profile also revealed that members had a higher rate of employment and voter registration than the African-American community as a whole. Though not all members could be classified as middle class, notes Eskew, they all appeared to accept middle-class values. But more importantly,

Through weekly mass meetings, protest demonstrations, and lawsuits, Shuttlesworth and the ACMHR soon became major irritants to the city's segregationist leaders, making them easy targets for both vigilante and police violence. Between 1956 and 1962, Shuttlesworth's church and home were bombed on three occasions, and he was frequently the target of retaliatory assaults and police arrests.[8] Shuttlesworth's protest activities especially incurred the wrath of Eugene "Bull" Connor, Birmingham's public safety commissioner.[9] A staunch segregationist with a short fuse, Connor's violence provided movement strategists the ideal antagonist to dramatize the plight of African Americans in the city.

Because Shuttlesworth and the ACMHR represented the most vocal, more militant voices of the African-American community, it was incumbent upon the SCLC to build a broader consensus with Birmingham's traditional African-American leadership before proceeding with "Project C."[10] Therefore, King enlisted the support of more moderate African-American leaders in Birmingham, including Lucius Pitts, president of Miles College; wealthy business leader A. G. Gaston; experienced Civil Rights attorney Arthur Shores; and

---

one common thread united all of these individuals: a deep faith and belief that God would help them destroy segregation" (Eskew, "The [ACMHR] and the Birmingham Struggle for Civil Rights," 46).

[8] White, ed., *A Walk to Freedom*, 10, 18, 30. Until 1961, Bethel Baptist Church also functioned as the headquarters and meeting place for the ACMHR; Shuttlesworth's parsonage was next to the church. By 1963 Shuttlesworth had been arrested nineteen times by Birmingham police on such charges as reckless driving, speeding, vagrancy, failure to obey an officer, disorderly conduct, and parading without a permit.

[9] For a perceptive treatment of Connor as the chief antagonist in the Birmingham movement, see William Nunnelley, *Bull Connor* (Tuscaloosa: University of Alabama Press, 1991).

[10] By traditional African-American leadership, I am referring to a contingent of middle-class leaders who advocated gradual change in the Jim Crow system through moral suasion, negotiation, and conventional political methods, as opposed to King's direct-action strategies. In other typologies of African-American leadership, these leaders have also been referred to as "moderates"; see, for example, Everett C. Ladd, *Negro Political Leadership* (Ithaca NY: Cornell University Press, 1966) 150–92; Donald R. Matthews and James W. Prothro, *The Negro and the New Southern Politics* (New York: Harcourt Brace and World, 1966) 186–90.

insurance broker and realtor John Drew.[11] In 1962 these leaders, joined by ACMHR vice-president Reverend Edward Gardner and student leader Frank Dukes, began negotiations with a coalition of white business leaders known as the Senior Citizens Committee.

Of the African-American leaders at the negotiating table, perhaps none had more at stake than President Pitts of Miles College, a small college affiliated with the CME Church. His students, inspired by the student activism erupting across the nation, were becoming restive with the slow pace of negotiations and were prepared to launch downtown demonstrations of their own. Pitts realized that if their demonstrations resulted in violent clashes with Bull Connor's police, he would be accountable to their parents, to the college's board of trustees (which was chaired by a CME bishop), and ultimately to his own conscience. "When I came here [Birmingham], I thought my involvement in civil rights was over," said Pitts.[12]

As a seasoned Civil Rights veteran who had devoted most of his life and ministry to the cause of racial reconciliation in Georgia, Pitts had accepted the presidency of Miles in 1961 to fulfill another lifelong passion: "I came to work on the education of black people, preparing them to move through the doors being opened by the foot soldiers of the movement."[13] Consequently, in 1958 Pitts declined Martin Luther King Jr.'s invitation to become the SCLC's first executive director to pursue a ministry focusing on educational opportunity and racial reconciliation. But if Pitts thought he could easily retreat from the movement into academia, he was in for a huge surprise: Birmingham in was about to erupt in a cauldron of Civil Rights activism, establishing itself as the new epicenter of the movement.

Pitts, however, should not be seen as a solitary CME voice in the Birmingham movement; there were other more radical and more conservative voices than his. But his was the firm but reassuring voice

---

[11]King, *Why We Can't Wait*, 52–53.
[12]Quoted in John Egerton, "Lucius Pitts and U. W. Clemon," *New South 25* (Summer 1970): 9.
[13]Ibid.

of good will and moderation, a soothing balm amidst the simmering shoals of racial antagonism.

This chapter examines the role of CMEs in this epicenter, primarily through the mediating influence of Pitts and other CME leaders and activists. Their participation in street demonstrations, mass meetings, and negotiating sessions helped to breathe new life into the movement, paving the way for the 1963 March on Washington and passage of the 1964 Civil Rights Act. In turn, the CME Church, both in Birmingham and across the nation, was revitalized as a movement church, consciously identifying with and endorsing the nonviolent goals, leadership, and tactics of the movement.

THE CME CHURCH IN BIRMINGHAM

The emergence of Lucius Pitts as a key leader in the Birmingham movement was partly the result of the force of his personality and commitment to racial reconciliation. It was also the result of both Miles College's strategic location as a movement base and the evolving social consciousness and activism of CMEs in Birmingham. The CME Church and Miles College had become an integral part of Birmingham's African-American community, providing both religious and educational leadership.

The founding of Birmingham in 1871 as an industrial city in the New South coincided with the rise of the Colored Methodist Church in 1870. The lure of jobs in a postbellum city with no history of slavery was especially attractive to the first African-American migrants to Birmingham. Most came from the so-called Black Belt of southern Alabama and Mississippi, where they had toiled unproductively as sharecroppers and tenant farmers.[14] Once they arrived, however, they were confronted with the harsh realities of racism in the New South, as they entered a new environment still permeated with the virulent

---

[14]On the history of African-American migrants to Birmingham in the nineteenth century, see Henry M. McKiven Jr., *Iron and Steel: Class, Race and Community in Birmingham, 1875–1920* (Chapel Hill: University of North Carolina Press, 1995); Fallin, *The African-American Church in Birmingham, Alabama*, 19–35.

racism of the Old South. African-American migrants were confined to segregated housing and inferior schools, denied equal access to social services and political franchise, and subjected to job discrimination in the steel industry. As largely unskilled laborers, African Americans found themselves "trapped in the dirtiest, most dangerous and lowest paying jobs."[15]

African-American churches responded to the plight of rural transplants by providing a range of spiritual and social services in this hostile environment. Like the migrants themselves, many of the city's first black congregations (Baptist, AME, AMEZ, CME, and others) were either transplanted from rural areas throughout the region or planted as new missions. Many of these churches were initially organized in company villages, in the downtown area, or in industrial towns bordering Birmingham. In some cases, churches of different denominations shared the same building.[16] Beginning in 1870 the North Alabama Conference of the CME Church began planting churches in the Birmingham area: St. Paul CME Church in Bessemer, Alabama (1870); Thirgood Memorial CME Church in Birmingham (1879); and Metropolitan CME Church in Ensley (1900).[17]

With the influx of rural African-Americans migrants to Birmingham in the twentieth century, the CME Church saw a steady growth of membership and churches during the Jim Crow era. Although CME churches had been a part of the Birmingham religious landscape since 1870, they seldom engaged in social activism prior to the 1960s.[18] For example, on 10 October 1961 when the Reverend L. S. Brannon, presiding elder of the Birmingham District Conference, made his annual report to the Birmingham Annual Conference, he commended each pastor for the church's accomplishments that

---

[15]Fallin, *The African-American Church in Birmingham, Alabama*, 24.

[16]Ibid., 29–30.

[17]Ibid., 26.

[18]One exception to this generalization was an effort in 1948 by several African-American leaders to organize an Urban League in Birmingham, for which Miles College president W. A. Bell and Henry Edmonds led a public fundraising drive; see LaMonte, *Politics and Welfare in Birmingham*, 148–49.

year.[19] At no point, however, did he mention the involvement of CME clergy or churches in the Birmingham Civil Rights movement or any other civic or political activities.[20]

With the initiation of "Project C" in 1963 by the SCLC and the ACMHR, CME clergy and churches began to take a more visible and active role in the movement, including Fifth Episcopal District bishop E. P. Murchison. For instance, several area clergy listed on the Birmingham Annual Conference appointment roster became active participants in various phases of "Project C." Among them were leading pastors N. L. Linsey of Thirgood CMEC, L. H. Whelchel of Metropolitan CMEC, J. E. Robinson of Miles Chapel CMEC, President Pitts of Miles College, and *Christian Index* editor M. C. Merriweather, who had been a pastor of several area churches. With the exception of Pitts, few of them had previous experience in nonviolent direct-action campaigns. Murchison and Merriweather were forceful advocates of Civil Rights activism while serving as editors of the *Christian Index*.

Merriweather's advocacy of the Civil Rights movement began while he was a pastor at various churches in Birmingham and escalated when he was elected editor of the *Christian Index*. In his monthly commentary on the Sunday school lesson, Merriweather often offered theological and sociological analyses of race relations in Birmingham and the South.

In a May 1959 column titled "A Nation Under God, or a People Under Prejudice?"[21] he invoked the warning Moses issued to the Hebrews after the deliverance from Egypt—"Beware lest you say...my power and the might of my hands have gotten me this wealth" (Deuteronomy 8:17)—to create an analogy with Jefferson County, Alabama (Birmingham). Though "one of the richest counties

---

[19]"Birmingham CME District's Report to the Birmingham CME Annual Conference, Held at Southside CME Church...October 10, 1961" *Christian Index*, 2 November 1961, 10–11.

[20]It is conceivable, though, that Brannon simply was following church protocol in highlighting strictly pastoral functions as prescribed in the CME *Discipline*—preaching, teaching, visitation, administration, and so forth.

[21]*Christian Index*, 2 July 1959, 5.

in America" (that is, in mineral deposits for steel production), it was also renowned for its deep-seated racial prejudices and tensions: "Doubtless we can find a place on earth where an iron curtain is drawn more tightly between the races than in Jefferson County, Alabama. Prosperity is a curse when it so heightens our ego, and blinds our eyes to the extent that we depreciate others."[22] Merriweather further commented on the relationship between America's manifest destiny and its racial dilemma:

> This nation was founded as a nation under God but today, our greatness problem is, the problem of race, notwithstanding all men were to find freedom and equality of opportunity upon these shores.... It is apparent that America has been chosen as God's instrument of human salvation. We can ill afford to forfeit this opportunity to the group of race haters and political demagogues whose success is due to preaching prejudice against the Negro or the Jew. Our national destiny may well depend upon our acknowledging that our hands have not gotten us this wealth but it is a gift from God for a purpose.[23]

As editor, Merriweather was in a position to influence both denominational policy and consciousness. He wrote biweekly commentaries and updates on the Civil Rights movement to a national constituency. In addition to exhorting CMEs to stand up for their rights, Merriweather also appealed to well-meaning whites to "speak up rather than be silent in the face of evil and injustice."[24] He urged them to let their voices be heard in opposition to "demigods and hatemongers who seek to get elected to public office," as had been the case with most of the governors in the South who opposed the 1954 Supreme Court decision.[25]

---

[22]Ibid.
[23]Ibid.
[24]"The Tragedy of Silence," *Christian Index*, 3–4. 27 September 1962
[25]Ibid.

Perhaps more than any other CME writer of his generation, Merriweather challenged the church to reflect on the deeper implications of the freedom movement for church and society. In an editorial titled "The Emerging New World Order," Merriweather quoted Ralph Waldo Emerson and Alfred North Whitehead on the need to confront the times.[26] He urged the church to "re-create and re-enact a new world in which we are reluctant to enter and unprepared to receive" and challenged it to re-examine some its "most cherished positions."[27] Moreover, he regarded the quest for human freedom as the "motivating dynamic" behind this "new world image," citing Gandhi's nonviolent philosophy and movement in India as a prime example.[28] He addressed the church's role in this new order:

> In dealing with the state we ought to remember that its institutions are not aboriginal, they are limited and alterable. The church cannot claim infallibility on the grounds of traditional orthodoxy. It must confirm, discipline and direct the inner structure of this new urge for freedom.... The church has both the power and the pattern to lead the world into a new experience of social and moral ethics in which the broken fabrics of human hopes and their most cherished ideas are brought together into a world community. This new world community must know no race, no class, neither can it be based on culture, only the Fatherhood of God and the Brotherhood of man is basic.[29]

PRESIDENT PITTS AND MILES COLLEGE ACTIVISM

Like other denominations, the CME Church in Alabama sought to provide educational opportunities to African Americans denied access

---

[26]*Christian Index*, 6 December. 1962, 3–4.
[27]Ibid.
[28]Ibid.
[29]Ibid.

to public schools. In 1898 the Alabama Conference of the CME Church organized a high school in Thomasville, and in 1902 established a high school in Booker City. In 1907 the two schools merged and moved to Birmingham, where a year later Miles Memorial College was chartered.[30] The school continued to function primarily as an elementary program, with a small enrollment in the secondary and college programs. By the 1930s Miles became the leading African-American college in Birmingham, with an average enrollment of several hundred students. Furthermore, Miles produced several generations of professional workers, teachers, and preachers, some of whom became active in the Birmingham Civil Rights struggle in the 1950s and 1960s.

An important precursor to student activism at Miles College came in 1956 when former Miles student Autherine Lucy defied massive resistance to become the first African-American student to be admitted to the University of Alabama.[31] Although she was expelled two weeks later, she remained optimistic about returning to the university. "I have no fear of going back. God will take care of me," said Lucy in an editorial in the *Christian Index*.[32] The editorial commended African Americans in Tuscaloosa and the NAACP for their support of Lucy: "Miles College and the [CMEC] have just reason to be proud of this young woman and Sunday School teacher.... Miss Lucy is right on her faith that God will take care of her. She is not alone in her struggle. Her battle is our battle."[33]

On 1 March 1960, inspired by Lucy's example and the rising tide of student activism at other colleges, students from Miles College and Daniel Payne College organized a "Prayer Vigil for Freedom" at Kelly

---

[30]On the founding and history of Miles College, see Othal H. Lakey, *The History of the CME Church* (Memphis: CME Publishing House, 1985) 339, 460–62; Fallin, *The African-American Church in Birmingham, Alabama*, 70–72.

[31]See chapters 1–6 of E. Culpepper Clark, *The Schoolhouse Door: Segregation's Last Stand at the University of Alabama* (New York: Oxford University Press, 1993).

[32]*Christian Index*, 1 March 1956, 3.

[33]Ibid.

Ingram Park near downtown.[34] Later that month, ten students, with the backing of Shuttlesworth and the ACMHR, launched Birmingham's student sit-ins at downtown lunch counters. They were promptly arrested and held for eighteen hours before being released on bail. Unlike campaigns in Nashville, Atlanta, and other southern cities, the Birmingham sit-in movement failed to desegregate lunch counters but succeeded in mobilizing the wider African-American community for action.

In 1961 the students joined the Jefferson County Voters League in a voter registration drive. While they frequently consulted Shuttlesworth for advice, the students maintained independence from both the ACMHR and SNCC. Led by Frank Dukes, the thirty-one-year-old president of the Miles College student government association, 700 Miles students met to adopt a statement titled "This We Believe," which listed seven specific grievances for which the students demanded immediate remedy.[35] "We do not intend to wait complacently for those rights which are already legally and morally ours to be meted out to us one at a time," said the students. "Today's youth will not sit by submissively while being denied all of the rights, privileges and joys of life."[36]

In January 1962, Dukes organized student leaders into the Anti-Injustice Committee to implement the demands of their manifesto. The first goal was to launch a "selective buying campaign" that month in downtown stores. The students were joined by Shuttlesworth and the ACMHR. President Pitts, however, expressed concern about the students' plans to demonstrate, fearing a major outbreak of violence by the police and the Ku Klux Klan. Seeking a less confrontational resolution, Pitts informed downtown merchants of the planned demonstrations and arranged a biracial meeting.[37] Pitts'

---

[34]Eskew, *But for Birmingham*, 148–51; on the role of Miles College students in the Birmingham movement, see King, *Why We Can't Wait*, 51–52; Eskew, *But for Birmingham*, 148–50, 194–202.

[35]Eskew, *But for Birmingham*, 194.

[36]Quoted in ibid.

[37]Eskew, *But for Birmingham*, 195; during the student protests, Pitts and other traditional African-American leaders engaged in negotiations with white business

behind-the-scenes intervention resulted in the cancellation of demonstrations, at least momentarily; it also came to characterize Pitts' moderate approach to Civil Rights. As a product of Paine College, Pitts sought to apply the "Paine College Ideal" of racial cooperation at a time when younger insurgents were advocating for more radical forms of protest.

Born in rural Georgia to tenant farmers, Pitts' matriculation at Paine was initially derailed by a serious eye injury. Three years later he returned to complete his degree in 1941.[38] From Paine the young CME minister enrolled in a master's program at Fisk University in Nashville, where he served as an assistant to the dean of the chapel. Unlike his mentor Channing Tobias, Pitts chose to remain in the South, where he devoted his life to ministry, education, and Civil Rights, mostly in Georgia and Alabama. Prior to becoming president of Miles College in 1961, Pitts honed his skills as a leader and negotiator in Georgia by serving as president of the interracial Georgia Council of Human Relations (an affiliate of the Southern Regional Council), vice-president of the Georgia state NAACP, and director of the Georgia Teachers and Education Association in Atlanta. Pitts remained at Miles ten years before accepting the presidency of his alma mater, Paine College, in 1970, becoming the school's first African-American president.

Pitts' background fully prepared him to negotiate with Birmingham's moderate white leadership, as well as to mediate the conflicting ideological tensions between traditional and activist African-American leaders in the meetings. The traditional elites included A. G. Gaston, Arthur Shores, John Drew, Earnest Taggart, and the Reverend J. L. Ware, while the activists included Dukes, Shuttlesworth, and Gardner. Cleavages between these two factions revolved largely around protest tactics and the charismatic leadership

---

executives, like Sid Smyer and James A. Head, and the Reverend Norman Jimmerson of the Alabama Council of Human Relations.

[38]This profile on Pitts is drawn from the following sources: Thomas Egerton, "Lucius Pitts and U. W. Clemon," in *A Mind to Stay Here* (New York: Macmillan, 1970) ; "A Tribute to Dr. Lucius Holsey Pitts, 1915–1974" *The Paineite*, 1 March 1974, Miles College Special Collection, Birmingham, Alabama.

of Shuttlesworth.[39] Affiliated with the outlawed NAACP chapter, traditional leaders advocated voter registration over direct-action campaigns, and were more willing to trust the good will of leaders. Siding with the traditional leaders, Pitts questioned the motives of ACMHR leaders when he inquired in a 22 January meeting, "How Christian is the Christian movement?" Pitts charged that if the ACMHR activists really had faith, they would focus on voting rights.[40] While Pitts' comments rankled Shuttlesworth and other members of the ACMHR, they succeeded in persuading Dukes to temporarily postpone demonstrations in January while a biracial committee attempted to negotiate an agreement.

In March 1962, Pitts could no longer persuade the students to delay their boycott, as they grew weary of the merchants' token concessions and stonewalling tactics. The Anti-Injustice Committee presented the merchants with a final list of demands, calling for the desegregation of stores, the hiring of African-American clerks, and the establishment of equal promotion policies.[41] This time the students were supported by Pitts and Shuttlesworth, as well as by other moderate groups like the Jefferson County Voters League.

By June 1962, the almost three-month-old boycott had lost its momentum under the combined pressure of white resistance, police intimidation, and dwindling community support. In a desperate effort to revive the momentum of the movement, Shuttlesworth invited the SCLC to Birmingham to assist its affiliate. Still reeling from the Albany campaign, the SCLC decided to table Shuttlesworth's invitation until its 1962 September convention, ironically slated for Birmingham.[42]

When Shuttlesworth announced that the SCLC planned to hold its annual convention in Birmingham, the chamber of commerce

---

[39]On the cleavages between traditional and activist leaders in Birmingham in the 1950s and 1960s, see Eskew, *But for Birmingham*, 121–51.

[40]Quoted in ibid., 197.

[41] White, ed., *A Walk to Freedom*, 38–39; Eskew, *But for Birmingham*, 194–99.

[42]See Thomas R. Peake, *Keeping the Dream Alive: A History of the Southern Christian Leadership Conference from King to the Nineteen Eighties* (New York: Peter Lang, 1987) 109–12.

became fearful that massive demonstrations would take place downtown. As a result, the chamber organized an eighty-nine-member group of business leaders called the Senior Citizens Committee to resolve the city's racial crisis. In September 1962, a subcommittee, headed by real estate executive Sidney Smyer, convened a biracial group of community and business leaders in an effort to stave off more demonstrations. Pitts and the Reverend Norman Jimmerson of the Alabama Council of Human Relations served as the chief moderators of these meetings between the white merchants and African-American leaders.[43] However, when Smyer realized neither Pitts nor Jimmerson wielded influence over the ACMHR–SCLC activists or the masses, he decided to negotiate directly with Shuttlesworth, just a few days prior to the start of the SCLC convention. The heated meeting resulted in a limited agreement by merchants to remove all Jim Crow signs from water fountains. Shuttlesworth agreed to call off the demonstrations. After the SCLC convention, Bull Connor harassed most merchants to replace their signs, thus prompting students to resume their demonstrations and widening the chasm between white leaders and Civil Rights activists.

For a second time Shuttlesworth invited Martin Luther King Jr. to Birmingham to join forces with the ACMHR. By doing so, Shuttlesworth reasoned that King could use his international reputation and nonviolent strategies to focus national media attention on the racial crisis in Birmingham, as well as mobilize the African-American community in an assault on racial segregation and injustice. Again, King postponed making a decision until after Christmas in order to make a full assessment of the crisis and to consult with the city's traditional African-American leadership who were generally opposed to King's intervention in local affairs. Finally, at the 1963 SCLC retreat in Dorchester, Georgia, King accepted Shuttlesworth's invitation to lead a campaign in Birmingham. King's strong ties with and deference to Birmingham's traditional African-American

---

[43]In addition to meeting with Smyer, Pitts also traveled to Washington, DC, in September to consult with U.S. Attorney General Robert F. Kennedy and other officials in the U.S. Department of Justice; see Garrow, *Bearing the Cross*, 220.

leadership assured Pitts a continuing role in the movement as a skilled mediator. But King's coming also opened the door for other CME pastors and members, who had heretofore sat passively on the sidelines, to demonstrate their commitment to the struggle for Civil Rights.

Of course not all CMEs in Birmingham were excited to see King and the SCLC; some, like Pitts, were wary about the outbreak of violent clashes and white backlash. But among those CMEs who gladly welcomed King's coming were M. C. Merriweather and James Armstrong. A former Birmingham pastor and now editor of the *Christian Index*, Merriweather characterized the mass demonstrations in Birmingham as the "determination on the part of Negro citizens to throw off the yoke of bigotry, prejudices and segregation which through the years has made Birmingham the most segregated city in the country."[44] Tracing the origins of segregation in the city to the racist and exploitive policies of the steel magnates and political elites, Merriweather exulted in the rise of an African-American insurgency that sought to "throw off the old image and to achieve...self dignity and self determination," with franchisement as the first step.[45] Blinded by bigotry and prejudice, the political establishment tried to block their path by reasserting "older patterns of white supremacy."[46] African Americans had no choice, argued Merriweather, but to "resort to mass demonstrations to secure rights guaranteed by the Constitution and the Supreme Court."[47]

As a flag bearer in World War II, James Armstrong was willing to sacrifice his life to preserve the freedoms enshrined in the Constitution. As a charter member of the ACMHR, the professional barber was prepared to support the SCLC's nonviolent war against segregation in Birmingham, still carrying the American flag and

---

[44]*Christian Index*, 23 May 1963, 3.
[45]Ibid.
[46]Ibid.
[47]Ibid.

serving as an ACMHR bodyguard.[48] In 1957 Armstrong joined seven other African-American families in an unsuccessful effort to integrate the city's public schools, and in April 1963 he joined Miles College students in their boycott of downtown stores. A member of Thirgood CME Church, where Merriweather was his former pastor, Armstrong represented a courageous minority of CME clergy and laypeople who publicly supported SCLC's direct-action campaigns in Birmingham.

"PROJECT C"

The SCLC targeted 14 March 1963 to begin the campaign in Birmingham. Reverend Wyatt Walker, SCLC's executive director, was assigned the task of mapping out the strategy, leaving the details to work out with Shuttlesworth.[49] On the advice of moderate African-American leaders in Birmingham, King was advised to delay protests until after the 5 March mayoral election, which featured a three-candidate race among Bull Connor, Albert Boutwell, and Tom King. African Americans anticipated the election of the moderate Boutwell over white supremacist Connor, leading to a reform of the current municipal system. King consented to this request but dispatched Walker to Birmingham to commence advance planning.

Arriving in Birmingham that February, Walker began preparing the African-American community for "Project C." He scheduled a series of meetings with community organizations with the goal of securing recruits and ministerial support. He also consulted with attorney Arthur Shores to familiarize himself with jail and bond procedures for mass arrests. Further, he mapped out a plan for sit-ins at primary and secondary sites downtown, mostly downtown restaurants. The SCLC's Leadership Training Committee began teaching volunteers the philosophy and tactics of nonviolent direct

---

[48]On Armstrong, see Townsend Davis, *Weary Feet, Rested Souls: A Guided Tour of the Civil Rights Movement.* (New York: W. W. Norton, 1998) 84–85; James Armstrong Papers, Martin Luther King Jr. Center for Nonviolent Change, Atlanta.

[49]The following chronology of "Project C" is reconstructed from the following sources: part 4 of LaMonte, *Politics and Welfare in Birmingham*; King, *Why We Can't Wait*, 59–95; White, ed., *A Walk to Freedom*, 50–56; Branch, *Parting the Waters*, 708–11, 725–54.

action. Leading the sessions were veteran activists James Lawson, James and Diane Bevel, Bernard Lee, Dorothy Cotton, and Andrew Young. Each volunteer was required to sign a commitment card that read,

I HEREBY PLEDGE MYSELF—MY PERSON AND BODY—TO THE NONVIOLENT MOVEMENT. THEREFORE I WILL KEEP THE FOLLOWING TEN COMMANDMENTS:
1. MEDITATE daily on the teachings and life of Jesus.
2. REMEMBER always that the nonviolent movement in Birmingham seeks justice and reconciliation—not victory.
3. WALK and Talk in a manner of love, for God is love.
4. PRAY daily to be used by God in order that all men might be free.
5. SACRIFICE personal wishes in order that all men might be free.
6. OBSERVE with both friend and foe the ordinary rules of courtesy.
7. SEEK to perform regular service for others and for the world.
8. REFRAIN from violence of fist, tongue, or heart.
9. STRIVE to be in good spiritual and bodily health.
10. FOLLOW the directions of the movement and of the captain of a demonstration.[50]

To the dismay of King and African Americans in Birmingham, Bull Connor finished a surprisingly close second in the 5 March mayoral race, prompting a run-off with Boutwell on 2 April 1963. Again, King, with Shuttlesworth's approval, agreed to postpone "Project C" until after the mayoral election, setting 3 April as the

---

[50]Reprinted in King, *Why We Can't Wait*, 63–64. CMEs and other Methodists may have been struck by the similarity of these commandments with moral precepts in the "General Rules" composed by John Wesley in 1743 and adopted by the Methodist Church in 1804.

new target date. Shuttlesworth suggested the delay could be used train Birmingham activists in nonviolent direct action, since only a small number of recruits had been trained. Furthermore, King needed time to counter the strong resistance from both black and white leaders.

King candidly admitted "there was tremendous resistance to our program from some of the Negro ministers, businessmen and professionals in the city." Frankly acknowledging this opposition, King suggested it was not because "these Negroes did not want to be free."[51] Rather, he suggested there were at least three reasons for their opposition. First, some of these leaders were "brainwashed" into accepting white domination and black subordination. Second, others were genuinely fearful that SCLC actions were "ill-timed and that we should have given the new Boutwell government a chance."[52] Third, some of these leaders felt resentment because they were left out of the planning and strategy sessions.[53] A fourth reason King did not mention was the cleavage between traditional leaders and Shuttlesworth, whom the former regarded as fanatical and autocratic.[54]

When the mayoral run-off occurred Connor was defeated, as anticipated by the thousands of African-American citizens who turned out to vote. But the hope of a new day in Birmingham politics was dashed again as Connor challenged the election results and set up a dual municipal government.

On the morning of 3 April 1963, "Project C" went into motion with simultaneous sit-ins at four downtown stores. At Britling's department store, James Armstrong joined a group of thirteen members of the ACMHR. They were refused service and immediately arrested. Thus, without King and with little preparation, the

---

[51]King, Why Can't we Wait, 63-64.

[52]Ibid.

[53]Ibid.

[54]See local antipathy toward Shuttlesworth in Fallin, *The African-American Church in Birmingham, Alabama,* 145–48; see also Andrew Manis, who attributes Shuttlesworth's combative style of leadership to his religious experience and sense of divine authority ("Religious Experience, Religious Authority, and Civil Rights Leadership," 143).

Birmingham campaign commenced with little fanfare. When King arrived later that day, he was dismayed at the lack of preparation and lukewarm community support for the demonstrations. From his headquarters at the A. G. Gaston Motel, King and his staff debated ways of mobilizing support for the campaign.

They agreed to build on the momentum of the ACMHR's weekly mass meetings that were coordinated by Reverend Edward Gardner. However, for the next five weeks the mass meetings were to be held daily at a rotating roster of churches. Beginning each evening at six o'clock and lasting about three hours, the meetings generally followed the same format: an opening devotion and freedom songs by the ACMHR choir, testimonials by activists recently released from jail, an offering, a major address by an SCLC official or supporter, an appeal for volunteers, and a concluding song and benediction.[55] Although King was greeted with enthusiastic support at the first mass meeting, he realized the SCLC still had not won over the majority of the African Americans. King especially saw the need to persuade moderate detractors—black and white—who charged that his coming to Birmingham was untimely in the wake of recent changes in city government, thus subverting recent progress in race relations.

As King struggled to mobilize support for the Birmingham movement, the SCLC shifted its initial focus from sit-in demonstrations to marching on city hall. At a mass meeting at St. James Baptist Church, King told demonstrators it was time to go to jail, King reminded the mass meeting that he had already been jailed twelve times, and Birmingham would make thirteen. Other leaders followed with public declarations of their willingness to go to jail. On 7 April Reverend A. D. King, King's younger brother and pastor of First Baptist Church in Ensley, led a group of nineteen marchers from St. Paul Methodist Church toward downtown. They were stopped by policemen lining the route of the march, who began arresting the demonstrators for marching without a permit. While King and other ministers bowed to pray, other African-American spectators were more vocal in their criticism of the police. A skirmish ensued between

---

[55]King, *Why We Can't Wait*, 60–62.

one of the spectators and the police, who ordered several police dogs to attack the young man before he was eventually subdued. By now other onlookers were involved in the melee as police unleashed snarling dogs to subdue the crowd and arrested seven spectators in addition to the nineteen activists already en route to jail.

This unplanned eruption of violence marked a turning point in the SCLC's strategy. SCLC now shifted its original strategy from an economic boycott through sit-ins to a direct confrontation with Bull Connor, with the intent of creating enough tension to draw media and federal attention to Birmingham. Beyond a faithful contingent of demonstrators from the ACMHR, SCLC staffers failed in their attempts to enlist large numbers of volunteers from the city's African-American community, either from the grass roots or from the traditional leadership. Consequently, without massive community support and media coverage, "Project C" began to unravel, threatening to become another Albany. The unleashing of Connor's snarling attack dogs unwittingly provided the ACMHR–SCLC strategists with a new strategy to invigorate the campaign.

Once again, King redoubled his efforts to convert lukewarm African-American clergy to the movement. In an 8 April meeting of 200 ministers, King chastised them for their indifference to the social conditions of their members. "I'm tired of preachers riding around in big cars, living in fine homes, but not willing to take their part in the fight.... If you can't stand up for your people, you are not fit to be a leader," charged King.[56] He implored them to provide strong, firm leadership for the mass meetings, since they as African-American clergy were "freer, more independent" than others in the community.[57] Although King's stinging diatribe failed to win over the majority of ministers, he was successful in securing the support of the Reverend John Cross, pastor of the prestigious Sixteenth Street Baptist Church. Located directly across the street from Kelly Ingram Park and only a few blocks from the A. G. Gaston Motel, the church became the movement center for the reinvigorated campaign. Still,

---

[56]Quoted in Eskew, *But for Birmingham*, 229.
[57]King, *Why We Can't Wait*, 67.

the majority of ministers remained unmoved by either King's rhetoric or Cross's conversion.

In a further effort to win over the traditional leadership, King met with African-American business and professional leaders at the A. G. Gaston Building. The meeting was convened by business leader Gaston in order to give King the opportunity to persuade his staunchest black opposition of the necessity of further demonstrations. While middle-class black leadership remained deeply divided over the campaign, one hopeful result of the discussions was the creation of the Central Committee, composed of thirty members of the ACMHR, the SCLC, and select members of the city's traditional leadership. Included among the latter were President Pitts, A. G. Gaston, Arthur Shoes, John Drew, and C. Herbert Oliver. Acting as advisers to the movement, the committee gave the perception of a united black front that had emerged from the bitter struggle of contending ideologies and conflicting strategies for racial justice. Both sides sought to put a positive spin on the meeting. Gaston, for example, issued a statement endorsing the goals of the protest movement while emphasizing the leadership role of local leaders. In contrast, King touted the agreement as a victory for a classless, nonviolent movement.

On 10 April, as mass meetings and demonstrations resumed with renewed intensity, the movement faced another crisis. Bull Connor obtained a court injunction from a state circuit judge that prohibited demonstrators from "engaging in, sponsoring, promoting or encouraging mass street parades, marches, picketing, sit-ins, and other actions likely to cause a breach of the peace."[58] Remembering the devastating effect of court injunction compliance during the Albany campaign, King promptly denounced the injunction and threatened to defy it with a march on Friday, 12 April.

In an early morning meeting that day, members of the Central Committee expressed concern about the impact of the injunction, specifically about the lack of financial reserves to cover bail for jailed activists. The committee debated whether the movement would be

---

[58]Eskew, *But for Birmingham*, 237.

better served by King's imprisonment for violation of the injunction or by his going north to raise funds for bail. Others, like Pitts and Gaston, remained adamant in their appeal to call off the march because of the impropriety of violating the sanctity of the Easter season by participating in acts of civil disobedience. Sensing a mood of despair, King broke away to pray for a solution to this impending crisis; upon his return he announced his decision to violate the injunction: "The path is clear to me. I've got to march. I've got so many people depending on me. I've got to march."[59]

On Good Friday, 12 April 1963, King, Abernathy, and Shuttlesworth, clad in gray work shirts and blue jeans, led a group of about fifty marchers from Zion Hill Baptist Church toward downtown. Directly behind them behind were two CME pastors, Nathaniel Linsey from Thirgood Memorial CME Church and J. E. Robinson from Miles Chapel CME Church.[60] Flanked by thousands of bystanders on the streets, they marched even more defiantly and sang freedom songs. Briefly eluding Connor's blockade with a detour, two motorcycle cops eventually brought the march to a halt near the federal building. As the marchers knelt in prayer, Connor ordered their arrest. King's decision to disobey the court injunction and his subsequent arrest transformed the previously lethargic Birmingham campaign in intended and unintended ways.

LETTERS AND VISIONS FROM A BIRMINGHAM JAIL

As expected, King's arrest focused the attention of the media and federal government officials on the Birmingham crisis. Part of the media attention was provoked by the publication of King's response to an editorial in both the *Birmingham Post-Herald* and *Birmingham News* by eight white clergymen who called the protests "unwise and

---

[59]Quoted in ibid., 240.

[60]Although neither Linsey nor Robinson was referred to by name, the two were included in a photograph appearing in the *Birmingham News*, 13 April 1963, marching behind King, Abernathy, and Shuttlesworth.

untimely."[61] Signed by two Episcopal bishops, two Methodist bishops, a Jewish rabbi, a Catholic bishop, a Presbyterian moderator, and the pastor of a prominent Baptist church, the statement accused "some local Negro citizens and outsiders of staging marches to incite hatred and violence."[62] The clergymen urged the city's African-American citizenry to withdraw support of the marchers and to support the peaceful efforts of "certain local Negro leadership" in the resolution of the crisis. Portraying themselves as moderates representing a wide spectrum of the religious community, the clergymen called for the resumption of peaceful negotiations between black and whites more intimately familiar with the local crisis: "When rights are consistently denied, a case should be pressed in the courts and negotiations among local leaders, and not in the streets."[63]

King's response to the clergymen—"Letter from a Birmingham Jail"[64]—respectfully yet forcefully responded to the clergymen's charge that he was an "outside agitator." By casting himself as a modern-day Apostle Paul, King carefully interpreted his call to Birmingham as a response to the "Macedonian call of aid" from the ACMHR:

> I cannot sit idly by in Atlanta and not be concerned about what happens in Birmingham. Injustice anywhere is a threat to justice everywhere. We are caught in an inescapable network of mutuality tied in a single garment of destiny. Whatever effects one directly affects all indirectly. Never again can we afford to live with the narrow, provincial "outside agitator" idea. Anyone who lives in the United States can never be considered as an outsider anywhere in this country.[65]

---

[61]*Birmingham Post-Herald*, 13 April 1963, 10, reprinted the next day in the *Birmingham News*.

[62]Quoted in Eskew, *But for Birmingham*, 244.

[63]Ibid.

[64]Reprinted in King, *Why We Can't Wait*, 76–95.

[65]Ibid.

To refute the accusation that his motive was to incite violence, King outlined the four steps to a nonviolent campaign: proof of injustice, negotiation, self-purification, and direct action. In his defense of direct action as a legitimate strategy for Christians in violating unjust laws, King eloquently cited biblical, philosophical, and historical precedents for civil disobedience. Having made his case for the legitimacy of civil disobedience, King expressed grave disappointment in the moderate white religious community in their opposition to the Civil Rights movement in Birmingham. By insisting on order at the expense of justice and gradualism at the expense of immediate action, they had become just as bad, if not worse, than the rabid segregationists in their opposition to racial justice. King's "letter" served not only as a powerful rebuttal to local and national white religious opposition, but also provided the movement with a theological and philosophical defense of nonviolent direct action.

Less philosophically, Nathaniel Linsey shared with readers of the *Christian Index* his own revelatory experience in the Birmingham jail, which he interpreted as a sign of divine providence:[66]

Nothing has been more revealing to me of God's providential care and divine presence in troubled times than the Stars. I could not help but think, as I looked at that shining Star, of the Saturday night before Easter in the Birmingham Jail we had been singing and praying prayers for deliverance (absolute) in an open "Snake" pit, similar to the den consigned to Daniel.

It was out doors between four walls of prison cells, and about four stories high. Iron bars lay across the top of the pit. The night air was cold; some of my fellow travelers were ill but no message could be gotten through for bond. Three or four benches were stationed around the walls; the floor was concrete; one wash basin and about five toilets were situated under a shelter at one end of the pit. This, too, was a black

---

[66]Nathaniel Linsey, "The Stars Still Shine in Birmingham," *Christian Index*, 10 October 1963, 6.

night in many ways, but before we ended our services, I looked up, and behold, there were Three Stars and no more, freely dressed in their magnificent beauty, representing the presence of the Father, the Son, and the Holy Spirit. They seemed to have been on an errand for God and had reached their destination. I could almost hear them singing the good news of the new birth of freedom. The thirty-two other prisoners rejoiced at this marvelous and eschatological sign.

Yes, the Stars Still Shine in Birmingham, and we are confident that God is working and will bring that day to pass when brotherhood will reign supreme here in this Magic City.[67]

Another short-term result from King's arrest on Good Friday was the escalation of protest demonstrations. On 14 April, Easter Sunday, Civil Rights activists led kneel-in demonstrations at segregated white churches across the city where ushers had blocked their entrance into worship services. That afternoon, an exuberant mass meeting at Thirgood CME Church in support of the jailed demonstrators erupted into violence as about fifty marchers spilled into the streets. Joined by 1,500 to 2,000 spectators they headed for the Southside jail. When police arrived to halt the march, they were greeted by angry bystanders. The police responded by turning on the crowd with their billy clubs and night sticks, swinging indiscriminately at nonviolent marchers and onlookers; twenty-six people were arrested. With the Birmingham movement spinning out of control, King and Abernathy decided to post bond and leave jail on Saturday, 20 April. Despite the escalation of protests from a dedicated cadre of activists, the movement still lacked a sufficient number of volunteers committed to nonviolent direct action.

---

[67]Ibid.

D-Day and the Children's Crusade

In early May, just as the Birmingham movement seemed ready to collapse, movement organizers discovered an untapped but controversial resource for reviving the movement—Birmingham's school children. First proposed by SCLC staffers James Bevel and Ike Reynolds, the idea for a children's march was flatly rejected by King and other members of the Central Committee. Eventually, King agreed to allow Bevel and the ACMHR–SCLC staff to host a meeting with high school students willing to demonstrate. Despite opposition from parents, principals, teachers, and community leaders, staff members set out to recruit and prepare students for a protest march on Thursday, 2 May.

On the day of the proposed march, students packed area churches. Singing freedom songs and waving picket signs, they were dispatched from the churches in orderly groups of ten to fifty students under the watchful eyes of the ACMHR–SCLC staff and a bewildered and enraged Bull Connor. He ordered his men to cordon off an eight-block area around Kelly Ingram Park and alerted area firemen to be on guard with high-pressure hoses. By that afternoon, hundreds of students were arrested, crammed into paddy wagons and school buses, and packed into overflowing jails. The success of the "children's crusade" breathed new life into the languid Birmingham movement but created a logistical nightmare for Connor. The next day Connor was prepared to meet the young demonstrators with a massive show of force.

On Friday morning, 3 May, Birmingham police erected barricades, positioned water hoses, and readied police dogs in preparation for demonstrations. More than 2,000 people gathered at Sixteenth Street Baptist Church to hear exhortations from King, comedian/activist Dick Gregory, and march coordinators. At one o'clock the students poured out of the church, singing, chanting, and heading toward Kelly Ingram Park. Again, police made numerous arrests. But Connor had seen enough; he ordered his officers to terminate the demonstrations by preventing marchers from leaving the church. For two hours, in front of a national and international television audience, firemen blasted marchers and onlookers alike with jolting streams of water. When angry onlookers retaliated with bricks and bottles, Connor ordered a squad of six police dogs to subdue the crowd. With the scene getting uglier by the minute, movement leaders called off the demonstrations around three o'clock that afternoon. By the end of the day more than 2,300 students and adults filled the jails of Birmingham and surrounding towns, including temporary shelters at the Alabama State Fairgrounds.

Reaction to the racial violence in Birmingham was immediate. The violence was televised across the world; Connor's brutality was condemned in both national and international media. Moreover, the Kennedy administration moved more decisively to intervene in the crisis by sending Burke Marshall, assistant attorney general for Civil Rights, to help mediate the crisis.[68] Meanwhile, Sid Smyer reconvened the dormant biracial group of business and community leaders in a secret meeting at the Birmingham Realty Board. Principal African-American leaders in this negotiation were Shores, Gardner, Shuttlesworth, Gaston, Drew, Pitts, Harold Long, and Andrew Young.[69]

Meanwhile, the protest marches and mass meetings continued to draw support. Although police continued to arrest marchers, they restrained from the use of violent force, partly in an effort to minimize negative publicity. But this respite from violence did not last long. On Tuesday, 7 May, Connor again unleashed dogs and fire hoses on the marchers and rioters, calling in support from the state troopers and neighboring police forces. Among the casualties of the day was Shuttlesworth, who was hospitalized after a fire hose slammed him against the door of a church. The negotiations, however, proceeded without him.

On Tuesday, 7 May, black and white negotiators met downtown to discuss a settlement, with Pitts, Shores, and Drew representing the traditional black leadership and Andrew Young the ACMHR–SCLC. After this meeting concluded a smaller group convened at the Drew

---

[68]LaMonte, *Politics and Welfare in Birmingham*, 180.
[69]Ibid., 181.

home to iron out the details of the settlement. Two main issues of debate centered, first, on how to word the agreement as not to embarrass the white negotiators while convincing African Americans of its value and, second, on how to deal with the arrest charges and bail bonds of thousands of young demonstrators.

On 8 May a settlement was announced on the following four points: desegregating lunch counters, restrooms, fitting rooms, and drinking fountains at downtown department and variety stores during the next ninety days; upgrading job opportunities for African Americans, including the hiring of a least one sales clerk within sixty days; releasing all those arrested during the disturbances either on bond or into their own custodies; and establishing communication between African-American leaders and the Senior Citizens Committee within the next two weeks.[70]

The next morning at an ACMHR–SCLC Central Committee meeting at the Gaston Motel, Pitts shared his realistic perceptions of the biracial settlement in a typed memo. He conceded that the white leaders had spoken in "good faith" because of pressure created by the demonstrations: "To say that they are frightened is an *understatement*; to say that we have completely won is an *overstatement*."[71] He recommended that the committee make further compromises on their demands. For example, Pitts was willing to accept a "tacit (if only verbal) agreement between our leaders and representatives of the city government that the charges against persons arrested during the demonstrations at the order of the Commissioners would be withdrawn."[72] In essence, Pitts advocated ending the demonstrations on the basis of verbal commitments and good faith of white leaders. After a period of debate on the Pitts memo, King expressed support for a moratorium on demonstrations and called for a vote. The traditional leaders, led by Pitts and Gaston, prevailed.

---

[70]Ibid.

[71]Quoted in Eskew, *But for Birmingham*, 285.

[72]Ibid.

Although no public officials were involved in the negotiations, King accepted the recommendation. In fact, Sidney Smyer, former head of the chamber of commerce, was the only white who openly identified himself with the negotiations.[73] Other movement activists, including Shuttlesworth, accused King of betraying the goals of the movement by agreeing to a moratorium on demonstrations. Shuttlesworth angrily denounced the moratorium and was prepared to lead a new wave of demonstrators that Wednesday before being persuaded by Young not to proceed. Two days later, however, Shuttlesworth appeared with King and Abernathy at a press conference at the Gaston Motel where he read from a prepared statement: "The city of Birmingham has reached an accord with its conscience. The acceptance of responsibility by local white leadership offers an example of a free people uniting to meet and solve their problems."[74] He then read the Four Points for the Progress, after which the weary leader collapsed in exhaustion.

But the brokered negotiation effected neither peace nor progress. On 11 May bombs exploded at the home of A. D. King and the Gaston Motel. The next day full-fledged riots erupted near the bombed hotel and elsewhere, even as the settlement was being explained to the community. In June 1963 Mayor Boutwell appointed a 212–member citizens committee to deal specifically with racial issues. Twenty-seven members were African American, including Pitts and at least three of the leaders from the demonstrations.[75]

On the national level, the most important impact of the Birmingham Civil Rights campaign, in conjunction with hundreds of other simultaneous campaigns, was that it forced a reluctant Kennedy administration to propose sweeping federal Civil Rights legislation. On 11 June 1963, as confrontation between African Americans and segregationists heightened on the streets of Birmingham and elsewhere, President Kennedy proposed the Civil Rights Act of

---

[73]LaMonte, *Politics and Welfare in Birmingham*, 184.
[74]Quoted in Eskew, *But for Birmingham*, 293–94.
[75]LaMonte, *Politics and Welfare in Birmingham*, 191–92.

1964.[76] Introduced in Congress on 23 June 1963, the bill carried eight provisions covering voting rights, school desegregation, desegregation of public accommodations and federally assisted programs, extension of the Civil Rights Commission, and equal employment opportunities.

The August 1963 March on Washington was in large part a celebration of the success of the Birmingham campaign and its promising repercussions for African Americans and the nation as a whole. Organized by veteran activists A. Phillip Randolph and Bayard Rustin, the march attracted 250,000 black and white citizens to the nation's capital. Standing at the foot of the Lincoln Memorial, King climaxed the three-hour event with his stirring "I Have a Dream" speech, celebrating the victories of freedom fighters and articulating a vision of a truly integrated America.

Despite the optimism expressed in King's speech, African Americans in Birmingham were less than jubilant about the state of racial progress in the "Magic City." In August and September a new wave of violence and terror struck, beginning with the bombing of attorney Arthur Shores' home and culminating with the 14 September bombing of Sixteenth Street Baptist Church, killing four young girls. The African-American community exploded with rage and grief, precipitating violent clashes between angry residents and police.

With the departure of King and the SCLC and the absence of Shuttlesworth, more traditional leaders stepped up to respond. For example, on 1 October the Jefferson Democratic Council presented a list of demands to Mayor Boutwell and the city council. Similar to the May ACMHR–SCLC demands, this new ten-point program of action included the hiring of minority policemen, the appointment of

---

[76]Kennedy announced his proposal on federal legislation for civil rights in a speech before the nation on the same day that Alabama governor George C. Wallace stood at the doors of the University of Alabama to block the entrance of two African-American students. Referring to the racial crisis as a "moral issue...as old as the Scriptures and...as clear as the American Constitution," Kennedy said the real issue was "whether all Americans are to be afforded equal rights and equal opportunities; whether we are going to treat our fellow Americans as we want to be treated" (quoted in "President John F. Kennedy Speaks to the Nation," in *A Walk to Freedom*, ed. White, 71).

African Americans to the city's independent boards and agencies, a nondiscriminatory city employment program, the reopening of parks, and the removal of segregation signs from municipal buildings.[77] Another group, the Inter-Citizens Committee, headed by the Reverend J. L. Ware and the Reverend C. Herbert Oliver, also petitioned the council over similar demands.

King and Shuttlesworth promised to resume demonstrations if there was not an immediate start of good-faith negotiations between political leaders and movement leaders.[78] On 20 October, 120 African-American leaders signed a petition publicly endorsing "Dr. King and Rev. Shuttlesworth as our leaders; their goals are ours, our struggle is theirs."[79] This statement counteracted an earlier statement by Gaston and Shores, urging the two leaders to stay away from the city in order to give negotiations a chance to work.[80] King and Shuttlesworth issued a 29 October ultimatum that the city hire African-American policemen or face new demonstrations. The tensions with themayor and city council, however, eased when King and Shuttlesworth backed down on their ultimatum. Once again, the city's traditional African-American leaders were left with the arduous responsibility of producing some tangible results from the negotiations. Although they, like their white moderate counterparts, regarded King as an "outside agitator," they had been transformed by a mass movement they had neither exclusively organized nor directed. Through their endorsement of King and Shuttlesworth they acknowledged their debt to this movement for their enhanced credibility with the African-American community and white power structure. They had now earned the epithet "inside agitator."

Earlier in September, King led a seven-member delegation of both inside and outside agitators to meet with President Kennedy about the crisis in the city. Two CME leaders were included in the delegation—President Pitts and Bishop E. P. Murchison, presiding

---

77LaMonte, *Politics and Welfare in Birmingham*, 188.
78Ibid.
79Quoted in Eskew, *But for Birmingham*, 325.
80*Birmingham Post-Herald*, 2 October 1963 and 18 October 1963, 188.

prelate of the Fifth Episcopal District, which included the Birmingham Annual Conference. Murchison described the substance of the meeting in a published report in the *Christian Index*[81]:

> We informed the President of the grave situation in Birmingham prior to and since the bombing on Sunday and the tragic death of the Negro children. We further informed him that the Negro citizens of Birmingham are frustrated, confused and almost on the verge of despair as a result of this reign of terror. We told him that there was widespread fear and public disorder and that the Negro population of the city did not have complete confidence in the existing law enforcement machinery there.... We discussed with the President the question of possible use of Federal troops to maintain order in Birmingham.... We closed the conference by assuring the president of our unswerving commitment to non-violence. We made it clear to him that we would not at any point encourage our people to engage in retaliatory violence. We are still convinced that violence in our struggle would be both impractical, immoral and harmful to the cause.[82]

Pitts and Murchison's inclusion in Civil Rights mainstream marked a critical stage in CME participation in the Civil Rights movement. Together they represented the institutional support that the CME Church in Alabama and Miles College gave the Birmingham movement. Although neither leader presumed to speak for his respective institution in support of the movement, their participation in various phases of the movement inspired their constituencies: other CME ministers and laypeople, Miles College students and alumni, and area high school students. Through their personal and

---

[81] 17 October 1963, Bishop E. P. Murchison, "Negro Leaders Confer with President on Birmingham Crisis, September 19, 1963," 3.
[82] Ibid.

collective participation in an ecumenical, mass-based freedom movement, they came to a fuller realization of the CME Church's role in the ongoing freedom struggle.

CHAPTER 7

"Implementing Justice and Righteousness": The Apex of CME Activism and Ecumenism, 1964–1968

The struggle in Birmingham had a radical, transformative effect on its CME participants, including traditional leaders like President Pitts. In a 26 January 1964 speech at the University of Oregon State, Pitts shared with the audience how his involvement in the Birmingham campaign reaffirmed his commitment to the freedom struggle. "As a black man I intend to have a hand in this freedom even if it means death," said Pitts.[1] "Patience—we've had too long. Young people are itchy for action in the face of human injustices that include poverty, unequal educational opportunities, beatings and harassments.[2]

In April 1964, Pitts expressed his growing frustration with the slow pace of progress made by the Boutwell mayoral administration, noting that more demonstrations were "waiting on the outskirts of our town," an apparent reference to the militancy of his students, many of whom had been active in the original marches.[3] By the end

---

[1]"Pitts Calls for Rebirth of Freedom," newspaper clipping in the Vertical File on Lucius Pitts (Henry C. Bunton Papers, Schomburg Center for Research in Black Culture, New York).

[2]Ibid.

[3]See *Birmingham Post-Herald*, 9 May 1964.

of the Birmingham campaign in 1963, Miles College students began channeling their discontent into community organizing and voter registration efforts. In a funded program called the Miles College Citizenship Project, about fifty students, under the direction of professor and ACMHR activist Abraham Woods, canvassed the Acipico and North Birmingham area and interviewed nonvoters. Woods proclaimed the project successful because some of the nonregistered voters did register as a result. An even larger group of students canvassed most of the Birmingham and outlying areas in December, and 851 more African Americans registered to vote. Altogether, between October 1963 and February 1964, approximately 3,840 African Americans registered to vote in Birmingham.[4]

Beyond student activism at Miles, CME churches in the Birmingham area began to reassess their commitment to the Civil Rights movements. Virtually silent and absent during the pivotal events of 1963, the Committee on Education of the Birmingham District CME Conference issued a report publicly affirming its support of school desegregation and the Civil Rights movement.[5] The report dealt primarily with the role of the church in both providing and supporting educational opportunities for students at private colleges like Miles and newly desegregated public schools like the University of Alabama:

> Ten years have after the passing of the School Desegregation Act of 1954, we find most of the schools in Alabama integrating only after specific court order and that to only a token extent. This conference should endorse without reservation the immediate implementation of this Act and the Civil Rights Act of 1964. The elimination of the dual system

---

[4]"Miles College Students on the Prowl for Non-Voters," *Christian Index*, 9 April 1964,12.

[5]"Report of the Committee on Education of the Birmingham District Conference of the [CMEC], Trinity CMEC, Pratt City, " *Christian Index*, 10 September 1964, 4–7.

of education in Alabama is the only and proper way to assure
equality in education for all children...without regard to race.[6]

Furthermore, the report called for members to support
organizations "whose mission is to carry the active campaign to get
for the Negro all of the rights and privileges to which he is entitled."
It encouraged local congregations to support especially the ACMHR,
its "parent body," the SCLC, and the NAACP when it would become
reactivated in Alabama: "In fact, every organization fighting for the
cause of the Negro should receive the support of the church."[7]

The responses of CMEs in Birmingham to the revitalized Civil
Rights movement are indicative of the transformation taking place in
the denomination itself, at local, regional, and connectional levels.
This chapter examines the responses of the CME Church at these
multiple levels between 1964 and 1968, the apex of the Civil Rights
movement and CME involvement. It explores how CME
involvement in national and global ecumenical bodies during this time
contributed to the church's social consciousness and activism,
culminating in an episcopal pronouncement in support of the Civil
Rights movement, a revival of merger dialogue with the AME and
AMEZ churches. The chapter closes with a discussion of CME
responses to the rise of the black power movement in the late 1960s
during the denouement of the Civil Rights movement. The CME
Church's engagement with Civil Rights, ecumenism, and black power
suggests that it was poised to enter what Merriweather referred to as
the "third phase of the Negro revolution."[8]

Phase one involved identifying the causes that gave rise to the
revolution: racial discrimination and segregation "designed to keep
the Negro minority at a substandard position and to deny him [sic]
the rights and privileges of first-class citizenship."[9] The second phase
involved devising and implementing the methods of the revolution, in

---

[6]Ibid.

[7]Ibid.

[8]"The Third Phase of Integration Is Upon Us," *Christian Index*, August 1964,
3–4.

[9]Ibid., 3.

this case the use of nonviolent direct action on the part of African Americans seeking equal justice and fairness. Merriweather pointed to Rosa Parks' actions on 1 December 1955 and the movement she ignited in Montgomery and the South as an example.

Out of this crucible emerged the representative leader, Dr. Martin Luther King Jr., who led the famous bus strike, the

> results of which triggered the second phase of this revolution. It was conceived and stemmed from the philosophy of Gandhi of India and it adopted a new concept in America known as non-violence. The immortal words of Dr. King became the battle cry of the movement of non-violence, "If the street must run with blood, let it be our blood and not that of our white brothers." The cause of this revolt and the methods used challenged the moral reserve of the American people as no event before had done since the Emancipation of slaves.[10]

From the Montgomery bus boycott came other "mass expressions of resentment" and movements: CORE, SNCC, and the "Alabama Non-violent movement, each having a peculiar method, all with one central purpose: "Freedom for the American Negro now" "The sophisticated Negro joined with ditch-diggers and scrub-women in the determination to secure freedom and human dignity. They found they were all common comrades in the ghetto and the Negro must turn to Negro leadership in the attempt to escape ghetto walls."[11]

After lauding the moral leadership of President Kennedy in the movement, Merriweather sketched the third phase of the revolution, namely, the "implementation of the stipulations of the mandate of the Civil Rights Act at the local level of labor, housing, public accommodations and education."[12] Once the door had been opened, he suggested, it "remains the duty of the oppressed to prepare

---

[10]Ibid.
[11]Ibid.
[12]Ibid., 4.

themselves to enter the open doors and to equip themselves as intelligent, worthy American citizens."[13]

In an earlier article, written at the height of the Birmingham campaign, Merriweather criticized CME leaders for remaining silent or indifferent about the Civil Rights struggle. "The American Negro is involved in a serious social revolution, the ramifications of which have claimed world attention. It seems reasonable that the CME Church should express a definite interest regarding this movement," suggested Merriweather.[14] In addition to Civil Rights, Merriweather advocated renewed interest in organic union, "one of the most urgent problems of our present day."[15] Between 1963 and 1968, CMEs responded to both of these concerns and other social issues with heightened interest and vigor.

CME SOCIAL ACTIVISM, 1964–1968

CME involvement in the ecumenical movement, predominantly through the NCC and WCC, opened new channels and resources for CME social activism. While CME affiliation with the Federal Council of Churches and the World Council of Churches predated the Civil Rights movement, it was only in the 1950s and 1960s that these ecumenical bodies gave serious attention to the issue of racial segregation in the United States.[16] However, at its 1946 biennial

---

[13]Ibid.

[14]"Are We Lacking in Co-Ordination, Aims and Objectives in the CME Church?" *Christian Index*, August 1964, 3–4.

[15]Ibid.

[16]This is not to suggest that either body had not attempted to address the racial crisis prior to the 1950s; both did, through the efforts of a vocal minority of African-American activists and their white allies. An early example of ecumenical advocacy for racial justice was the FCC's Department of Race Relations, created in 1921. In 1950, this department was renamed the Department of Racial and Cultural Relations when the FCC merged to become the NCC. The department published a bi-monthly newsletter, *Interracial News Service*, and promoted such educational activities as Race Relations Sunday and annual institutes on race relations; see James F. Findlay Jr., *Church People in the Struggle: The National Council of Churches and the Freedom Movement, 1950–1970* (New York: Oxford University Press 1994) 17–19. Like the FCC, the World Council of Churches condemned racism at its inaugural assembly in 1948, identifying "prejudice based upon race or colour

meeting in Columbus, Ohio, the FCC issued the following condemnation of racial segregation:

> The Federal Council of Churches of Christ in America hereby renounces the pattern of segregation as unnecessary and undesirable and a violation of the Gospel of love and human brotherhood. Having taken this action, the Federal Council requests its constituent communions to do likewise. As proof of their sincerity in this renunciation they will work for a non-segregated church and a nonsegregated society.[17]

The FCC's "request" was taken up by several denominations issuing similar pronouncements, including the General Council of the Congregational Churches, the General Assembly of the Presbyterian Church in the USA, the International Convention of the Disciples of Christ, and the Northern Baptist Convention. For the most part, the FCC and its constituent members emphasized a cautious, gradualist approach to the solution of racial problems. In 1954 the NCC supported the Supreme Court's decision outlawing segregation in public schools and stressed the responsibility of churches in securing compliance to this ruling. The 1954 ruling opened new opportunities for mainline denominations seeking to address the race problem.

For example, in 1955 the NCC General Board authorized the "Southern Project," an experimental program designed to help

---

and practices of discrimination and segregation as denials of justice and human dignity." But it was not until 1969, when the council's central committee established the Program to Combat Racism (PCR), that the WCC moved beyond mere denunciation of racism and developed concrete programs to eliminate it. Two fundamental principles of the PCR were, first, the acknowledgment that"racism is not an unalterable feature of human life, and, second, that the creation of racial justice would involve a redistribution of political power and economic wealth; see WCC Central Committee, 1969, "Plan for an Ecumenical Programme to Combat Racism," reprinted in *The Ecumenical Movement: An Anthology of Key Documents*, ed. Michael Kinnamon and Brian E. Cope (Grand Rapids MI: William B. Eerdmans, 1997) 218–20.

[17]Quoted in Samuel M. Cavert, *The American Churches in the Ecumenical Movement, 1900–1968* (New York: Association Press, 1968) 190.

southern communities respond to the crisis precipitated by the Supreme Court ruling. The project was headed by Will Campbell, a Southern Baptist minister from Mississippi, who crisscrossed the South to mediate racial conflicts in Montgomery, Alabama; Little Rock, Arkansas; Nashville, Tennessee; and Birmingham, Alabama. Through his ministry Campbell maintained a relatively close relationship with Martin Luther King Jr. and other Civil Rights activists. By 1963, however, the "Southern Project" was phased out and Campbell left the NCC to work as a freelance writer.[18] By the early 1960s a new generation of NCC leaders wanted to implement even bolder initiatives to confront the nation's racial crisis, which had begun spilling over into people's living rooms. One such leader was J. Irwin Miller, an industrialist from Columbus, Indiana, and lay leader in the Christian Church (Disciples of Christ), who was elected president of the NCC at its 1960 assembly. Miller was committed to aligning mainline churches more closely with Civil Rights organizations and channeling more direct support to the movement.

Along these lines, in 1963 the NCC enthusiastically supported a national, ecumenical, interfaith Conference on Religion and Race, joining hundreds of Catholics, Protestants, and Jews for a three-day conference in Chicago. Designed to commemorate the centennial of the signing of the Emancipation Proclamation by President Lincoln, the conference was chaired by President Benjamin Mays of Morehouse College, with Bishop B. Julian Smith of the CME Church, Archbishop Paul Hallinan of the Catholic Church, and Rabbi Ferdinand Isserman of St. Louis serving as vice-chairmen.[19] The conference included keynote addresses by Rabbi Abraham Heschel, Martin Luther King Jr., J. Irwin Miller and Robert Sargent Shriver.

Representing the NAACP, Reverend Edward Odoms recorded his observations of the conference in the *Christian Index*. He noted, first, a mood of contrition over the failure of organized religion to confront segregation and discrimination; second, a focus on concrete

---

[18]Findlay, *Church People in the Struggle*, 22–26.

[19]"Bishop B. J. Smith Selected Co-Chairman for National Interreligious Conference on Race...," *Christian Index*, August 1964, 1.

issues beyond pious generalities; and, third, a procedure for follow-up activities, including the selection of target cities for pilot programs.[20] In addition to Bishop Smith, the CME Church was represented by four bishops and nine delegates.[21]

Although based in Chicago at the time, Smith's selection as co-chair of the conference represented another step forward in the CME Church's participation in the Civil Rights and ecumenical movements. Smith not only represented an African-American Methodist tradition among the four chairs of the commission, but also served as a member of the NCC's newly created Commission on Religion and Race.[22] Moreover, Smith had firsthand knowledge of the racial crisis in the South, having been reared in Barnesville, Georgia, and having served as episcopal leader of the First Episcopal District, which included CME churches in Tennessee and Arkansas.

Bishop Smith was not hesitant about protesting racial discrimination in his own episcopal district. For example, at the June 1963 convocation at Lane College, Smith and other CMEs in attendance drafted "An Open Letter to the City Official, Business, Civic and Religious Leaders of the City of Jackson [Tennessee]."[23] The statement identified Jackson as one of three cities in Tennessee with a population over 100,000 that lagged in providing "democracy to all its citizens, especially in the area of employment...motel accommodations, theaters, recreational facilities, restaurants, educational opportunities and churches."[24] The statement implored religious leaders in particular to help "eliminate all forms of discrimination and segregation based on race" and encouraged all

---

[20]"Surveying Social Action: Religion and Race," *Christian Index*, August 1964, 6.

[21]Amos Ryce II, "CMEs Send Nine Official Delegates to the National Conference of Religion and Race: A Report by Amos Ryce, II," *Christian Index*, August 1964, 4.

[22]Smith served as the lone African American on the commission's Anti-Segregation Committee, which adopted a resolution endorsing the use of economic boycotts as a protest tactic against segregation. See "The National Council of Churches Spark Drive Against Segregation," *Christian Index*, 27 June 1963, 2.

[23]*Eastern Index*, Spring 1963, 3.

[24]Ibid.

people of good will to work toward this goal. The statement, however, stopped short of threatening economic boycotts or direct-action protest, relying more on moral suasion:

> We implore the city official, business, civic and religious leaders to take cognizance of the injustices, indignities and inequities suffered by some of the citizens of this city.
> We call upon these leaders to eradicate these evils so that all citizens of Jackson may walk in dignity and enjoy the freedom guaranteed by the Constitution of the United States.[25]

While this statement appears mild compared to the demands made by activists in other southern communities, it represents a radical shift from the accommodationist strategies of the first generation of CMEs who convened in Jackson almost a century earlier.

The shift from CME accommodationism during the Reconstruction era to social activism during the Civil Rights movement reached a high point on 23 July 1963 in a special session of the College of Bishops at Collins Chapel CMEC in Memphis, Tennessee. Here, for the first time, the bishops issued a public pronouncement committing the CME Church to "direct participation in the Civil Rights movement, from the local church to the general church."[26] With Bishop Smith serving as host and coordinator of the session, representatives from each of the church's nine episcopal districts met on various committees to examine critically every phase of the Civil Rights problem and to review carefully President Kennedy's proposed Civil Rights legislation. Each committee was charged with suggesting ways in which local CME churches could participate in the movement. In a closing worship service, almost 600 people flocked

---

[25]Ibid.

[26]Reported by M. C. Merriweather, "Bishops of the CME Church Offer Hope and Give Direction as the They Rise to the Occasion," *Christian Index*, 8 August 1963, 3–4.

to Collins Chapel to hear Senior Bishop Bertram Doyle read the official pronouncement. Merriweather's report in the *Christian Index* attempted to capture the historic import of the bishop's pronouncement:

> The statement comprehended the historical responsibility of the CME Church as an entity in the solution of this problem by virtue of the fact the [c]hurch originated in the very heart of the Old Confederacy and should confront its responsibility with a deep sense of urgency.... It is quite difficult to give here a detail [sic] report in such a limited space. Suffice it to say, the philosophical, the spiritual and moral elements of the address lifted the audience into a state of awe and silent rapture. It was significant, however, that [Bishop Doyle] closed his statement with these words, "That we commit our sacred honors, our total resources and our lives to the solution of the Civil Rights problem, and the ultimate triumph of the Kingdom of God in the world."[27]

For Merriweather, who for years lobbied for more church involvement in the movement, the bishop's statement "presented a challenge to all the members of the CME Church and to Negroes determined to secure human rights and dignity."[28] For other CME activists, like Charles Gomillion, B. Julian Smith, Ruby Doris Smith, Donald Holowell, Henry Bunton, and Lucius Pitts, the statement was a belated endorsement of their involvement in the movement. For Bunton the meeting at Collins Chapel marked a homecoming to the city where he helped sparked the Civil Rights struggle in the 1950s. As the bishop of the Seventh Episcopal District, which comprised the eastern seaboard coast from Maine to South Carolina, Bunton assumed

---

[27]Ibid. Although Merriweather did not include a full transcript of the pronouncement, it is very likely the statement was strongly influenced by such contemporaneous events as the Birmingham campaign, the March on Washington, and President Kennedy's proposal of a civil rights act.

[28]Ibid., 4.

the challenge of coordinating the denomination's implementation of the bishop's pronouncement.

CME Social Action Commission

The creation of a denominational Commission on Social Action was one of the first steps the CME Church took toward implementing the bishop's pronouncement. On 18 November 1964, Bishop Bunton convened a planning meeting in Memphis to discuss the formation and agenda of the commission. The consensus of those in attendance was to elevate the commission to departmental status at the 1966 General Conference.[29] A more formal organizational meeting took place in January 1965.[30] The main agenda for this meeting centered on a discussion of the following six imperatives: the purpose of the committee; the educational program of the church; "the image of the church as an agency in creating a program of wholesome recreation for youth and adults"; "the church's responsibility in the implementation of the Civil Rights Bill"; the church's role in implementing the provisions of the War Against Poverty; and the church's relation to the other "great movements."[31]

After hearing a description of the Methodist Church's program of social concern, the committee divided into three working groups: a committee on purpose, a committee on guidelines, and a committee on program of action. The committee on purpose, chaired by Dean M. L. Darnell of Phillips School of Theology in Atlanta, crafted the following brief theological statement to undergird the commission's purpose:

> The Christian meaning of God, Man and the World has been revealed to us in the fact of Jesus, the gospel and the activity of the Holy Spirit; and preserved for and to us in and

---

[29]"Bishop Bunton Holds Important Meeting on Social Action," *Christian Index*, 3 December 1964, 2.

[30]"Committee on Christian Social Action and Concern," *Christian Index*, 14 January 1965, 11–13.

[31]Ibid.

through the witness of believers, the biblical records, and the organization, program and fellowship of the Christian Church.

Our servant Lord and the Gospel declare this meaning to be the loving God supremely and our neighbors as ourselves. Whenever this love is real it is expressed in the whole of human relations. In light of the above principles—the [CMEC] organized an instrument, "The Commission of Christian Social Action and concern," in which to call the attention of man and society to the role of the church in Social Action and Concern.

Therefore, we propose and recommend that it shall be the purpose of the Commission to relate the gospel to the total man in such areas as peace, war, United Nations [and] temperance in tobacco, drugs, gambling, human relations and the economic affairs of youth and the aged.[32]

This working draft became the basis for the CME Social Creed adopted by the CME General Conference in 1966.[33] As such, it contained little that was original in theological conception or social outlook, borrowing freely from other denominational and ecumenical social pronouncements. More surprisingly, though, the CME draft made no explicit reference to the Civil Rights struggle for racial equality, either as a theological imperative of the gospel or a particular social concern.

---

[32]Ibid., 11–12.

[33]Dean M. L. Darnell headed the special committee that drafted the creed at the 1966 General Conference. In the section titled "Theological Perspective," the creed affirmed Jesus' concern for human well-being and justice: "For the Church to be silent in the face of need, injustice and exploitation is to deny the Lord of the Church.... We believe that whatever is of interest and concern to people—physical, intellectual, social, economic and political—should also be of interest to the Church." See *Journal of the General Conference 1966*, 90; Othal H. Lakey, *The History of the CME Church* (Memphis: CME Publishing House, 1985) 588–90; Luther E. Smith, "To Be Untrammeled and Free: The Urban Ministry Work of the CME Church: 1944–90," in *Churches, Cities and Human Community*, ed. Clifford J. Green (Grand Rapids MI: William B. Eerdmans, 1996) 66–67.

The committee on program of action, chaired by Reverend Cleo McCoy of Greensboro, North Carolina, proposed a list of immediate and long-range issues for "concentration, study and action." While Civil Rights concerns were conspicuously absent from the above theological statement, they were more explicitly highlighted by this committee. For example, the committee's first recommendation was "that the church become increasingly active in the areas of political action—including registration, voting and political education in general."[34] Related to this recommendation, the committee also urged "immediate and aggressive implementation of the recently passed Civil Rights Law."[35]

The committee on guidelines proposed regulations for the commission's chairperson (to be appointed by the College of Bishops), officers, membership, meetings, commissions (for annual and district conferences), and bylaws.[36]

The creation of the church's Commission on Social Concerns stemmed primarily from the 1966 Social Creed, but its evolution took much longer. The 1970 General Conference established the Department of Christian Social Action and Concerns but granted it no budget and no full-time director. The commission largely functioned as an advisory committee to the College of Bishops and the General Conference at the connectional level. In 1982, the General Conference expanded the commission into the Department of Social Concerns, an independent department with its own budget (though partial) and general secretary, Dr. Mance Jackson.[37]

The creation of the CME Social Creed and the Commission on Social Concerns in the 1960s at the zenith of the Civil Rights

---

[34]"Committee on Christian Social Action and Concern," *Christian Index*, 14 January 1965, 12.

[35]Ibid.

[36]Ibid., 12.

[37]In 1986, however, the General Board of Social Concerns was disbanded as a result of denominational restructuring; consequently, the board merged with two other boards to become the Board of Social Concerns, Missions, and Evangelism. For the origins and demise of the Commission of Social Concerns, see Lakey, 589; Smith, Dedicated...Committed 67–69.

movement is a prime expression of CME social consciousness and activism at the denominational level. Although it took some time for these denominational statements and actions to filter down the various episcopal districts and local congregations, CME "social concern" could be seen in at least three other areas: increased participation and visibility in major Civil Rights campaigns in Selma (1965), Memphis (1968), and Washington, DC (1968); increased focus on electoral politics as a result of the Civil Rights Act of 1964; and expanded emphasis on the global dimensions of poverty and injustice.

After the Civil Rights victories of 1963 and 1964 the CME Church no longer vacillated between its public support of Martin Luther King Jr.'s SCLC and the NAACP. After 1964 CMEs more vigorously supported the SCLC's last major civil campaigns in Selma,[38] Memphis, and Washington, DC. In his 1978 autobiography, Bishop Smith proudly recalled his and his district's participation in Civil Rights struggles of the 1960s:

> We marched with Dr. Martin Luther King Jr. and the sanitation workers of Memphis and Nashville. We marched for other causes in Forrest City, Arkansas, Clarksville, Mississippi and elsewhere. We participated in the Meirdeth [sic] March in Mississippi.
>
> We participated in the freedom thrusts of the National Council of Churches for voter registration in Mississippi. Some of our leaders worked in the Freedom School and took the brunt of insults and injury...as we supported the Delta Ministry....
>
> We marched in Memphis and sat-in for the rights of all citizens to eat anywhere they might choose. We joined hands with other church leaders in meeting with President John F.

---

[38]On 25 September 1965, the College of Bishops sent a letter to President Lyndon B. Johnson expressing their outrage at the brutality inflicted on marchers at the Edmund Pettus Bridge in Selma, Alabama ("Statement from the College of Bishops...," *Christian Index*, 25 March 1965, 2).

Kennedy concerning civil and other social problems affecting our nation.[39]

After King's assassination on 4 April 1968, his successor Ralph Abernathy was committed to implementing King's plans for a Poor People's March to Washington. "We sat where they sat," wrote Bishop Smith of CME support for the residents of Haywood and Fayette counties in Arkansas who made the trek to the nation's capital. Smith's episcopal district established a fund to support the residents of "tent city."[40]

CMEs AND THE BALLOT

If the 1963 Birmingham campaign paved the way for the passage of the 1964 Civil Rights Act, then the 1965 Selma crusade led to the passage of the 1965 Voting Rights Act.[41] The congressional debate leading up to the bill's passage produced more than its share of political commentary in the *Christian Index*. As usual, Merriweather led the charge in support of the bill, praising President Johnson for his courage in introducing it to Congress and lambasting southern politicians who were bent on defeating it. After Kennedy's assassination in 1963, Merriweather praised president-elect Johnson as a worthy successor to Kennedy because Johnson had the advantage of being "well-versed in the civil rights problem.... Coming from the South, he has doubtless known this problem from childhood."[42] Then, drawing an analogy from the Bible, Merriweather made the following

---

[39]Bishop Benjamin Julian Smith, *Dedicated...Committed: The Autobiography of Bishop Benjamin Julian Smith* (Nashville: Hemphill Press, 1978) appendix.

[40]Ibid., 66.

[41]For historical accounts of the 1965 Selma Crusade and the Voting Rights Act of 1965, see David J. Garrow, *Protest at Selma: Martin Luther King Jr. and the Voting Rights Act of 1965* (New Haven CT: Yale University Press, 1978) 133–61; Albert P. Blaustein and Robert L. Zangrando, eds., *Civil Rights and African Americans* (Evanston IL: Northwestern University Press, 1968.) 566–72; Charles E. Fager, *Selma 1965: The March that Changed the South*, 2d ed. (Boston: Beacon Press, 1985) 219–29.

[42]"A Brief Look at Our New President, Lyndon B. Johnson," *Christian Index*, 16 January 1964, 3.

prediction about Johnson's presidential potential: "Like Lincoln, let us hope that he was awaiting the day when he could deal a decisive blow to this problem of human inequities.... Moses our leader is dead. We must go over this Jordan under new leadership whose wealth of experience and sense of justice in respect of human dignity of all men adequately prepares him to conquer the land of Canaan and put to flight the Son of Anak."[43]

Furthermore, Merriweather interpreted Johnson's landslide victory in the 1964 election as "conclusive evidence that the American people were in search of a greater way of life in the ideals of American Democracy, justice, freedom, and opportunity advantaged may be shared by all alike."[44] He astutely noted three salient points about this election. First, sectionalism and party affiliation did not seem to prevail over individual voting; more than 61 percent of voters cast their ballots for Johnson. Second, he underscored Johnson's willingness to confront controversial problems at home and abroad, especially Civil Rights issues and the escalating war in Vietnam. Third, Merriweather observed that the four or five states Goldwater won were deep southern states that traditionally voted Democrat. They were motivated by sectional prejudice, according to Merriweather: "They voted their protest against the Civil Rights of the American Negro."[45] Johnson's victory represented "the hand of retribution against the Republican Party for having betrayed the confidence of the American Negro and abandoning him at the time of his most crucial needs. [They had] repudiated the spirit of Lincoln to which many American Negroes had looked for hope."[46] But African Americans also played a crucial role in the defeat of the Republican Party, concluded Merriweather:

> The Negro played a conspicuous part in the final verdict
> of the campaign, because it was his vote in strategic areas

---

[43]Ibid., 3.
[44]"In Quest of the Great Society," *Christian Index*, 19 November 1964, 3.
[45]Ibid.
[46]Ibid.

[Tennessee, Virginia, Texas, Illinois, Pennsylvania] that turned the tide at critical points in the nation.... We hope that the American white politicians have learned that the Negro element in America must be reckoned with, his rights respected, his dignity safeguarded and his influence recognized.[47]

Other CME leaders, such as Reverend Lymell Carter, urged readers to exercise fully their newly gained right to vote: "And now we have an opportunity through the ballot, not only to be effective participants in the restoration of freedom, human dignity and good government, but we have an opportunity to be workers together with God."[48] Carter squarely confronted the question that many first-generation CMEs evaded: Why should we have anything to do with politics? First, politics is a means of expressing Christian love, responded Carter. He compared the ballot to a physician using a scalpel to remove cancerous tissue from the body, describing the ballot as a necessary tool to "remove from our government the malignant growth of injustice and evil corruption. We are endeavoring to save the body of our government through love."[49] Second, voting is a means of expressing Christian conviction and taking a stand on issues by making our voices heard. Third, using the power of the ballot is a "means of instituting justice and righteousness," so long denied African Americans.[50]

Despite their impassioned pleas for CMEs to take full advantage of the rights guaranteed and protected by the 1965 Voting Rights Acts, neither Merriweather nor Carter commented on another important effect of the new laws: the candidacy and election of African Americans, especially in the South. In the 1960s a handful of CME leaders in the Midwest and North had been elected or appointed to municipal offices, but the number remained relatively small in the

---

[47]Ibid.

[48]Reverend Lymell Carter, "Crisis 64—Register and Vote," *Christian Index*, 24 September 1964, 6–7.

[49]Ibid.

[50]Ibid.

South. Three examples from the South were the Reverend David Cunningham, who was elected chair of the War on Poverty Committee of Memphis; the Reverend William Johnson, who was appointed to the Community Relations Commission of Memphis; and the Reverend J. Lorenza Key, who served on the administrative staff of the Housing and Urban Renewal Agency of Macon, Georgia.[51]

CME ECUMENISM IN THE CIVIL RIGHTS ERA

This study has argued that the evolution of CME social consciousness and activism, expressed in the Social Creed and the Social Action Commission, was a direct byproduct of CME involvement in the Civil Rights movement. An equally important factor in the growth of CME social consciousness and activism is the influence of ecumenism. In fact, the ecumenical context of the Civil Rights movement is often overlooked or downplayed. While scholars of the movement have rightly underscored the role of African-American religion and churches as major factors in the movement, they have not adequately interpreted the ecumenical dimensions and legacy of the Civil Rights movement.

It is often assumed that since the leadership of the Civil Rights mainstream was dominated by Baptist ministers, the dominant ethos of the movement was Baptist. But studies of the major movement centers reveal the remarkable ecumenical make-up of local leadership and constituencies.[52] Baptists, Methodists, Holiness-Pentecostals, Presbyterians, and Catholics joined one another in mass meetings, sit-ins, and marches across the South. What is often obscured, though, is

---

[51]Smith, Dedicated...*Committed*, 63.

[52]See, for example, Mary R. Sawyer, "Black Ecumenical Movements: Proponents of Social Change," in *Review of Religious Research* 30 (12 December 1988): 151–61; Sawyer, *Black Ecumenism: Implementing the Demands of Justice* (Valley Forge PA: Trinity Press International, 1994) 35–65; Sawyer, "Black Protestantism as Expressed in Ecumenical Activity," in *Reforming the Center: American Protestantism, 1900 to the Present*, ed. Douglass Jacobsen and William Vance Trollinger Jr. (Grand Rapids MI: William B. Eerdmans, 1999) 284–99; William D. Watley, *Singing the Lord's Song in a Strange Land: The African-American Churches and Ecumenism* (Grand Rapids MI: William B. Eerdmans, 1993).

how these distinctive religious traditions were empowered and enriched by their participation in these ecumenical contexts. The CME Church, then, represents a case study of how one denomination was radically shaped and transformed by its participation in two sometimes overlapping movements, the Civil Rights and ecumenical movements.

CMEs entered the Civil Rights struggle of the 1950s and 1960s already immersed in the ecumenical movement. The CME Church had fully participated in international and national ecumenical bodies throughout much of its history, beginning with the first Ecumenical Methodist Conference in 1881. Moreover, the CME Church became a charter member of both the Federal Council of Churches (later the NCC) in 1950 and the World Council of Churches in 1948, even before these bodies established the pursuit of racial justice as a mission priority. In fact, it was because these ecumenical bodies neglected the race problem that the CME Church became a charter member of the Fraternal Council of Negro Churches in 1934. Finally, by the 1960s CMEs had engaged other African-American Methodist bodies in conversations on organic merger. The sheer dynamism generated by the Civil Rights movement contributed a renewed sense of urgency and vitality to CME ecumenism at local, regional, national, and global levels.

At the denominational level, M. C. Merriweather wrote numerous editorials accentuating the connections between the Civil Rights and ecumenical movements. In an editorial published during the 1963 Birmingham campaign, Merriweather directed the following question to church leadership: "We are standing at the point of critical involvement and the question in the minds of the general public at the moment is: what does my Church have to say about these problems or to what extent are we involved in these changes?"[53] He noted that the problems of race relations, church mergers, and the question of ecumenicity were on the agendas of all denominations and interdenominational groups: "We cannot escape the question (why?) when other denominations are uniting their

---

[53]"Broadening the Bases of Freedom," Christian Index 2 May 1963, 2-4.

forces and facilities for more effective work to the Kingdom of God. The question of ecumenicity is upon us, and we should confront it with open minds and with long range planning."[54]

Perhaps no two people took the question of ecumenicity more seriously than Bishops B. Julian Smith and Henry Bunton.[55] Their Civil Rights ecumenism dated back to the mid-1950s when Smith invited Bunton to transfer from Denver to Memphis to work with the CME Board of Christian Education, of which Smith served as general secretary. Shortly thereafter, Bunton was appointed pastor of Mt. Olive Cathedral CME Church in Memphis. After their respective elections to the episcopacy, their ecumenical endeavors diverged into two mutually related directions: Smith devoted his energies to the NCC and its programs for racial justice while Bunton devoted his energies toward effecting organic merger with other African-American Methodist bodies.

During the 1960s Smith kept the issue of ecumenism before the CME Church by holding positions in three ecumenical bodies: vice-president of the NCC, president of the Tennessee Council of Churches, and member of the Central Committee of the WCC. During his tenure at the NCC, Smith often represented the NCC at national meetings, Civil Rights marches, and press conferences.[56] For example, in June of 1963, Smith served as the NCC's key spokesperson in Mississippi at the funeral of slain Civil Rights leader Medgar Evers.[57]

Within his own episcopal district, Smith sought to implement the same style of Civil Rights ecumenism he advocated and embodied at the WCC and the NCC. In a New Year's greeting to "fellow Christians

---

[54]Ibid.

[55]This is not to suggest that other CME leaders were neither interested nor involved in ecumenism at various levels.

[56]For example, the cover of the 23 January 1964 edition of the *Christian Index* featured a photo of Smith and four other NCC leaders meeting with President Johnson in the White House; see also "The National Council of Churches Sparks Drive Against Segregation," *Christian Index*, 27 June 1963, 2; "Our Fellowship: National Council of Churches—Civil Rights Workers," *Christian Index*, 12 December 1963.

[57]"Statement by Bishop B. Julian Smith...," *Eastern Index*, Spring 1963, 2.

in Arkansas and Tennessee," Smith displayed his ecumenical activism by reviewing the Civil Rights struggles of the year 1963.

> During 1963, which marked the hundredth anniversary of the signing of the Emancipation Proclamation,...Negro citizens...have been engaged in a struggle for first class citizenship.... This struggle to walk in dignity has taken place in places of public accommodations, on public carriers, in the streets, in educational institutions, in factories, in the building industries...and even in churches.
>
> After waiting patiently for one hundred years, we the Negroes, feel that the time has arrived for us to have equal opportunity for employment, apprenticeship, union membership, job training and promotion based upon merit and not race.... We want equal access to education, the right to vote and equal protection of the law.[58]

Smith mentioned a number of groups that had made contributions to the Civil Rights movement, including student groups, Civil Rights organizations, and ecumenical bodies. However, he sharply criticized white Christians for their "appalling silence" in addressing racial inequities in their towns: "As one Christian to another, would you like to exchange places with us, or would you like for other Christians to be silent in the face of such injustices?"[59] Yet Smith closed his greetings with this positive appeal to white Christians in Tennessee and Arkansas:

> At the beginning of this new year we come to seek your help as Christians in our struggle. We are convinced that our cause is just and right. We are seeking only that which a just and loving Father desires for all of his children and not just some of them. The race problem can be solved if we as

---

[58]Bishop B. Julian Smith, "New Year's Greeting to Fellow Christians in Arkansas and Tennessee," *Christian Index*, 16 January 1964, 2, 4.
[59]Ibid., 4.

Christians have a will to solve it. Can we depend upon you to witness to the Fatherhood of God and to work for justice for all his children in your church and community? We need your help.[60]

As the former general secretary for the CME Department of Christian Education, Smith also included ecumenical programs as part of his district's educational ministry, thus promoting ecumenical dialogue at the local level. Two concrete examples of these ecumenical encounters were the Joint Pastor's and the Woman's Missionary Institutes hosted annually at Lane College and co-sponsored by the CME, AME, and AMEZ churches.[61] The institutes were designed to aid local pastors and missionaries in continuing their education and sharpening their tools for ministry. Each year, the institutes' pan-Methodist planning committee met to adopt a theme, approve courses, select faculty, and plan worship and extracurricular activities. "Many of the most distinguished pastors, theologians and Bible scholars from across the nation, without regard to race, joined us from year to year in making this Institute one of the unique ecumenical efforts of this century," said Smith.[62]

ORGANIC MERGER *RECIDIVOUS*

Bishop Smith's ecumenical institutes at Lane College were a harbinger of the kind of fruitful ecumenical dialogue and cooperative actions that resulted among African-American Methodists in the mid-1960s. Bishop Bunton became the CME catalyst for reviving the spirit of organic union that lay dormant since the 1930s. A symbolic move in this direction came in February of 1965 when Bunton moved his episcopal offices into the Methodist Building in Washington, DC, where he joined two other African-American bishops, AME bishop

---

[60]Ibid.
[61]Smith, De*dicated...Committed*, 70–71.
[62]Ibid., 71.

George Barber and AMEZ bishop Raymond Jones.[63] In a joint statement the three bishops lauded the opening of joint offices as an expression of their interest in greater cooperation among their respective communions and a "willingness to enter into a large church union."[64]

What the three bishops meant by their "willingness to enter into a large church union" is not entirely clear from their statement, but during the 1960s two proposals for union were discussed. The first proposal involved renewed interest in organic merger among all or some of the historically black Methodist denominations, including those African Americans who comprised the Central Jurisdiction of the Methodist Church. The second proposal explored by African-American Methodists was the 1962 initiative of the Consultation on Church Union (COCU) to create a church in the United States that was "truly catholic, truly evangelical, and truly reformed."[65]

---

[63]"Bishop Henry C. Bunton Moves His Office to Methodist Building, Washington D. C.," *Christian Index*, 25 February 1965, 1–2. The building also included the regional and national offices of several agencies of the Methodist Church, the National Council of Churches, the United Presbyterian Church, the Church of the Brethren, and the United Churches of Christ (UCC).

[64]Ibid., 2.

[65]The idea to create a "truly catholic, truly evangelical and truly reformed" church was sparked by a sermon preached by Eugene Carson Blake, stated clerk of the United Presbyterian Church, on 4 December 1960 at Grace Cathedral (Episcopal) in San Francisco, titled "A Proposal Toward the Reunion of Christ's Church." He suggested the time was right for churches in the United States to transcend their historic and theological divisions; see Eugene Carson Blake, *A Proposal Toward the Reunion of Christ's Church* (Philadelphia: General Assembly of the United Presbyterian Church, USA, 1961). In April 1962, forty-two representatives from four denominations—the United Presbyterian Church, the Methodist Church, the Episcopal Church, and the United Church of Christ—met at an exploratory plenary session in Washington, DC, where they constituted themselves as the "Consultation on Church Union." The Christian Church (Disciples of Christ) and the Evangelical United Church joined the union later that year; the African-American Methodist bodies joined as observant-participants and subsequently as full members; for the origins and development of COCU, see Paul A. Crow Jr., "The Church—A New Beginning," in *Church Union at Midpoint*, ed. Paul A. Crow Jr. and William J. Boney (New York: Association Press, 1972) 20–40; for African-American Methodist participation in COCU, see Mary R. Sawyer, "Blacks in White Ecumenism," *Midstream: The Ecumenical Movement Today* 31/3 (July 1992): 222–36; Frederick

In January 1964, eighty-eight representatives from the CME, AME, and AMEZ churches gathered at Wesley Theological Seminary in Washington, DC, to re-open discussion on organic union among their respective bodies.[66] Serving as co-conveners for the conference were Wesley professor of ecumenics John Satterwhite (AMEZ), Dean Charles S. Spivey of Payne Theological Seminary (Wilberforce, Ohio), and CME presiding elder C. N. Reed of the New York–Washington District. A total of six bishops were present, with Bunton as the lone bishop from the CME Church. Of the nineteen CME delegates in attendance, five were from movement centers in the South, including M. C. Merriweather (Memphis), L. H. Pitts (Birmingham), and Cleo McCoy (Greensboro). African-American Methodist women, however, were conspicuously underrepresented among the delegates; only five attended the sessions, none of whom were CME.[67]

The conference deliberations produced no significant break-throughs in the elusive quest for organic merger. Like earlier discussions, the conferences committed the implementation of the merger process into the hands of the bishops' councils of each denomination, namely to designate committees "vested with the authority to draw up a Plan of Union,"[68] to hold joint sessions among themselves to discuss the issue, and to promote the idea in their general conferences and episcopal addresses.[69] The delegates left the door open for other African-American Methodists to join future consultations. Although no explicit mention was made to the COCU

D. Jordan, "COCU and the Black Churches," in *Church Union at Midpoint*, 113–17; John E. Brandon, "Three Black Methodist Churches in the Consultation on Church Union: Problems and Prospects for Union" (DMin diss., Boston University, 1986).

[66]See Virgil E. Lowder, "Negro Methodists Consider Union," *Christian Century* (19 February 1964): 250–51; Mary R. Sawyer, "Efforts at Black Merger," *Journal of the Interdenominational Theological Seminary* 8/2 (Spring 1986): 305–15.

[67]See statement from "Consultation on AMEZ, AME, CME Church Union," Wesley Theological Seminary, 23 January 1964 (Henry C. Bunton Papers).

[68]Ibid., 2.

[69]Ibid.

plan of union, the delegates acknowledged openness to "the larger goal of union among all churches."[70]

In April of 1965, the bishops followed up on the 1964 consultation's recommendation for a trilateral meeting of bishops to chart a course for organic union. The so-called "tri-council of bishops" convened at Lane Tabernacle CME Church in St. Louis to weigh the prospects of organic union. All three senior bishops were present, along with their designated "secretariats" (other bishops). Here they targeted 1972 as the year for the consummation of their union. In the meantime, the three denominations agreed to establish a general commission, made up of representatives from each church, to study the following areas: structure and polity, theological and doctrinal foundations, liturgy, missions, publications, educational systems, evangelism, public relations, pension programs, and legal procedures.[71]

After the 1965 St. Louis consultation, the general commission met three times—Atlanta in 1965; Washington, DC, in 1968; and Chicago in 1969.[72] After 1969, however, the thrust for union among the three denominations appeared to dissipate, although the CME and AMEZ churches continued to pursue merger.[73] Two factors may account for the breakdown in merger talks in the 1960s.

The first factor was the competing vision of the COCU for a more expansive form of merger, one that proposed to unite multiple Protestant traditions into a single, racially integrated church. On 28 March 1968 COCU agreed to draft an ambitious plan of union for ten Protestant denominations, four of which were Methodist.[74] This

---

[70]Ibid.

[71]Committee memo from Bishop Frederick D. Jordan to Bunton, secretary, 31 March 1965 (Henry C. Bunton Papers).

[72]For reports on these meetings see *Christian Index* 3 February 1966, 3–4 on the Atlanta meeting; see *Christian Index*, 4 January 1968, 2–3 on the Washington, DC, meeting.

[73]A resolution for merger was adopted by the general conferences of the AMEZ and CME churches in 1978 and 1980, respectively.

[74]These Methodist bodies were the AME, AMEZ, CME, and the newly constituted United Methodist Church; on the 1968 meeting in Dayton, Ohio, see "The Editor's Notebook," *Christian Index*, 11–18 April 1968; "The Editor's

vision was particularly attractive to many African-American Methodists who were committed to the ideal of racial integration promoted by the Civil Rights movement. In 1965 the AME Church became the first of those three denominations to join COCU, followed by the AMEZ Church in 1967 and the CME Church in 1968.[75] For AME ecumenists like Charles Spivey, membership in COCU did not preclude organic union with the AME, CME, and AMEZ churches. Merger was still a "desirable, attainable step in the direction of this larger merger [with the Methodist Church]. Union of these three bodies anticipates in part the Methodist [sic] Church."[76]

Several CMEs wrote editorials to the *Christian Index* endorsing the position that organic merger with the African Methodists was mutually compatible with the goals of COCU.[77] But others, like Bunton, expressed caution about COCU and merger with the Methodist Church. In a May 1968 address before the AME General Conference in Philadelphia, Bunton warned that independent African-American Methodists "should think long and hard before they surrender their autonomy to any organization in which they will become an ineffective minority."[78] Bunton, however, reaffirmed his and the CME Church's commitment to working out a plan of union

---

Notebook," *Christian Index*, 25 April–2 May 1968, 2, 5; *Christian Index*, "Consultation on Church Union Roundup," 25 April–2 May 1968, 7, 14. The plan was adopted two years later in Atlanta; see *A Plan of Union for the Church of Christ Uniting* (Princeton NJ: Consultation on Church Union, 1970).

[75]For an explanation of the AME Church's reasons for joining COCU, see Charles Spivey, "Why the AME Church Joined the Consultation on Church Union," *Christian Index*, 26 May 1966, 7, 11, 14.

[76]Ibid., 11; Throughout this article, Spivey refers to the union of the Methodist Church with the black Methodist bodies as the "United Church" rather than the "Methodist Church."

[77]See, for example, S. J. Laws, "The Imperative for Union," *Christian Index*, 3–4; Marshall Gilmore, "Reflection of Merger," *Christian Index*, 24 February 1966, 2, 4; R. Theodore Cunningham, "Ecumenism and Organic Union," *Christian Index*, 26 October 1967, 11; see also the short-lived journal, *The Christian Call*, published by Rev. Robert Tieuel Jr., a CME pastor in Texas who pledged "to devote the rest of his life to leading [the] Negro Methodist Union Movement," Spring 1964, 1.

[78]Reprinted in Henry C. Bunton, *In Quest of a Savior: Selected Sermons from a Rugged Preacher* (1966) 100–101; see also, Henry C. Bunton, "The Urgency of the Time—The Irresistible Call to Action," *Christian Index*, 12 October 1967, 6.

with the AME and AMEZ churches. Only a minority of CMEs expressed outright opposition to merger. Ervin Miller, a layperson from Augusta, Georgia, regarded the recent discussions among AMEs, AMEZs, and CMEs as a sham. After so many aborted efforts in the past, "why would anyone have any more faith in their merging now than they did in previous years?" he asked.[79] "I will believe in merger when I see it and not before. By all means I want it, but history gives me no present foundation for faith."[80]

THE CHALLENGE OF BLACK POWER

A second factor for the breakdown of merger talks was the rise of black consciousness and militancy among African-American clergy in the 1960s. Distancing themselves from the integrationist goals of Martin Luther King Jr. and the Civil Rights mainstream that now dominated the denominational hierarchies, these leaders became increasingly critical of the paternalism and racism in the ecumenical churches. The precursors of black theology, this younger generation of clergy was more likely to form broad-based coalitions with other African-American clergy/activists, including those in predominantly white denominations and church agencies, than to promote organic union among their respective denominations. One early expression of African-American clergy advocacy of black power was the northern-based National Committee of Negro Churchmen (NCNC), formed in 1966. On 31 July 1966 the NCNC issued a full-page statement in the *New York Times* addressing the issue of black power, with the intention of clarifying African-American clergy's positions and pointing to the theological implications of black power.[81] Only two CME ministers, the Reverend Caesar Coleman of Memphis and the

---

[79]Henry C. Bunton, "Matters of Concern," *Christian Index*, 12 May 1966, 14.

[80]Ibid.

[81]The statement is reprinted in vol. 1 of *Black Theology: A Documentary History,* James H. Cone and Gayraud S. Wilmore (Maryknoll NY: Orbis Books, 1993) 19–26; for a discussion of the NCNC and subsequent evolution into the National Conference of Black Christians, see Sawyer, *Black Ecumenism*, 66–89; Mark L. Chapman, *Christianity on Trial: African-American Religious Thought Before and After Black Power* (Maryknoll NY: Orbis Books, 1996) 75–91.

Reverend Joseph Coles of New York, were listed among its forty-two signatories.[82] The statement evoked no official response from the CME College of Bishops.[83]

Although only two CMEs signed the 1966 NCNC statement, other CME leaders sought to respond to the social and theological issues raised by black power advocates. Among them was Bishop Joseph Johnson Jr., who, along with Preston Williams of Boston University, served as co-chair of the NCNC's commission on theology, which was charged with the task of clarifying the theological meaning and implications of black power. Prior to his death in 1978, Bishop Johnson published a series of writings that contributed to the foundational corpus of black theology.[84] But like other CME leaders, Johnson was reluctant to support black power

---

[82]Coleman served as executive secretary of the CME Board of Christian Education in Memphis, and Coles was pastor of the Williams Institutional CMEC Church in New York.

[83]The *Christian Index*, however, kept CME readers fully abreast of the NCNC's subsequent meetings, activities, and statements; see "National Committee of Negro Churchmen," *Christian Index*, 7 September 1967, 2, 4; "National Committee of Negro Churchmen Meets at Crispus Attucks' Monument," *Christian Index*, 7 September 1967, 2; "National Committee of Negro Churchmen Meet in St. Louis...," *Christian Index*, 29 June 1967, 2, 4; "National Committee of Negro Churchmen Meet in St. Louis...," *Christian Index*, 7 November 1968, 5.

[84]See especially "Jesus Christ, the Liberator," in *Quest for a Black Theology*, ed. James J. Gardiner and J. Deotis Roberts Sr. (Philadelphia: United Church Press, 1971); *The Soul of the Black Preacher* (Philadelphia: United Church Press, 1971); and *Proclamation Theology* (Shreveport LA: Fourth Episcopal District Press, 1977), which includes a harsh critique of Cone's seminal works, *Black Theology and Black Power* (Philadelphia and New York: Seabury Press, 1969), *A Black Theology of Liberation* (New York: J. B. Lippincott, 1970), and *God of the Oppressed* (New York: Seabury Press, 1974). Johnson criticized two elements in James Cone's theology: (1) his tendency to absolutize blackness as the norm for interpreting Christianity and (2) his negative evaluation of the role of African-American churches in the historic struggle for black freedom (*Proclamation Theology*, 144–49). While Johnson acknowledged his own indebtedness to Cone's theology and applauded his recovery of the liberation motif in contemporary theology, he was nonetheless "disturbed at the 'passionate' language used in [his] writings. Whereas this language reflects commitment and deep concern in the process of communicating the Christian message, it also adumbrates the feeling of deep anger, raw emotions and reckless phraseology" (*Proclamation Theology*, 151–52).

militancy and rhetoric and continued to embrace integrationist and ecumenical goals.

In 1967, the "Committee on Response to the Black Manifesto,"[85] chaired by the Reverend James Cummings, drafted an official CME response.[86] While the committee substantively agreed with the manifesto's analysis of racism in the United States, it disagreed with the manifesto's theological assumptions, ideological commitments, and programmatic solutions. First, speaking from an integrationist perspective, the committee regarded race relations as a "moral issue" that needed to be confronted by the totality of black and white institutions, not just by white religious bodies.[87] Second, the committee rejected the presumption of any one person or group to speak for all African Americans: "For too long, whites have decided what was just and right for black persons. What we now refuse whites to do we will not permit a few self-selected blacks to do either! Thus, the principle of self-determination which we deem essential to the present struggle of black people in American [sic] is grossly violated

---

[85]For a full text of the "Black Manifesto," see Cone and Wilmore, vol. 1 of *Documentary History of Black Theology,* 327–336. The "Manifesto" was first issued by James Forman, a black nationalist and former executive secretary of SNCC, on 26 April 1969 at the National Black Economic Development Conference at Wayne State University in Detroit. The conference was sponsored by the Interreligious Foundation for Community Organizations (IFOC) to locate funding sources for urban development. Black nationalist and stridently anti-capitalist in tone, the "Manifesto" demanded $500 million in reparations from white Christian churches and synagogues for their complicity in the economic exploitation of African Americans. The "Manifesto" received massive publicity on 4 May 1969 when Forman interrupted services at Riverside Church in New York City to present the "Manifesto"; for accounts of the ensuing controversy and responses of churches and synagogues, see Robert S. Lecky and H. Elliot Wright, eds., *The Black Manifesto* (New York: Sheed and Ward, 1969); Arnold Schuster, *Reparations: The Black Manifesto and Its Challenge to White America* (Philadelphia and New York: J. B. Lippincott, 1970); James Forman, *The Making of Black Revolutionaries,* 2d ed. (Washington DC: Open Hand Publishing, 1985) 543–53. Gayraud S. Wilmore, *Black Religion and Black Radicalism: An Interpretation of the Religious History of Afro-American People,* 2d rev. ed. (Maryknoll NY: Orbis Books, 1983) 233–42.

[86]"The Black Manifesto: A Response from the Christian Methodist Episcopal Church," undated mimeographed copy (Henry C. Bunton Papers).

[87]Ibid.

by the Black Manifesto." Reflecting the CME Church's adoption of King's nonviolent philosophy and strategy, the committee also renounced the manifesto's threat of violence and "any means necessary" to effect its demands: "Now not only are we, as a Church of Jesus Christ, opposed to the violence in obedience to the command of Christ, but we oppose it as a strategy for achieving the legitimate goals and aspirations of black people."[88]

Fourth, the committee rejected the manifesto's explicit Marxist analysis of racism and critique of capitalism in the United States, affirming that "all human economic systems are evil and that no system should be held up as that desired by the black people of America."[89] Here again, the committee acknowledged racism as a manifestation of human sin that "afflicts black people as well as white."[90] Therefore, the manifesto's call for a "black-controlled government" was not only impractical but an "uninhibited expression of black racism."[91] Fifth, the committee objected to the arbitrary amount of reparation money the manifesto demanded from white religious institutions. Sixth, the committee rejected the manifesto's critique of African-American Christianity for its uncritical acceptance of Euro-American Christianity.[92]

In summary, the decade of the 1960s proved to be a climactic chapter not only in the course of the Civil Rights movement but also in the development of CME social consciousness, activism, and ecumenism. Galvanized by the 1963 Civil Rights unrest in Birmingham and the 1963 March on Washington, the CME College of Bishops unabashedly pronounced the church's support of the Civil Rights movement, thereby giving belated sanction and support to a small contingent of CMEs who had already immersed themselves in local and regional Civil Rights campaigns.

---

482 Ibid.

[88]Ibid., 3.

[89]Ibid., 4.

[90]Ibid.

[91]Ibid., 4–5.

[92]Ibid., 6.

The CME Church's endorsement of the Civil Rights movement coincided with its expanding involvement in regional, national, and global ecumenism, including the NCC, WCC, COCU, and pan-Methodist ventures. When these ecumenical bodies themselves placed racial justice at the forefront of their agenda, largely in response to the demands of African-American Christians, CMEs discovered an ever-widening circle of ecumenical partners. These mutually related movements provided CMEs with a plethora of new insights, resources, and partners in mission. But with the denouement of the Civil Rights movement and the rise of black power militancy in the late 1960s, CMEs faced new challenges to their Civil Rights activism, challenging but not subverting their support of integration, ecumenism, and racial justice.

CHAPTER 8

Summary and Conclusion

The purpose of this study has been to examine CME involvement in the Civil Rights movement and to assess the impact of this movement on the church's evolving social and ecumenical consciousness. CME involvement in the ecumenical and Civil Rights movements of the mid-twentieth century precipitated a painful but invigorating shift in denominational identity, ecumenism, and social activism. Although CMEs were not the most visible leaders in the movements, they were represented at multiple levels. Moreover, their participation in the Civil Rights movement was preceded by decades of involvement in local and regional struggles for racial justice throughout the South, which resulted in closer cooperation and solidarity with other African-American Methodists, ecumenical bodies, and Civil Rights organizations.

Beginning with the "rise of Colored Methodism" during the aftermath of slavery, this study has emphasized the distinctive religious and social character of first-generation colored Methodists and their relationship with their southern white benefactors in the MECS. Although the relationship between white and colored members changed after emancipation, it was governed by a code of racial etiquette that assumed white dominance and colored insubordination. Consequently, the quest for full CME autonomy in the New South was circumscribed by a system that perpetuated social distinctions on the basis of race.

In an effort to survive within this system, colored Methodists embraced Booker T. Washington's pragmatic approach to racial progress, which emphasized racial uplift through hard work and education, as well as social and political accommodation to the Jim Crow system. CMEs, however, added a religious and theological dimension to their accommodation in that they endeavored to maintain close ties with southern Methodists. By doing so the CME Church not only sought to secure legitimacy as an authentic Wesleyan church, but also to receive property, financial support, and consultation from its parent church. More ambiguously, though, CMEs adopted the MECS's notion on the "spirituality" of the church, a doctrine promulgated by southern evangelicalism that narrowly confined the church's mission to religious matters rather than social or political ones.

Whether the first generation of CMEs adopted this doctrine as an article of faith or an interim strategy of survival is debatable. What is clear, however, is that by the early twentieth century CMEs began to challenge this doctrine in their public discourse and social witness. This fundamental shift in CME social consciousness can be attributed partly to the church's wider exposure to and participation in more progressive movements, especially the Civil Rights and ecumenical movements. Consequently, in the four decades leading up to the 1955 Montgomery bus boycott and the emergence of Martin Luther King Jr., the CME Church became an active partner and power broker in such socially progressive organizations as the NAACP, the Fraternal Council of Negro Churches, the World Methodist Council, the Federal (National) Council of Churches, and the World Council of Churches. In other words, the CME Church was primed for the coming social revolution in the 1950s and 1960s.

One major indicator of CME preparedness for social change in the 1950s was the denomination's name change from "Colored" to "Christian" Methodist Episcopal Church, initiated at the 1954 General Conference. The name change reflected the church's deepening commitment to ecumenism and Civil Rights. From an ecumenical perspective, the name "Christian" connoted a more prescriptive designation of the church's essential nature and unity, now predicated on religious rather than racial identity. From a Civil Rights perspective, the rejection of the name "Colored" implied an outright repudiation of Jim Crow classifications of white and colored and a firmer commitment to racial equality.

After the historic 1954 *Brown v. Board of Education* Supreme Court decision, CMEs intensified their support of desegregation and Civil Rights, primarily through the legal strategies of the NAACP, the nation's oldest Civil Rights organization. Consequently, CMEs were less reluctant to support the nonviolent direct-action strategies of Martin Luther King Jr. and other activists in Montgomery, Alabama, as well as subsequent crusades. However, a few CME activists did embrace King and the SCLC's philosophy and strategies by leading similar campaigns in their own locales (e.g., Henry Bunton in Memphis, Tennessee, and Charles Golmillion in Tuskegee, Alabama). Their success in galvanizing local churches to support local struggles set a precedent for subsequent CME involvement in Civil Rights campaigns and electoral politics.

Thus, with a heightened sense of social and ecumenical consciousness during the 1960s, a growing contingent of CME leaders participated in the Civil Rights movement and encouraged their local congregations, conferences, and denominational hierarchy to do likewise. CMEs made significant but largely unheralded contributions to the Civil Rights struggle in movement centers in Nashville, Atlanta, Birmingham, and Memphis, where there were heavy concentrations of CME churches and members.

Joining an ecumenical and religiously based movement of local people, a growing contingent of CME ministers and laypeople attended mass meetings, marched in demonstrations, sat-in at lunch counters, negotiated settlements, and performed countless other deeds for the cause of freedom. Nowhere was this broad-based support for the movement more evident than in the Birmingham campaign, where a coalition of the ACMHR and the SCLC confronted the nation's "most segregated city." Here, traditional leaders like President Lucius Pitts of Miles College joined forces with ministers and students in confrontations with Birmingham's white power structure.

Regarded as a major turning point in the Civil Rights movement, the Birmingham campaign was instrumental in revitalizing the momentum of the movement after the SCLC's 1962 Albany debacle and in initiating federal legislation of a comprehensive Civil Rights bill. Moreover, national and global media coverage of the Birmingham campaign influenced black and white religious bodies to support the movement and to place racial justice on their agenda. For a brief period after the Birmingham campaign and the March on Washington, the Civil Rights movement evolved into more of an interracial, ecumenical, and interfaith movement.

With its strategic location in the South and its long history of ecumenical involvement, the CME Church was at the forefront of this emerging ecumenical Civil Rights activism. The participation of CMEs in the Birmingham campaign paved the way for wider CME participation at local, regional, and national levels. During the apex of the movement, between 1964 and 1968, CME involvement in national and global ecumenical bodies contributed to the church's social consciousness and activism, leading to an episcopal endorsement of the movement, adoption of a CME Social Creed, and formation of a Social Action Commission. Furthermore, CME Civil Rights ecumenism led to a revival of merger dialogue with the AME and AMEZ churches and participation in the Consultation on Church Union. By the denouement of the Civil Rights movement in 1968 and the subsequent rise of the black power movement, CME social consciousness and activism had reached a new level of maturity. Almost 100 years old, the Colored Methodist Church that was born from the biracial union of colored and white Methodists in the South had evolved from its social and religious captivity in the New South into a national and ecumenical church that was now at the forefront for racial justice.

Consequently, as the CME Church braced itself to enter what M. C. Merriweather called the "third phase of the revolution," it did so with a transformed identity and mission. As far as its identity, the church painfully shed its "colored" name, with all its connotations of racial ambiguity, separation, and inferiority. The name "colored" had originally signified African-American autonomy and freedom in the aftermath of slavery, but both were circumscribed by white racism and paternalism in the New South. By replacing "colored" with

"Christian," the CME Church asserted its freedom and autonomy by renaming itself to reflect a changing social reality, as well as to signify a hopeful move toward Christian unity.

The quest for human dignity became one of the dominant themes to emerge in the CME quest for freedom and autonomy. For CMEs the quest for dignity meant nothing less than respect for African-American personhood and equal treatment under the law. The daily indignities of living under Jim Crow segregation worked to strip African Americans of their self-worth and full potential as human beings created in the image and likeness of God. That Christian churches in the South sanctioned such a system with racist dogma and separatist practices only confirmed the captivity of the gospel to the prevailing culture. Consequently, through such bold acts as changing their denominational name, supporting Civil Rights organizations like the NAACP, and participating in local campaigns, CMEs individually and collectively asserted their demand for human dignity.

In addition to the quest for basic human dignity, participation in the Civil Rights and ecumenical movements helped CMEs recover neglected and undeveloped elements of their Wesleyan identity, particularly Wesleyan social ethics and the doctrine of sanctification. After emancipation from slavery, colored Methodists were eventually exposed to the more radical dimensions of John Wesley's social teachings, including his repudiation of slavery and his concern for the poor. Moreover, in the late nineteenth and early twentieth centuries, CMEs came in contact with Methodist seminaries, thinkers, and social agencies espousing the social gospel, in almost direct opposition to the doctrine of the "spirituality of the church" of southern evangelicalism.

CME appropriation of the social gospel differed, however, in at least two respects from more liberal white Methodists counterparts. First, CME leaders like Channing Tobias and Henry Bunton, both of whom attended Methodist seminaries outside the South, included the racial problem as a fundamental concern of the social gospel. Second, for these and other CME leaders, the appropriation of social gospel did not lead to a repudiation or diminution of other distinctive Methodist doctrines or practices. Subsequently during the first five decades of the twentieth century, the CME Church made no major changes in the doctrinal standards or polity of the church but established a more holistic connection between spiritual and social witness. Although CMEs tended to avoid the term "sanctification" to describe this connection, they articulated elements of Wesley's understanding of sanctification and social holiness. Going beyond Wesley, though, CMEs came to embrace an even more radical understanding of the church's involvement in the transformation of social and political structures, with CME involvement in the Civil Rights movement being the prime example.

If the rediscovery and transformation of Wesleyan social ethics marked a major development within the CME Church during the Civil Rights movement, the rediscovery of other African-American Methodists in the struggle was another turning point. Although CMEs and other African-American Methodist bodies had been in dialogue with each other since the late nineteenth century and had proposed several merger plans, the Civil Rights and ecumenical movements provided new momentum for cooperation and merger. Not only did these bodies share Wesleyan roots, doctrine, and polity within an African-American "sacred cosmos," but they also shared an ongoing quest for racial justice and equality within American society. Consequently, renewed conversations between CMEs, AMEs, and AMEZs in the 1960s placed Civil Rights high on their agenda, seeing their merger as a way of further mobilizing resources for the movement.

The consummate goal of organic merger among these and other African-American Methodists remains elusive for a variety of reasons. One major complication was the meaning of racial integration for African-American Methodists and the relationship between integration and ecumenism. As their 1954 name change indicated, CMEs were inclined to see integration and ecumenism as parallel movements toward a fully integrated society and church; thus, they remained more ambiguous about the meaning of racial specificity and consciousness. Such ambiguity could be seen in the CME Church's debate in the 1960s whether to pursue organic merger with the African-American Methodists, the United Methodist Church, and/or the Consultation of Church Union. This debate took place during the rise of the black power movement in the 1960s, which forced the CME Church to reassess its understanding of racial integration and to affirm its distinctive African-American identity. By its first centennial in 1970, the social and ecumenical consciousness of the Colored Methodist Episcopal Church had been radically transformed since its inception as a church of former slaves whose social progress was circumscribed by the narrow constraints of white racism and paternalism. In its place emerged the Christian Methodist Episcopal Church, fully committed to Civil Rights and ecumenism and ready to confront the bittersweet legacies of the post-Civil Rights era.

Bibliography

Archival Sources

Department of Archives and Manuscripts, Birmingham Public and Jefferson County Free Library, Linn-Henly Research Library, Birmingham.
Special Collections, Fisk University Library, Nashville, Tennessee.
Special Collections, Lane College Library, Jackson, Tennessee.
King Library and Archives, Martin Luther King Jr. Center for Nonviolent Social Change, Inc., Atlanta.
Special Collections, C.A. Kirkendoll Learning Resource Center, Miles College, Birmingham, Alabama.
Race Relations Information Center, Nashville Public Library, Nashville.
Henry C. Bunton Papers. Schomburg Center for Research in Black Culture, New York Public Library, New York.
Manuscript Division, Tennessee State Library and Archives, Nashville.

Newspapers

Atlanta *Constitution*
Atlanta *Daily World*
Birmingham *News*
Birmingham *Post-Herald*
Birmingham *Times*
Birmingham *World*
Memphis *Commercial Appeal*
Memphis *Press-Scimitar*
Nashville *Globe*
Nashville *Tennessean*
SCLC Newsletter

Periodicals

A.M.E. Church Review
A.M.E.Z. Church Quarterly Review
Central Christian Advocate (MEC)
Christian Index (CME)

Christian Recorder (AME)
Daily Christian Advocate (MECS)
Gammon Theological Seminary Bulletin
Journal of Religious Thought
Missionary Messenger (CME)
Phylon
Southern Christian Recorder (MECS)
Star of Zion (AMEZ)

PRIMARY SOURCES

Bell, W. A., ed. *Missions and Cooperation of the Methodist Episcopal Church, South with the Colored Methodist Episcopal Church*. Nashville: Board of Missions, MECS, 1923.
Bunton, Henry C. *The Challenge to Become Involved*. 1966.
————. *A Dreamer of Dreams: An Autobiography*. Memphis: CME Publishing House, 1998.
————. *In Quest of a Savior: Selected Sermons from a Rugged Preacher*.
Carson, Eugene Blake. *A Proposal Toward the Reunion of Christ's Church*. Philadelphia: General Assembly of the United Presbyterian Church, USA, 1961.
Colclough, J. C. *The Spirit of John Wesley Gilbert*. Nashville: Cokesbury Press, 1925.
Culp, D. W., ed. *Twentieth-Century Negro Literature: Or a Cyclopedia of Thought*. Atlanta: J. L. Nichols and Company, 1902.
Curry, Norris S. *The Methodist Preacher: Prophet, Priest and Pastor: An Experience, a Call, a Preparation, an Appointment, a Retirement*. MC Publishing House, 1977.
Du Bois, W. E. B. *The Souls of Black Folk*. In *W. E. B. Du Bois: Writings*, ed. Nathan L. Huggins. New York: Library of America, 1986.
Du Bois, W. E. B., ed. *The Negro Church: Report of a Social Study Made under the Direction of Atlanta University*. Atlanta: Atlanta University, 1903.
Finklestein, Louis, ed. *Thirteen Americans: Their Spiritual Autobiographies*. New York: Institute for Religious and Social Studies, 1953.
Harrison, W. P., ed. *The Gospel among Slaves: A Short Account of Missionary Operations among the African Slaves of the Southern States*. Nashville: Publishing House of the ME Church, South, 1893.
Holsey, Lucius H. *Autobiography, Sermons, Addresses, and Essays*. 2d ed. Atlanta: The Franklin Printing and Publishing Company, 1899.
Johnson, Joseph A. *Basic Christian Methodist Beliefs*. Shreveport LA: Fourth Episcopal District Press, 1978.

———. "Jesus Christ, the Liberator." In *Quest for a Black Theology*, ed. James J. Gardiner and J. Deotis Roberts Sr. Philadelphia: United Church Press, 1971.

———. *Proclamation Theology*. Shreveport LA: Fourth Episcopal District, 1977.

———. *The Soul of the Black Preacher*. Philadelphia: United Church Press, 1971.

Lane, Isaac. *Autobiography of Bishop of Issac Lane, LL.D. With a Short History of the C.M.E. Church in America and of Methodism*. Nashville: Publishing House of the ME Church, South, 1916.

Logan, Rayford, ed. *What the Negro Wants*. Chapel Hill: University of North Carolina Press, 1944.

McTyeire, Hollis T., C. F. Sturgis, and A. Holmes. *Duties of Masters to Servants: Three Premium Essays*. Charleston: 1851.

Murray, Florence, ed. *The Negro Handbook, 1946–47*. New York: Current Books, 1947.

Parkhurst, Jessie G., ed. *Negro Yearbook; A Review of Events Affecting Negro Life, 1941–1946*. Tuskegee AL: Tuskegee Institute, 1947.

Payne, Daniel. *Alexander. History of the African Methodist Episcopal Church*. New York: Arno Press, 1969.

Phillips, Charles H. *From the Farm to the Bishopric: An Autobiography*. Nashville: Parthenon Press, 1932

———. *History of the Colored M.E. Church*. Jackson TN: Publishing House of the CME Church, 1898.

Ransom, Reverdy C. *The Negro: The Hope or the Despair of Christianity*. Boston: Ruth Hill, 1935.

Spivey, Charles S. *A Tribute to the Negro Preacher and Other Sermons and Addresses*. Wilberforce OH: Charles Spivey, 1944.

Washington, Booker T. "Address Delivered at the Opening of the Cotton States' Exposition in Atlanta, Georgia" (1895). Reprinted in *The Negro Orators and their Orations*, ed. Carter G. Woodson. New York: Russell and Russell, 1925.

Wesley, John. *Thoughts on Slavery*. In vol. 11 of *The Works of John Wesley*, ed. Thomas Jackson. Oxford: Clarendon Press, 1975–1983.

SECONDARY WORKS

Abbey, Merril R. *The Epic of United Methodist Preaching: A Profile in American Social History*. Lanham MD: University Press of America, 1984.

Ahlstrom, Sidney A. *A Religious History of the American People*. New Haven CT: Yale University Press, 1972.

Albert, Peter J. and Ronald Hoffman, eds. *We Shall Overcome: Martin Luther King Jr. and the Black Freedom Struggle.* New York: Parthenon Books, 1990.

Angell, Stephen. *Bishop Henry McNeal Turner and African-American Religion in the South.* Knoxville: University of Tennessee Press, 1992.

Ansbro, John J. *Martin Luther King Jr.: The Making of a Mind.* Maryknoll NY: Orbis Books, 1982.

Avis, Joel Jr. *Religion and Race: Southern Presbyterians, 1946–1983.* Tuscaloosa: University of Alabama Press, 1994.

Ayers, Edward L. *The Promise of the New South: Life after Reconstruction.* New York: Oxford University Press, 1992.

Bacote, Clarence. *The Story of Atlanta University.* Atlanta: Atlanta Univeristy Press, 1969.

Baer, Hans A. and Merrill Singer. *African-American Religion in the Twentieth Century: Varieties of Protest and Accommodation.* Knoxville: University of Tennessee Press, 1992.

Bailey, Kenneth K. *Southern White Protestantism in the Twentieth Century.* New York: Harper & Row, 1964.

Baldwin, Lewis V. *"Invisible" Strands in African Methodism: A History of the African Union Methodist Protestant and Union American Methodist Episcopal Churches.* Metuchen NJ: Scarecrow Press, 1983.

Baldwin, Lewis V. *The Legacy of Martin Luther King, Jr.: The Boundaries of Law, Politics, and Religion.* With Rufus Burrow Jr., Barbara Holmes, and Susan Holmes Winfield. South Bend IN: University of Notre Dame Press, 2002.

———. *The Mark of a Man: Peter Spencer and the African Union Methodist Tradition.* Lanham MD: University Press of America, 1987.

———. *There Is a Balm in Gilead: The Cultural Roots of Martin Luther King Jr.* Minneapolis: Fortress Press, 1991.

———. *To Make the Wounded Whole: The Cultural Legacy of Martin Luther King Jr.* Minneapolis: Fortress Press, 1992.

Barclay, Wade C. *History of Methodist Mission.* 4 vols. New York: Board of Missions, Methodist Church, 1949–1973.

Banner-Haley, Charles T. *The Fruits of Integration: Black Middle-class Ideology and Culture, 1960–1990.* Jackson: University Press of Mississippi, 1994.

Bartley, Numan V. *The Rise of Massive Resistance: Race and Politics in the South during the 1950s.* Baton Rouge: Louisiana State University Press, 1969.

Beifuss, Joan. *At the River I Stand: Memphis, the 1968 Strike and Martin Luther King.* Memphis: B & W Books, 1985.

Bennett, Lerone Jr. *Before the Mayflower: A History of Black America*. 6th rev. ed. New York: Penguin Books, 1987.

Blaustein, Albert P. and Robert L. Zangrando, eds. *Civil Rights and the American Negro: A Documentary History*. Evanston IL: Northwestern University Press, 1968.

Bloom, Jack M. *Class, Race and the Civil Rights Movement* Bloomington: Indiana University Press, 1987.

Blumberg, Rhoda Lois. *Civil Rights: The 1960's Freedom Struggle*. Rev. ed. New York: Twayne Publishers, 1991.

Boles, John H. *The Great Revival, 1787–1805: The Origins of the Southern Evangelical Mind*. Lexington: University of Kentucky Press, 1972.

———. *The Irony of Southern Religion*. New York: Peter Lang, 1994.

Born, Ethel W. *By My Spirit: The Story of Methodist Protestant Women in Mission, 1879–1939*. New York: Women's Division of the General Board of Global Ministries, 1990.

Boxill, Bernard R. *Blacks and Social Justice*. Rev. ed. Lanham MD: Rowan and Litterfield Publishers, 1992.

Bradley, David H. *A History of the AME Zion Church, 1796–1968*. 2 vols. Nashville: Parthenon Press, 1956–1970.

Branch, Taylor. *Parting the Waters: America in the King Years, 1954–1963*. New York: Touchstone Books, 1988.

———. *Pillar of Fire: America in the King Years, 1963–65*. New York: Simon & Schuster, 1998.

Brandon, John E. "Three Black Methodists Churches in the Consultation on Church Union: Problems and Prospects for Union." DMin diss., Boston University, 1986.

Brawley, James P. *Two Centuries of Methodist Concern: Bondage, Freedom and Education of Black People*. New York: Vantage Press, 1974.

Brisbane, Robert H. *The Black Vanguard: Origins of the Negro Social Revolution*. Valley Forge PA: Judson Press, 1970.

Broderick, Francis L. and August Meier, eds. *Negro Protest in the Twentieth Century*. Indianapolis: Bobbs-Merrill Company, 1965.

Bruce, Dickson D. Jr. *And They All Sang Hallelujah: Plain-Folk Camp-Meeting Religion, 1800–1845*. Knoxville: University of Tennessee Press, 1974.

Bucke, Emory S., ed. *History of American Methodism*. 3 vols. Nashville: Abingdon Press, 1964.

Bulluck, Henry Allen. *A History of Negro Education in the South from 1619 to the Present*. New York: Praeger, 1967.

Burkett, Randall K. *Black Redemption: Churchmen Speak for the Garvey Movement*. Philadelphia: Temple University Press, 1978.

Burns, Stewart, ed. *Daybreak of Freedom: The Montgomery Bus Boycott*. Chapel Hill: University of North Carolina Press, 1997.

Burrow, Rufus Jr. *Personalism: A Critical Introduction.* St. Louis: Chalice Press, 1999.

Button, James W. *Blacks and Social Change: Impact of the Civil Rights Movement in Southern Communities.* Princeton NJ: Princeton University Press, 1989.

Cameron, Richard M. Vol. 1 of *Methodism and Society in Historical Perspective*, ed. the Board of Social and Economic Relations of the Methodist Church. Nashville: Abingdon Press, 1961.

Campbell, Daniel M. and Rex R. Johnson. *Black Migration in America: A Social Demographical History.* Durham NC: Duke University Press, 1981.

Campbell, Ernest Q. *Christians in Racial Crisis: A Study of Little Rock's Ministry.* Washington, DC: Public Affairs Press, 1959.

Carmichael, Stokley and Charles V. Hamilton. *Black Power.* New York: Vintage Press, 1967.

Carson, Clayborne. *In Struggle: SNCC and the Black Awakening of the 1960s.* Cambridge MA: Harvard University Press, 1981.

Carson, Clayborne, senior ed. *Called to Serve.* Vol. 1 of *The Papers of Martin Luther King Jr.* Berkeley: University of California Press, 1992.

———. *Recovering Precious Values.* Vol. 2 of *The Papers of Martin Luther King Jr.* Berkeley: University of California Press, 1994.

———. *Birth of a New Age.* Vol. 3 of *The Papers of Martin Luther King Jr.* Berkeley: University of California Press, 1997.

———. *The Student Voice, 1960–1965: Periodical of the Student Nonviolent Coordinating Committee.* Westport CT: Meckler Corporation, 1990.

Carson, Clayborne, David J. Garrow, Vincent Harding, and Darlene Clark Hine, eds. *The Eyes on the Prize Civil Rights Reader.* New York: Penguin Books, 1991.

Cartwright, Joseph H. *The Triumph of Jim Crow: Tennessee Race Relations in the 1880s.* Knoxville TN: University of Tennessee Press, 1976.

Cauthen, Kenneth. *The Impact of American Religious Liberalism,* New York: Harper and Row Press, 1976.

Cavery, Samuel M. *Church Cooperation and Unity in America: A Historic Review.* New York: Association Press, 1968.

Cell, John W. *The Highest Stage of White Supremacy: The Origins of Segregation in South Africa and the American South.* New York: Cambridge University Press, 1982.

Chafe, William H. *Civilities and Civil Rights: Greensboro, North Carolina, and the Black Struggle for Freedom.* New York: Oxford University Press, 1980.

Chalmers, David. *And the Crooked Places Made Straight: The Struggle for Social Change in the 1960s*. Baltimore: Johns Hopkins University Press, 1991.

Chapman, Mark L. *Christianity on Trial: African-American Religious Thought Before and After Black Power*. Maryknoll NY: Orbis Books, 1996.

Chappell, David. *Inside Agitators: White Southerners in the Civil Rights Movement*. Baltimore: Johns Hopkins University Press, 1994.

Childs, John Brown. *The Political Black Minister: A Study in Afro-American Politics and Religion*. Boston: G. K. Hall, 1980.

Chiles, Robert E. *Theological Transition in American Methodism, 1790–1935*. Lanham MD: University Press of America, 1984.

Clark, E. Culpepper. *The Schoolhouse Door: Segregation's Last Stand at the University of Alabama*. New York: Oxford University Press, 1993.

Clary, George E. Jr. "The Founding of Paine College—A Unique Venture in Inter-Racial Cooperation in the New South (1882–1903)." EdD diss., University of Georgia, 1965.

Colburn, David R. *Racial Change and Community Crisis: St. Augustine, Florida, 1877–1980*. New York: Columbia University Press, 1985.

Cone, James H. *Black Power and Black Theology*. New York: Seabury Press, 1969.

———. *For My People: Black Theology and the Church*. Maryknoll NY: Orbis Books, 1984.

---*God of the oppressed*. New York: Seabury Press, 1974.

———. *Martin and Malcolm in America: A Dream or a Nightmare*. Maryknoll NY: Orbis Books, 1991.

Cone, James H. and Gayraud S. Wilmore, eds. *Black Theology: A Documentary History*. 2 vols. 2d rev. ed. Maryknoll NY: Orbis Books, 1993.

Conkin, Paul K. *Cane Ridge: America's Pentecost*. Madison: University of Wisconsin Press, 1990.

———. *Gone with the Ivy: A Biography of Vanderbilt University*. Knoxville: University of Tennessee Press, 1985.

Couto, Richard A. *Lifting the Veil: A Political History of Struggles of Emancipation*. Knoxville: University of Tennessee Press, 1993.

———. *Ain't Gonna Let Nobody Turn Me Around: The Pursuit of Justice in the Rural South*. Philadelphia: Temple University Press, 1991.

Crawford, Vicki L., Jacqueline A. Rouse, and Barbara Woods, eds. *Women in the Civil Rights Movement*. Vol. 16 of *Black Women in United States History*. Brooklyn: Carlson Publishing, 1990.

Creel, Margaret Washington. *"A Peculiar People": Slave Religion and Community-Culture among the Gullahs*. New York: New York University Press, 1988.

Crow, Paul A. Jr. and William J. Boney, eds. *Church Union at Midpoint*. New York: Association Press, 1972.

Crum, Mason. *The Negro in the Methodist Church*. New York: Division of Education and Cultivation, Board of Missions and Church Extension, The Methodist Church, 1951.

Cruse, Harold. *The Crisis of the Negro Intellectual*. New York: William Morrow, 1967.

Culver, Dwight. *Negro Segregation in the Methodist Church*. New Haven CT: Yale University Press, 1953.

Curtis, Olin A. *A Christian Faith*. New York: Eaton and Manis, 1905.

Daniel, Pete. *The Shadow of Slavery: Peonage in the South, 1901–1969*. Urbana: University of Illinois Press, 1990.

Davis, Allison, Burleigh B. Gardner, and Mary R. Gardner. *Deep South*. New forward by Claudia Mitchell-Kernan. Los Angeles: The Center for Afro-American Studies, University of California, 1988.

Davis, Townsend. *Weary Feet, Rested Souls: A Guided Tour of the Civil Rights Movement*. New York: W. W. Norton, 1998.

Del Pino, Julius E. "Black Leadership in the United Methodist: A Historical Review and Empirical Study." PhD diss., Northwestern University, 1976.

D'Emilio, John, ed. *The Civil Rights Struggle: Leaders in Profile*. New York: Facts on File, 1979.

Dodd, Donald B. and Wynelle S. Dodd. *Historical Statistics of the South, 1954–1968*. Tuscaloosa: University of Alabama Press, 1973.

Dollard, John. *Caste and Class in a Southern Town*. Garden City NY: Doubleday, 1957.

Doyle, Bertram. *The Etiquette of Race Relations: A Study in Social Control*. New York: Schocken Books, 1971.

Doyle, Don H. *Nashville since the 1920s*. Knoxville: University of Tennessee Press, 1985.

Dvorak, Katherine L. *An African-American Exodus: The Segregation of the Southern Churches*. Brooklyn: Carlson Publishing, 1991.

Eagles, Charles W., ed. *The Civil Rights Movement in America*. Jackson: University Press of Mississippi, 1986.

Egerton, John. *A Mind Here to Stay: Profiles from the South*. New York: McMillan, 1970.

———. *Speak Now Against the Day: The Generation Before the Civil Rights Movement*. New York: Alfred A. Knopf, 1994.

Eskew, Glenn T. *But for Birmingham: The Local and National Movements in the Civil Rights Struggle*. Chapel Hill: University of North Carolina Press, 1997.

Essien-Udom, E. U. *Black Nationalism: A Search for an Identity in America*. Chicago: University of Chicago Press, 1972.

Evans, James H. *We Have Been Believers: An African-American Systematic Theology*. Minneapolis: Fortress Press, 1992.

Everett, Carl Jr. *Negro Political Leadership in the South*. Ithaca NY: Cornell University Press, 1966.

Fager, Charles E. *Selma 1965: The March that changed the South*. 2nd ed. Boston: Beacon Press, 1985.

Fallin, Wilson Jr. *The African-American Church in Birmingham, Alabama, 1815–1963: A Shelter in the Storm*. New York: Garland Publishing, 1997.

Fairclough, Adam. *To Redeem the Soul of America: The Southern Christian Leadership Conference and Martin Luther King Jr*. Athens: University of Georgia Press, 1987.

————. *Race and Democracy: The Civil Rights Struggle in Louisiana, 1915–1972*. Athens: University of Georgia Press, 1995.

Farish, Hunter D. *The Circuit Rider Dismounts: A Social History of Southern Methodism, 1865–1900*. Richmond VA: Exposition Press, 1938.

Felton, Ralph A. *The Ministry of the Central Jurisdiction of the Methodist Church*. Madison NJ: Drew Theological Seminary, 1951.

Findlay, James F. Jr. *Church People in the Struggle: The National Council of Churches and the Black Freedom Movement, 1950–1970*. New York: Oxford University Press, 1993.

Flemming, Cynthia Griggs. *Soon We Will Not Cry: The Liberation of Ruby Doris Smith*. Boston: Rowman and Littlefield, 1998.

Fluker, Walter E. *They Looked for a City: A Comparative Analysis of the Ideal of Community in the Thought of Howard Thurman and Martin Luther King Jr*. Lanham MD: University Press of America, 1989.

Foner, Eric. *Freedom's Lawmakers*. New York: Oxford University Press, 1993.

————. *Reconstruction: America's Unfinished Revolution*. New York: Harper & Row, 1988.

Foner, Philip S. and Robert James Branham, eds. *Lift Every Voice: African-American Oratory, 1787–1900*. Tuscaloosa: University of Alabama Press, 1998.

Forman, James. *The Making of Black Revolutionaries*. 2d ed. Washington, DC: Open Hand Publishing, 1985.

Franklin, Jimmie Lewis. *Back to Birmingham: Richard Arrington Jr. and His Times*. Tuscaloosa: University of Alabama Press, 1989.

Franklin, John Hope. *Reconstruction after the Civil War*. 2d ed. Chicago: University of Chicago Press, 1994.

Franklin, John Hope and August Meier, eds. *Black Leaders of the Twentieth Century*. Urbana: University of Illinois Press, 1982.

Franklin, John Hope and Alfred A. Moss Jr. *From Slavery to Freedom*. 7th ed. New York: McGraw-Hill, 1994.

Franklin, Michael Robert. *Liberating Visions: Human Fulfillment and Social Justice in African-American Thought*. Minneapolis: Fortress Press, 1990.

Franklin, V. P. *Black Self-Determination: A Cultural History of African-American Resistance*. New York: Lawrence Hill Books, 1984.

Frazier, E. Franklin and C. Eric Lincoln. *The Negro Church in America: The Black Church since Frazier*. New York: Schocken Books, 1974.

Fredrickson, George M. *Black Liberation: A Comparative History of Black Ideologies in the United States and South Africa*. New York: Oxford University Press, 1995.

Fredrickson, GS. *The Black Image in the White Mind: The Devate on Afro-American Character and Destiny*. New York: Harper and Row, 1971.

Fullinwider, S. P. *The Mind and Mood of Black America: 20th Century Thought*. Homewood IL: Dorsey, 1969.

Gadsen, James S. *Experiences, Struggles and Hopes of the Black Church*. Nashville: Tidings, 1974.

Garrow, David J. *Bearing the Cross: Martin Luther King Jr. and the Southern Christian Leadership Conference*. New York: William Morrow & Company, 1986.

Garrow, David J., ed. *Atlanta, Georgia, 1960–1961: Sit-Ins and Student Activism*. Brooklyn: Carlson Publishing, 1989.

———. *Birmingham, Alabama, 1956–1963: The Black Struggle for Civil Rights*. Brooklyn: Carlson Publishing, 1989.

———. *The Walking City: The Montgomery Bus Boycott, 1955–1956*. Brooklyn: Carlson Publishing, 1989.

———. *We Shall Overcome: The Civil Rights Movement in the United States in the 1950s and the 1960s*. 3 vols. Brooklyn: Carlson Publishing, 1989.

———. *Protest at Selma: Martin Luther King Jr. and the Voting Rights Act of 1965*. New Haven CT: Yale University Press, 1978.

Gatewood, Willard B. *Aristocrats of Color: The Black Elite, 1880–1920*. Bloomington: Indiana University Press, 1990.

Genovese, Eugene. *Roll, Jordan, Roll: The World the Slaves Made*. New York: Vintage Books, 1976.

Giddings, Paula. *When and Where I Enter In: The Impact of Black Women on Race and Sex in America*. New York: William Morrow & Company, 1984.

Goen, C. C. *Broken Churches, Broken Nation: Denominational Schisms and the Coming of the War*. Macon GA: Mercer University Press, 1985.

Goldfield, David R. *Promised Land: The South since 1945*. American History Series. Arlington Heights IL: Harlan Davidson, 1987.

Gorrell, Donald K. *The Age of Social Responsibility: The Social Gospel in the Progressive Era*. Macon GA: Mercer University Press, 1988.

Graham, Hugh Davis. *Crisis in Print: Desegregation and the Press in Tennessee*. Nashville: Vanderbilt University Press, 1967.

Graham, John H. *Black United Methodists: Retrospect and Prospect*. New York: Vantage Press, 1979.

———. *The Role of Gammon Theological Seminary in Ministerial Training and Services for the Negro Churches, 1940–1954*. Atlanta: Gammon Theological Seminary, 1956.

Graham, William L. "Patterns of Intergroup Relations in the Cooperative Establishment Control, and Administration of Paine College (Georgia) by Southern Negro and White People: A Study of Intergroup Process." PhD diss., New York University, 1955.

Grant, Joanne. *Ella Baker: Freedom Bound*. New York: John Wiley and Sons, 1998.

Grantham, Dewey W. *The South in Modern History: A Region at Odds*. New York: Harper Collins, 1994.

———. *Southern Progressivism: The Reconciliation of Progress and Tradition*. Knoxville: University of Tennessee Press, 1983.

Gray, C. Jarrett Jr., comp. *The Racial and Ethnic Presence in American Methodism: A Bibliography*. Madison NJ: General Commission on Archives and History, UMC, 1993.

Gregg, Howard D. *History of the African Methodist Episcopal Church: The Black Church in Action*. Nashville: AME Church Sunday School Union, 1980.

Gregg, Robert. *Sparks from the Anvil of Oppression: Philadelphia's African Methodists and Southern Migrants, 1890–1940*. Philadelphia: Temple University, 1993.

Grier, William H. and Price M. Cobbs. *Black Rage*. New York: Bantam Books, 1968.

Griffin, Paul R. *Black Theology as the Foundation of Three Methodist Colleges: The Educational Views and Labors of Daniel Payne, Joseph Price, and Isaac Lane*. Lanham MD: University Press of America, 1984.

Haines, Herbert H. *Black Radicals and the Civil Rights Mainstream, 1954–1970*. Knoxville: University of Tennessee Press, 1988.

Halberstam, David. *The Fifties*. New York: Villard Books, 1993.

———. *The Children*. New York: Random House, 1998.

Hall, Jacquelyn Dowd. *Revolt against Chivalry: Jessie Daniel Ames and the Women's Campaign against Lynching*. New York: Columbia University Press, 1979.

Hall, Kermit L., ed. *Civil Rights in American History: Major Historical Interpretations*. New York: Garland Publishers, 1987.

Hall, Raymond L. *Black Separatism in the United States*. Hanover NH: University Press of New England, 1978.

Hamilton, Charles V. *The Black Preacher in America*. New York: William Morrow, 1972.

Hampton, Henry and Steve Fayer, eds. *Voices of Freedom: An Oral History of the Civil Rights Movement from the 1950s through the 1980s*. New York: Bantam Books, 1990.

Harding, Vincent. *Hope and History: Why We Must Share the Story of the Movement*. Maryknoll NY: Orbis Books, 1990.

————. *The Other American Revolution*. Los Angeles: Center for Afro-American Studies, UCLA, 1980.

————. *There Is a River: The Black Struggle for Freedom in America*. New York: Harcourt Brace Jovanovich, 1981.

Harlan, Louis R. *Booker T. Washington: The Making of a Black Leader, 1856–1901*. New York: Oxford University Press, 1972.

————. *Booker T. Washington: The Wizard of Tuskegee*. New York: Oxford University Press, 1983.

Harmon, Nolan B., ed. *Encyclopedia of World Methodism*. Nashville: United Methodist Publishing House, 1974.

Harris, Eula Wallace and Maxine Harris Craig. *Christian Methodist Episcopal Church: through the Years*. Rev. ed. Jackson TN: 1965.

Harris, Forrest E. Jr. *Ministry for Social Crisis: Theology and Praxis in the Black Church Tradition*. Macon GA: Mercer University Press, 1993.

Harris, Frederick C. *Something Within: Religion in African-American Political Activism*. New York: Oxford University Press, 1999.

Henri, Florette. *Black Migration: Movement North, 1900–1920*. Garden City NY: Anchor/Doubleday Books, 1976.

Higginbotham, Evelyn Brooks. *Righteous Discontent: The Women's Movement in the Black Baptist Church, 1880–1920*. Cambridge MA: Harvard University Press, 1993.

Hilderbrand, Reginald F. *The Times Were Strange and Stirring*. Durham NC: Duke University Press, 1995.

Hill, Samuel S. *Southern Churches in Crisis*. New York: Holt, Rinehart, and Winston, 1969.

Hine, Darlene Clark and Kathleen Thompson. *A Shining Thread of Hope: The History of Black Women in America*. New York: Broadway Books, 1998.

Hollowell, Louise and Martin C. Lehfeldt. *The Sacred Call: Tribute to Donald L. Hollowell—A Civil Rights Champion*. Winter Park FL: FOUR-G Publishers, 1997.

Hough, Joseph C. Jr. *Black Power and White Protestants*. New York: Oxford University Press, 1968.

Howard-Pitney, David. *The Afro-American Jeremiad: Appeals for Justice in America*. Philadelphia: Temple University Press, 1990.

Hutchison, William R. *The Modernist Impulse in American Protestantism.* New York: Oxford Univeristy Press, 1976.

Jacoway, Elizabeth and David Colburn, eds. *Southern Businessmen and Desegregation.* Baton Rouge: Louisiana State University Press, 1982.

Jaynes, Gerald D. and Robin M. Williams, eds. *A Common Destiny: Blacks and American Society.* Washington, DC: National Academy Press, 1989.

Jennings, Theodore W. Jr. *Good News to the Poor: John Wesley's Evangelical Economics.* Nashville: Abingdon Press, 1990.

Johnson, Charles A. *The Frontier Camp Meeting.* Dallas: Southern Methodist University Press, 1955.

Jones, Donald G. *The Sectional Crisis and Northern Methodism: A Study in Piety.* Metuchen NJ: Scarecrow Press, 1979.

Jones, Jacqueline. *Labor of Love, Labor of Sorrow: Black Women, Work, and the Family from Slavery to the Present.* New York: Basic Books, 1985.

Jordan, Winthrop D. *White over Black: American Attitudes toward the Negro, 1550-1812.* Chapel Hill NC: University of North Carolina Press, 1968.

Kapur, Sudarshan. *Raising Up a Prophet: The African-American Encounter with Gandhi.* Boston: Beacon Press, 1992.

Kellogg, Charles Flint. *NAACP: A History of the National Association for the Advancement of Colored People.* Baltimore: Johns Hopkins University Press, 1967.

Kelsey, George D. *Racism and the Christian Understanding of Man.* New York: Charles Scribner's Sons, 1965.

King, Martin Luther Jr. *Strength to Love.* New York: Harper & Row, 1963.

————. *Stride toward Freedom.* New York: Harper & Row, 1958.

————. *The Trumpet of Conscience.* New York: Harper & Row, 1967.

————. *Where Do We Go From Here: Chaos or Community?* Boston: Beacon Press, 1968.

————. *Why We Can't Wait.* New York: The New American Library, 1963.

King, Richard H. *Civil Rights and the Idea of Freedom.* New York: Oxford University Press, 1992.

Kinnamon, Michael and Brian E. Cope, eds. *The Ecumenical Movement: An Anthology of Key Documents.* Grand Rapids MI: William B. Eerdmans, 1997.

Kirby, James E., Russell E. Richey, and Kenneth E. Rowe, eds. *The Methodists.* Westport CT: Greenwood Press, 1996.

Kluger, Richard. *Simple Justice: The History of Brown v. Board of Education and Black America's Struggle for Equality.* New York: Vintage Books, 1975.

Knotts, Alice G. *Fellowship of Love: Methodist Women Changing American Racial Attitudes, 1920–1968.* Nashville: Kingwood Books, 1996.

Ladd, Everett C. *Negro Political Leadership*. Ithaca NY: Cornell University Press, 1966.

Lakey, Othal H. *The History of the CME Church*. Memphis: CME Publishing House, 1985.

————. *The Rise of "Colored Methodism": A Study of the Background and the Beginnings of the Christian Methodist Episcopal Church*. Dallas: Crescendo Book Publications, 1972.

Lakey, Othal H. and Betty Beene Stephens. *God in My Mama's House: The Women's Movement in the CME Church*. Memphis: CME Publishing House, 1994.

Lamon, Lester C. *Blacks in Tennessee, 1791–1970*. Knoxville: University of Tennessee Press, 1981.

————. *Black Tennesseans, 1900 – 1930*. Knoxville: University of Tennessee Press, 1977.

LaMonte, Edward S. *Politics and Welfare in Birmingham, 1900–1975*. Tuscaloosa: University of Alabama Press, 1995.

Larkin, William C. *The E. P. Murchinson Story*. Decatur GA: William C. Larkin, 1990.

Lerner, Gerda, ed. *Black Women in White America: A Documentary History*. New York: Vintage Books, 1973.

Lawson, Steven F. *Black Ballots: Voting Rights in the South, 1944–1969*. New York: Columbia University Press, 1976.

————. *Running for Freedom: Civil Rights and Black Politics since 1941*. Philadelphia: Temple University Press, 1991.

Lecky, Robert S. and H. Elliot Wright, eds. *The Black Manifesto*. New York: Sheed and Ward, 1969.

Levine, Lawrence W. *Black Culture and Black Consciousness: Afro- American Folk Thought from Slavery to Freedom*. New York: Oxford University Press, 1977.

Lincoln, C. Eric. *The Black Church Since Frazier*. New York: Schocken Books, 1974.

————. *Race, Religion, and the Continuing American Dilemma*. New York: Hill and Wang, 1984.

————. *Sounds of the Struggle: Persons and Perspectives in Civil Rights*. New York: William Morrow and Company, 1971.

Lincoln, C. Eric, ed. *The Black Experience in Religion*. Garden City NY: Anchor/Doubleday Books, 1974.

————. *Martin Luther King Jr.: A Profile*. Rev. ed. American Century Series. New York: Hill and Wang, 1984.

Lincoln, C. Eric and Lawrence H. Mamiya. *The Black Church in the African-American Experience*. Durham NC: Duke University Press, 1990.

Litwack, Leon. *Been in the Storm So Long: The Aftermath of Slavery*. New York: Vintage Books, 1980.

———. *Trouble in Mind: Black Southerners in the Age of Jim Crow*. New York: Alfred A. Knopf, 1998.

Logan, Rayford and Michael R. Winston, eds. *The Dictionary of American Negro Biography*. New York: W. W. Norton, 1982.

Lovett, Bobby Lee. *The Negro in Tennessee, 1961-1970: A Socio-Military History of the Civil War Era*. PhD diss., Universtiy of Arkansas, 1978.

Luker, Ralph E. *The Social Gospel in Black and White: American Racial Reform, 1885–1912*. Chapel Hill: University of North Carolina Press, 1991.

Manis, Andrew Michael. *Southern Civil Religions in Conflict: Civil Rights and the Culture Wars*. Macon: Mercer University Press, 2001.

———. *A Fire You Can't Put Out: The Civil Rights Life of Birmingham's Reverend Fred Shuttlesworth*. Tuscaloosa: University of Alabama Press, 1999.

Marable, Manning. *Race, Reform and Rebellion: The Second Reconstruction in Black America, 1945–1982*. 2nd ed. Jackson: University Press of Mississippi, 1991.

Marquardt, Manfred. *John Wesley's Social Ethics: Praxis and Principles*. Nashville: Abingdon Press, 1992.

Marsh, Charles. *God's Long Summer: Stories of Faith and Civil Rights*. Princeton NJ: Princeton University Press, 1997.

Marx, Gary. *Protest and Prejudice*. Rev. ed. New York: Harper & Row, 1969.

Mathews, Donald G. *Religion in the Old South*. Chicago: University of Chicago Press, 1977.

———. *Slavery and Methodism*. Princeton NJ: Princeton University Press, 1965.

Matthews, Donald R. and James W. Prothro. *The Negro and the New Southern Politics*. New York: Harcourt Brace and World, 1966.

Mays, Benjamin E. *Born to Rebel*. New York: Charles Scribner's Sons, 1971.

———. *The Negro's God*. Boston: Chapman and Grimes, 1938.

Mays, Benjamin E. and Joseph W. Nicholson. *The Negro's Church*. New York: Arno Press, 1969.

McAdam, Doug. *Freedom Summer*. New York: Oxford University Press, 1988.

McAfee, Sara Jane. *History of the Woman's Missionary Society in Colored Methodist Episcopal Church*. Rev. ed. Phenix City AL: Phenix City Herald 1945.

McCartney John T. *Black Power Ideologies: An Essay in African-American Political Thought*. Philadelphia: Temple University Press, 1992.

McClain, William B. *Black People in the Methodist Church*. Cambridge MA: Schenkman Publishing Company, 1984.

McCulloh, Gerald O. *Ministerial Education in the American Methodist Movement*. Nashville: United Methodists Board of Higher Education, 1980.

McDowell, John Patrick. *The Social Gospel in the South: The Woman's Home Mission Movement in the Methodist Episcopal Church, South, 1886–1939*. Baton Rouge: Louisiana State University Press, 1982.

McGary, Howard and Bill E. Lawson. *Between Slavery and Freedom*. Bloomington: University of Indiana Press, 1992.

McKiven, Henry M. Jr. *Iron and Steel: Class, Race and Community in Birmingham, 1875–1920*. Chapel Hill: University of North Carolina Press, 1995.

McMillen, Neil R. *The Citizens' Council: Organized Resistance to the Second Reconstruction, 1954–1964*. Urbana, IL: University of Illinois Press, 1994.

McNeill, Genna Rae. *Groundwork: Charles Hamilton Houston and the Struggle for Civil Rights*. Philadelphia: Temple University Press, 1983.

Meier, August. *Negro Thought in America, 1880–1915*. Ann Arbor: University of Michigan Press, 1963.

Meier, August and Elliot Rudwick. *Along the Color Line: Explorations in the Black Experience*. Urbana: University of Illinois Press, 1976.

———. *Black Protest in the Sixties*. Chicago: Quadrangle Books, 1970.

———. *Core: A Study in the Civil Rights Movement 1942–1968*. Urbana IL: University of Chicago Press, 1975

Miller, Floyd. *The Search for a Black Nationalism: Black Colonization and Emigration, 1787–1863*. Urbana: University of Illinois Press, 1975.

Miller, Keith D. *Voice of Deliverance: The Language of Martin Luther King Jr. and Its Sources*. New York: Free Press, 1992.

Mjagkij, Nina. *Light in the Darkness: African Americans and the YMCA, 1852–1946*. Lexington: University of Kentucky Press, 1994.

Montgomery, William E. *Under Their Own Vine and Fig Tree: The African-American Church in the South, 1865–1900*. Baton Rouge: Louisiana State University Press, 1993.

Morris, Aldon D. *The Origins of the Civil Rights Movement: Black Communities Organizing for Change*. New York: Free Press, 1984.

Morris, Aldon D. and Carol M. Mueller, eds. *Frontiers in Social Movement Theory*. New Haven CT: Yale University Press, 1992.

Morris, Calvin S. *Reverdy C. Ransom: Black Advocate of the Social Gospel*. Lanham MD: University Press of America, 1990.

Moses, Wilson Jeremiah. *Black Messiahs and Uncle Toms: Social and Literary Manipulations of a Religious Myth*. University Park: Pennsylvania State University Press, 1982.

————. *The Golden Age of Black Nationalism: Classical Black Nationalism, 1850–1925*. New York: Oxford University Press, 1988.

Moses, Wilson Jeremiah, ed. *Classical Black Nationalism: From the American Revolution to Marcus Garvey*. New York: New York University Press, 1996.

Morrow, Ralph E. *Northern Methodism and Reconstruction*. East Lansing: Michigan State University Press, 1956.

Mukenge, Ida Rousseau. *The Black Church in Urban America: A Case Study in Political Economy*. Lanham MD: University Press of America, 1983.

Murphy, Larry J., Gordon Melton, and Gary L. Ward, eds. *Encyclopedia of African American Religions*. New York: Garland Publishing, 1993.

Murray, Peter C. "Christ and Caste in Conflict: Creating a Racially Inclusive Methodist Church." PhD diss., Indiana University, 1985.

Muse, Benjamin. *The American Negro Revolution: From Nonviolence to Black Power, 1963–1967*. Bloomington: Indiana University Press, 1968.

Myrdal, Gunnar. *An American Dilemma: The Negro Problem and Modern Democracy*. 2 vols. New York: Harper & Row, 1944.

Nelsen, Hart M. and Anne K. Nelsen. *Black Church in the Sixties*. Lexington, KY, University of Kentucky Press, 1975.

Neverdon-Morton, Cynthia. *Afro-American Women of the South and the Advancement of the Race, 1895–1925*. Knoxville: University of Tennessee Press, 1989.

Niebuhr, H. Richard. *The Kingdom of God in America*. New York: Harper & Row, 1937.

————. *The Social Sources of Denominationalism*. New York: World Publishing, 1957.

Norrell, Robert J. *Reaping the Whirlwind: The Civil Rights Movement in Tuskegee*. New York: Vintage Books, 1986.

Norwood, Frederick A. *The Story of American Methodism*. Nashville: Abingdon Press, 1974.

Norwood, Frederick A., ed. *Sourcebook of American Methodism*. Nashville: Abingdon Press, 1982.

Nunnelley, William. *Bull Connor*. Tuscaloosa: University of Alabama Press, 1991.

Oakes, Henry Nathaniel. "The Struggle for Racial Equality in the Methodist Episcopal Church: The Career of Robert E. Jones." PhD diss., University of Iowa, 1973.

Oppenheimer, Martin. *The Genesis of the Southern Student Movement: A Case Study in Conemporary Negro Protest*. PhD diss., University of Pennsylvania, 1963.

Owen, Christopher H. *The Sacred Flame of Love: Methodism and Society in Nineteenth-Century Georgia*. Athens: University of Georgia Press, 1998.

Paris, Peter J. *The Social Teachings of the Black Churches*. Philadelphia: Fortress Press, 1985

Parks, Rosa. *Rosa Parks: My Story*. New York: Dial Books, 1992.

Payne, Daniel Alexander. *History of the African Methodist Episcopal Church*. New York: Arno Press, 1969.

Payne, Wardell J., ed. *Directory of African American Religious Bodies*. Washington, DC: Howard University Press, 1991.

Peake, Thomas R. *Keeping the Dream Alive: A History of the Southern Christian Leadership Conference from King to the Nineteen Eighties*. New York: Peter Lang, 1987.

Peck, James. *Freedom Ride*. New York; Simon and Schuster, 1962.

Powdermaker, Hortense. *After Freedom: A Cultural Study in the Deep South*. New introductory essay by Brackette F. Williams and Drexel G. Woodson. Madison: University of Wisconsin Press, 1993.

Rabinowitz, Howard N. *Race Relations in the Urban South, 1865–1890*. Urbana IL: University of Illinois Press: 1980.

Rabinowitz, Howard N., ed. *Southern Black Leaders of the Reconstruction Era*. Urbana: University of Illinois Press, 1982.

Raboteau, Albert J. *A Fire in My Bones: Reflections on African-American Religious History*. Boston: Beacon Press, 1995.

———. *Slave Religion: The "Invisible Institution" in the Antebellum South*. New York: Oxford University Press, 1978.

Raines, Howell, ed. *My Soul Is Rested: Movement Days in the Deep South Remembered*. New York: Penguin Books, 1983.

Reimers, David M. *White Protestantism and the Negro*. New York: Oxford University Press, 1965.

Richardson, Harry V. *Dark Glory: A Picture of the Church among Negroes in the Rural South*. New York: Friendship Press, 1947.

———. *Dark Salvation: The Story of Methodism as it Developed among Blacks in America*. Garden City NY: Anchor/Doubleday Books, 1976.

Richey, Russell E. *Denominationalism*. Nashville: Abingdon Press, 1977.

———. *Early American Methodism*. Bloomington: Indiana University Press, 1991.

———. *The Methodist Conference in America*. Nashville: Kingwood Books, 1996.

Richey, Russell E., ed. *Rethinking Methodist History*. Nashville: Kingwood Books, 1985.

Richey, Russell E. and Kenneth E. Rowe, eds. *Reimagining Denominationalism: Interpretive Essays*. New York: Oxford University Press, 1994.

Richey, Russell E., Kenneth E. Rowe, and Jean Miller Schmidt, eds. *Perspectives on American Methodism: Interpretive Essays*. Nashville: Abingdon Press, 1993.

Robinson, Jo Ann Gibson. *The Montgomery Bus Boycott and the Women Who Started It: The Memoir of Jo Ann Gibson Robinson*, ed. David J. Garrow. Knoxville: University of Knoxville Press, 1987.

Robnett, Belinda. *How Long? How Long? African-American Women in the Struggle for Civil Rights*. New York: Oxford University Press, 1997.

Rogers, Kim Lacy. *Righteous Lives: Narratives of the New Orleans Civil Rights Movement*. New York: New York University Press, 1993.

Rouse, Ruth and Stephen Neill, eds. *A History of the Ecumenical Movement, 1517-1948*. Philidelphia: Westminster Press, 1967.

Runyon, Theodore. *The New Creation: John's Wesley's Theology Today*. Nashville: Abingdon Press, 1998.

Runyon, Theodore, ed. *Sanctification and Liberation*. Nashville: Abingdon Press, 1981.

Savage, Horace C. *The Life and Times of Bishop Isaac Lane*. Nashville: National Publication Company, 1958.

Sawyer, Mary R. *Black Ecumenicism: Implementing the Demands of Justice*. Valley Forge PA: Trinity Press International, 1994.

Schuster, Arnold. *Reparations: The Black Manifesto and Its Challenge to White America*. Philadelphia: J. B. Lippincott, 1970.

Sernett, Milton C. *Black Religion and American Evangelicalism: White Protestants, Plantation Missions, and the Flowering of Negro Christianity, 1787–1865*. Metuchen NJ: Scarecrow Press, 1975.

———. *Bound for the Promised Land: African-American Religion and the Great Migration*. Durham NC: Duke University Press, 1997.

Sernett, Milton C., ed. *Afro-American Religious History: A Documentary Witness*. Durham NC: Duke University Press, 1985.

Shaw, James B. F. *The Negro in the History of Methodism*. Nashville: Parthenon Press, 1954.

Shockley, Grant S., ed. *Heritage and Hope: The African Presence in United Methodism*. Nashville: Abingdon Press, 1991.

Singleton, George A. *The Romance of African Methodism: A Study of African Methodism: A Study of the African Methodist Episcopal Church*. New York: Exposition Press, 1952.

Shaw, Stephanie J. *What a Woman Ought to Be and Do: Black Professional Women Workers during the Jim Crow Era*. Chicago: University of Chicago Press, 1996.

Sitkoff, Harvard. *The Struggle for Black Equality: 1954–1980*. New York: Hill and Wang, 1981.

Sledge, Robert Watson. *Hands of the Ark: The Struggle for Change in the Methodist Episcopal Church, South 1914–1939*. Lake Junaluska NC: General Commission on Archives and History, 1975.

Smith, Bishop B. Julian. *Dedicated...Committed: The Autobiography of Bishop B. Julian Smith*. Hemphill Press, 1978.

Smith, H. Shelton. *In His Image, But...:Racism in Southern Religion, 1780–1910*. Durham NC: Duke University Press, 1972.

Smith, John Abernathy. *Cross and Flame: Two Centuries of United Methodism in Middle Tennessee*. Nashville: United Methodist Publishing House, 1984.

Smith, Kelly Miller. *Social Crisis Preaching*. Macon GA: Mercer University Press, 1983.

_____. *The Pursuit of a Dream (The Nashville Story)*. Unpublished. Kelly Miller Smigh Papers, Vanderbilt University.

Smith, R. Drew, ed. *New Day Begun: African American Churches and Civic Culture in Post-Civil Rights America*. Vol. 1 of The Public Influences of African American Churches. Durham NC: Duke University Press, 2003.

Smith, Warren Thomas. *John Wesley and Slavery*. Nashville: Abingdon Press, 1986.

Smock, Raymond W., ed. *Booker T. Washington in Perspective*. Jackson: University Press of Mississippi, 1988.

Sparks, Randy J. *On Jordan's Stormy Banks: Evangelicalism in Mississippi, 1773–1876*. Athens: University of Georgia Press, 1994.

Spencer, Jon Michael. *Protest and Praise: Sacred Music of Black Religion*. Minneapolis: Fortress Press, 1990.

Stevens, Thelma. *Legacy for the Future: The History of Christian Social Relations in the Woman's Division of Christian Service, 1940–1968*. Cincinnati: Women's Division, General Board of Global Ministries, United Methodist Church, 1978.

Stoper, Emily. *The Student Nonviolent Coordinating Committee: The Growth of Radicalism in a Civil Rights Organization*. Brooklyn: Carlson Publishing, 1989.

Stuckey, Sterling. *Slave Culture: Nationalist Theory and the Foundations of Black America*. New York: Oxford University Press, 1987.

Stuckey, Sterling, ed. *The Ideological Origins of Black Nationalism*. Boston: Beacon Press, 1976.

Sullivan, Patricia. *Days of Hope: Race and Democracy in the New Deal Era*. Chapel Hill: University of North Carolina Press, 1995.

Sumner, David E. "The Local Press and the Nashville Student Movement, 1960." PhD diss., University of Tennessee Press 1989.

Sweet, William Warren. *Methodism in America*. Rev. ed. Nashville: Abingdon Press, 1953.

Taylor, Sandra A. "The Nashville Sit-In Movement." Master's thesis, Fisk University, 1973.

Thomas, James S. *Methodism's Racial Dilemma: The Story of the Central Jurisdiction*. Nashville: Abingdon Press, 1992.

Thornbrough, Emma Lou, comp. *Booker T. Washington*. Englewood Cliffs NJ: Prentice-Hall, 1969.

Tindall, George B. *The Emergence of the New South, 1913–1945*. Baton Rouge: Louisiana State University Press, 1967.

_____.*Too Secure These Rights: The Report of the President's Committee on Civil Rights*. New York: Simon and Schuster, 1947.

Toulouse, Mark G. and James O. Duke, eds. *Makers of Christian Theology in America*. Nashville: Abingdon Press, 1997.

Trotter, Joe William. *The Black Migration in Historical Perspective*. Urbana: University of Illinois Press, 1985.

Tucker, David. *Black Pastors and Leaders: Memphis, 1819–1972*. Memphis: Memphis State University Press, 1975.

_____. *Lieutenant Lee of Beale Street*. Nashville: Vanderbilt University Press, 1971.

————. *Memphis Since Crump: Bossism, Blacks, and Civic Reformers, 1948–1968*. Knoxville: University of Tennessee Press, 1980.

Van der Bent, Ans J. *Breaking Down the Walls: World Council of Churches Statements and Actions on Racism, 1948–1985*. Geneva: World Council of Churches, 1986.

Van Deberg, William L. *New Day in Babylon: The Black Power Movement and American Culture, 1965–1975*. Chicago: University of Chicago Press, 1992.

Van Deberg, William, ed. *Modern Black Nationalism from Marcus to Louis Farrakhan*. Philadelphia: Temple University Press, 1997.

Walker, Clarence E. *A Rock in a Weary Land: The African Methodist Episcopal Church During the Civil War and Reconstruction*. Baton Rouge: Louisiana State University Press, 1982.

Walker, Wyatt T. *Somebody's Calling My Name: Black Sacred Music and Social Change*. Valley Forge PA: Judson Press, 1979.

Walls, William J. *The African Methodist Episcopal Zion Church: Reality of the Black Church*. Nashville: AME Zion Publishing House, 1974.

Ward, Brian and Tony Badger. *The Making of Martin Luther King Jr. and the Civil Rights Movement*. New York: New York University Press, 1996.

Washington, Booker T., with W.E.B. DuBois. *The Negro in the South: His Economic Progress to His Moral and Religious Development*. Philadelpia: G.W. Jacobs and Company, 1907.

Washington, James Melvin, ed. *A Testament of Hope: The Essential Writings of Martin Luther King Jr.* San Francisco: Harper & Row, 1986.

Washington, Joseph R. Jr. *Black Religion: The Negro and Christianity in the United States*. Boston: Beacon Press, 1964.

Watley, William D. *Roots of Resistance: The Nonviolent Ethic of Martin Luther King Jr.* Valley Forge PA: Judson Press, 1985.

———. *Singing the Lord's Song in a Strange Land: The African- American Churches and Ecumenism*. Grand Rapids MI: William. B. Eerdmans, 1993.

Wells-Barnett, Ida B. Edited by Alfreda M. Duster. *Crusader for Justice: The Autobiography of Ida B. Wells*. Chicago: University of Chicago Press, 1970.

Wheeler, Edward L. *Uplifting the Race: The Black Minister in the New South, 1865–1902*. Lanham MD: University Press of America, 1986.

Whelchel, Love Henry Jr. *Hell without Fire: Conversion in Slave Religion*. Nashville: Abingdon Press, 2002.

White, Marjorie L., ed. *A Walk to Freedom: The Reverend Fred Shuttlesworth and the Alabama Christian Movement for Human Rights, 1956-1964*. Birmingham: Birmingham Historical Society, 1998.

Wigger, John H. *Taking Heavenly Storm: Methodism and the Rise of Popular Christianity in America*. New York: Oxford University Press, 1998.

Williams, Juan. *Eyes on the Prize: America's Civil Rights Years, 1954–1965*. New York: Penguin Books, 1986.

Williamson, Joel. *The Crucible of Race: Black-White Relations in the American South since Emancipation*. Berkeley: University of California Press, 1984.

Wilmore, Gayraud S. *Black Religion and Black Radicalism: An Interpretation of the Religious History of Afro-American People*. 2d rev. ed. Maryknoll NY: Orbis Books, 1983.

Wilmore, Gayraud S., ed. *African-American Religious Studies: An Interdisciplinary Anthology*. Durham NC: Duke University Press, 1989.

Wilson, Charles Reagan. *Judgment and Grace in Dixie*. Athens: University of Georgia Press, 1995.

Wogaman, J. Philip. *Methodism's Challenge in Race Relations: A Study of Strategy*. Boston: Boston University Press, 1960.

Wolfe, Miles. *Lunch at the Five and Ten: The Greensboro Sit-ins, A Contemporary History*. New York: Stein and Day, 1970.

Wood, Forrest G. *The Arrogance of Faith: Christianity and Race in America from the Colonial Era to the Twentieth Century*. New York: Alfred A. Knopf, 1990.

Woodson, Carter G. *The History of the Negro Church*. Washington, DC: The Associated Publishers, 1921.

Woodward, C. Vann. *The Origins of the New South*. Baton Rouge: Louisiana State University Press, 1971.

————. *The Strange Career of Jim Crow.* 3rd rev. ed. New York: Oxford University Press, 1974.

Wright, Richard R. Jr. *The Bishops of the African Methodist Episcopal Church.* Nashville: AME Sunday School Union, 1963.

Wuthnow, Robert. *The Restructuring of American Religion: Society and Faith since World War II.* Princeton NJ: Princeton University Press, 1988.

Young, Henry J. *Major Black Religious Leaders: 1755–1940.* Nashville: Abingdon Press, 1977.

————. *Major Black Religious Leaders since 1940.* Nashville: Abingdon Press, 1979.

Yrigoyen, Charles Jr. and Susan E. Warrick, eds. *Historical Dictionary of Methodism.* Lanham MD: Scarecrow Press, 1996.

Zinn, Howard. *Albany: A Study in National Responsibility; SNCC, The New Abolitionists.* Atlanta: Southern Regional Council, 1962.

————. *SNCC: The New Abolitionists.* Westport CT: Greenwood Press, 1964.

ARTICLES

Baer, Hans A. "Black Mainstream Churches; Emancipatory or Accommodative Responses to Racism and Social Stratification in American Society. " *Review of Religious Research* 30 (December 1988): 162–76.

Baer, Hans and Merril Singer. "Toward a Typology of Black Sectarian Response to Racial Stratification." *Anthropological Quarterly* 54 (1981): 1–14.

Bailey, Kenneth K. "The Post-Civil War Separations in Southern Protestantism: Another Look." *Church History* 46 (December 1979): 453–73.

Baker, Ella. *Developing Community Leadership In Black Women in White America: A Documentary History,* ed. Gerda Lerner. New York: Vintage Books, 1973.

Baldwin, Lewis V. "Martin Luther King Jr. and Black Methodists: Historical Reflections." *AME Church Review* 107 (1992).

————. "The Minister as Preacher, Pastor, and Prophet: The Thinking of Martin Luther King Jr." *America Baptist Quarterly* 7 (June 1988): 79–97.

Berenson, William M., Kirk W. Elifson, and Tandy Tollerson III. "Preachers in Politics: A Study of Political Activism among the Black Ministry. " *Journal of Black Studies* 24 (June 1976): 373–92.

Berkeley, Kathleen C. "Colored Ladies Also Contributed: Black Women's Activities from Benevolence to Social Welfare, 1866–1896." In *The Web of Southern Relations: Women, Family, and Education,* ed. Walter Fraser Jr., R. Frank Saunders Jr., and Jon L. Wakelyn. Athens: University of Georgia Press, 1985. 181–203.

Braden, Anne. "Birmingham, 1956–1979: The History that We Made. " *Southern Exposure* 7/2 (January 1979): 48–54.

Catchings, L. Maynard. "Interracial Activities in Southern Churches." *Phylon*
13 (March 13): 54–56.

Corley, Robert G. "In Search of Racial Harmony: Birmingham Business
Leaders and Desegregation, 1950–1963." In *Southern Businessmen and
Desegregation*, ed. Elizabeth Jacoway and David Colburn. Baton Rouge:
Louisiana State University Press, 1982.

Crowther, Edward R. "Holy Honor: Sacred and Secular in the Old South."
Journal of Southern History 58 (November 1992): 619–36.

Dalfiume, Richard M. "The Forgotten Years of the Negro Revolution." *Journal
of American History* 55/1 (June 1968): 90–106.

Dickerson, Dennis C. "Black Ecumenism: Efforts to Establish a United
Methodist Episcopal Church, 1918–1932." *Church History* 52 (December
1983): 479–91.

Egerton, John. "Lucius Pitts and U. W. Clemon." *New South* 25 (Summer
1970): 9–20.

Eskew, Glenn T. "Black Elitism and the Failure of Paternalism in Postbellum
Georgia: The Case of Bishop Lucius Henry Holsey." *Journal of Southern
History* 58/4 (November 1992): 637–66.

_____. *The Alabama Christian Movement for Human Rights and the
Birmingham Struggle for Civil Rights, 1956-1963, in Birmingham*, ed.
David J. Garrow. Brooklyn: Carlson Publishing, 1989.

Fairclough, Adam. "The Southern Christian Leadership Conference and the
Second Reconstruction, 1957–1973." *South Atlantic Quarterly* 80 (1981):
177–94.

———. "The Preachers and the People: The Origins and Early Years of the
Southern Christian Leadership Conference, 1955–1959." *Journal of
Southern History* 52/3 (August 1986): 403–40.

Fendrich, James M. "Keeping the Faith or Pursing the Good Life: A Study of
the Consequences of Participation in the Civil Rights Movement."
American Sociological Review 42 (February 1977): 144–57.

Flemming, Cynthia Griggs. *More than a Lady: Ruby Doris Smith Robinson
and Black Women's Leadership in the Standent Nonviolent Coordinating
Committee, In Hidden Histories of Women in the New South*, ed. *Virginia
Bernhard et. al.* Columbia: University of Missouri Press, 1994.

_____. "'More Than a Lady': Ruby Doris Smith Robinson and Black
Women's Leadership in the Student Nonviolent Coordinating
Committee." In *Hidden Histories of Women in the New South*, ed.
Virginia Bernhard et al. Columbia: University of Missouri Press, 1994.

Franklin, Jimmie Lewis. *Black Southerners, Shared Experience, and Place: A
Reflection Journal of Southern History 60:1* February 1994: 3-18.

Franklin, Robert Michael. "Religious Belief and Political Activism in Black
    America: An Essay." *Journal of Religious Thought* 43/1 (Fall/Winter
    1986–1987): 63–72.
Frederickson, Mary E. "'Each One Is Dependent on the Other': Southern
    Churchwomen, Racial Reform, and the Progress of Transformation,
    1880–1940." In *Visible Women: New Essays on American Activism*, ed.
    Nancy A. Hewitt and Suzanne Lebsock. Urbana: University of Illinois
    Press, 1993.
Garrow, David J. "Black Ministerial Protest Leadership, 1955–1970." In
    Encyclopedia of Religion in the South, ed. Samuel S. Hill. Macon GA:
    Mercer University Press, 1984.
Gorrell, Donald K. "The Social Creed and Methodism through Eighty Years."
    Methodist History 26 (July 1988): 213–28.
Graham, W.L. *An Historic Instance of Mutual Involvement of the Negro.*
    Journal of Educational Sociology (28 October 1954): 83-87.
Gravely, Will B. "African Methodism and the Rise of Denominationalism." In
    Rethinking Methodist History, ed. Russell E. Richey and Kenneth E.
    Rowe. New York: Oxford University Press, 1994.
————. "The Social, Political and Religious Implications of the Formation of
    the Colored Methodist Episcopal Church (1870)." *Methodist History* 18
    (October 1979): 3–25.
Griffin, Paul R. "The Black Rational Orthodox Impulse in the Post Civil
    African-American Religious Experience." *Fides et Historia* 23 (Fall 1991):
    43–56.
Hadden, Jeffery K. "Clergy Involvement in Civil Rights." *Annals of the
    American Academy of Political and Social Science* 387 (January 1970):
    118–27.
Harding, Vincent. "A Beginning in Birmingham." *The Reporter* 6 (June 1963):
    13–19.
Hunt, Larry L. and Janet Hunt. "Black Religion as Both Opiate and Inspiration
    of Civil Right Militance: Putting Marx to the Test." *Social Forces* 56/1
    (1977): 1–14.
Jackson, W. Sherman. "The Civil Rights Movement and the Black Churches."
    Negro History Bulletin 36 (1984): 41–42.
Johnson, Stephen D. "The Role of the Black Church in Black Civil Rights
    Movements." In *The Political Role of Religion in the United States*, ed.
    Stephen D. Johnson and Joseph Tamey. Boulder CO: Westview Press,
    1986.
Johnstone, Ronald L. "Negro Preachers Take Sides." *Review of Religious
    Research* 2 (Fall 1969): 81–88.

Jones, Jacqueline Royster. *A Heartbeat for Liberation: The Reclamation of Ruby Doris Smith. Sage: A Scholarly Journal on Black women* Student Supplement 1988: 64-65.

_____. "A 'Heartbeat' for Liberation: The Reclamation of Ruby Doris Smith." *Sage: A Scholarly Journal on Black Women* (Student Supplement 1988): 64–65.

King, Richard H. "Citizenship and Self-Respect: The Emergence of Politics in the Civil Rights Movement." *Journal of American Studies* 22 (April 1988): 7–22.

King, Slater. "The Bloody Battleground of Albany." *Freedomways* 4/1 (1964): 93–101.

———. "Our Main Battle in Albany." *Freedomways* 5/3 (1965): 417–23.

Kirby, Jack T. "The Southern Exodus: 190–1960." *Journal of Southern History* 49/4 (November 1983): 585–600.

Lee, Oscar J. "The Freedom Movement and the Ecumenical Movement." *Ecumenical Review* 17 (January 1965): 8–28.

Lawson, Steven F. "Freedom Then, Freedom Now: The Historiography of the Civil Rights Movement." *American Historical Review* 94 (April 1991): 456–71.

Lomas, Louis. "Freedom Rides." *In the Civil Rights Reader*, ed. Leon Friedman. New York: Walker and Company, 1962.

Lowder, Virgil E. "Negro Methodists Consider Union." *Christian Century* (19 February 1964): 250-251.

Maffly-Kipp, Laurie F. "Denominationalism and the Black Church." In *Rethinking Denominationalism*, ed. Robert Bruce Mullin and Russell E. Richey. New York: Oxford University Press, 1994.

Maldron, Thomas W., Hart M. Nelsen, and Raytha L. Yokley. "Religion as a Determinant of Militancy and Political Participation among Black Americans." *American Behavioral Scientist* 17 (July-August 1974): 783–97.

Manis, Andrew Michael. "Religious Experience, Religious Authority, and Civil Rights Leadership: The Case of Birmingham's Fred Shuttlesworth." In vol. 5 of *Cultural Perspectives on the American South*, ed. Charles Reagan Wilson. New York: Gordon and Breach, 1986.

Marx, Gary T. "Religion: Opiate or Inspiration of the Civil Rights Militancy among Negroes?" *American Sociological Review* 32/1 (February 1976): 64–72.

Matthews, Donald G. "The Methodist Mission to Slaves, 1829-1844." *Journal of American History 51* (March 1965) 615-631.

Meier, August and Elliot Rudwick, "The First Freedom Ride." *Phylon* 30/3 (1969), 213–22.

Miller, Robert Moats, "Southern White Protestantism and the Negro, 1865–1965." In *The Negro in the South since 1865: Selected Essays in American History*, ed. Charles E. Wynes. Southern Historical Publication, n. 10. Tuscaloosa: University of Alabama Press, 1965.

Murray, Peter C. "The Racial Crisis in the Methodist Church." *Methodist History* 26/1 (October 1987): 3–14.

Nelsen, Hart M., Thomas W. Maldron, and Raytha L. Yokley. "Black Religion's Promethean Motif: Orthodoxy and Militancy." *American Journal of Sociology* 81 (1975): 139–46.

Nelson, Harold A. "Leadership and Change in an Evolutionary Movement: An Analysis of Change in the Leadership Structure of the Civil Rights Movement." *Social Forces* 49 (1971): 353–71.

Orser, W. Edward. "Racial Attitudes in Wartime: The Protestant Churches during World War I." *Church History* 41/3 (September 1972): 337–53.

Ricks, John A. "'De Lord' Descends and Is Crucified: Martin Luther King Jr. in Albany, Georgia." *Journal of Southwest Georgia History* (Fall 1984): 3–14.

Ritchey, Russell E. "The Southern Accent of American Methodism." *Methodist History* 27 (October 1988): 3–24.

Satterwhite, John H. "African Methodist Episcopal Zion Theology for a Uniting Church." *Journal of Religious Thought* 22 (Autumn/Winter 1972): 61–67.

Sawyer, Mary R. "Black Ecumenical Movements: Proponents of Social Change." *Review of Religious Research* 30/2 (December 1988): 151–61.

———. "Black Protestantism as Expressed in Ecumenical Activity." In *Reforming the Center: American Protestantism, 1900 to the Present*, ed. Douglas Jacobsen and William Vance Trollinger Jr. Grand Rapids MI: William B. Eerdmans, 1999.

———. "Blacks in White Ecumenism." *Midstream: The Ecumenical Movement Today* 31/3 (July 1992): 222–36.

———. "Efforts at Black Church Merger." *Journal of the Interdenominational Theological Seminary* 8/2 (Spring 1986): 305–316.

Shuttlesworth, Fred. "Birmingham Relisted." *Ebony* (August 1971): 114–18.

———. "Birmingham Shall Be Free Some Day." *Freedomways* 4 (1964): 16–19.

Smith, Luther E. "To Be Untrammeled and Free: The Urban Ministry Work of the CME Church: 1944–90." In *Churches, Cities and Human Community*, ed. Clifford J. Green. Grand Rapids MI: William B. Eerdmans, 1996.

Sumner, David E. "The Publisher and the Preacher: Racial Conflict at Vanderbilt University." *Tennessee Historical Quarterly* 56 (Spring 1997): 34–43.

Trueblood, Roy W. "Union Negotiation between Black Methodists in America." *Methodist History* 3/4 (July 1970): 18–29.

Trulear, Harold Dean. "The Role of the Church in Black Migration: Some
    Preliminary Observations." *Journal of the Afro-American Historical and
    Genealogical Society* 8 (Summer 1987): 51–56.
Walker, Jack L. "Functions of Disunity: Negro Leadership in a Southern City."
    Journal of Negro Education 32 (Summer 1963): 227–36.
Walker, Wyatt T. "Albany, Failure or First Step?" *New South* 18 (June 1963):
    3–8.
Wills, David W. "Beyond Commonality and Plurality: Persistent Racial
    Polarity in American Religion and Politics." In *Religion and American
    Politics*, ed. Mark Noll. New York: Oxford University, 1990.
———. "An Enduring Distance: Black Americans and the Religious
    Establishment." *Between the Times: The Travail of the Protestant
    Establishment in America, 1900–1960*, ed. William Hutchinson.
    Cambridge: Cambridge University Press, 1989.
Wood, James R. "Unanticipated Consequences of the Organizational Coalitions:
    Ecumenical Cooperation and Civil Rights Policy." *Social Forces* 50
    (1971): 512–21.
Wynn, Linda T. "The Dawning of a New Day: The Nashville Sit-Ins, February
    13–May 10, 1960." *Tennessee Historical Quarterly* 50 (1991): 42–54.

Index